The Flaw
of
Averages

The Flaw
of
Averages

WHY WE UNDERESTIMATE RISK IN
THE FACE OF UNCERTAINTY

Sam L. Savage

WILEY

John Wiley & Sons, Inc.

For general information on our other products and services or for technical support, please contact our Customer Care Department within the United States at (800) 762-2974, outside the United States at (317) 572-3993 or fax (317) 572-4002.

Wiley also publishes its books in a variety of electronic formats. Some content that appears in print may not be available in electronic books. For more information about Wiley products, visit our web site at www.wiley.com.

Library of Congress Cataloging-in-Publication Data:

Savage, Sam L., 1944–
 The flaw of averages : why we underestimate risk in the face of uncertainty / Sam L. Savage.
  p. cm.
 Includes bibliographical references and index.
 ISBN 978–0–471–38197–6 (cloth)
  1. Risk. 2. Uncertainty. I. Title.
 HB615.S313 2009
 338.5—dc22

2008052144

Printed in the United States of America
10 9 8 7 6 5 4 3 2 1

For Daryl, Jacob, and Russell, and in memory of Fruipit, our beloved dog

Contents

You cannot learn to ride a bicycle from a book, and I claim the same is true for coping with uncertainty. Paradoxically, this book attempts to do what it claims is impossible.

FOUNDATIONS

In planning for the future, uncertain outcomes are often replaced with single, so-called average numbers. This leads to a class of systematic errors that I call the Flaw of Averages, which explains among other things why forecasts are always wrong.

The electronic spreadsheet brought the power of business modeling to tens of millions. In so doing, it also paved the way for an epidemic of the Flaw of Averages.

APPLICATIONS

Preface

The Flaw of Averages describes a set of common avoidable mistakes in assessing risk in the face of uncertainty. It helps explain why conventional methods of gauging the future are so *wrong* so *often*, and is an accessory to the recent economic catastrophe. Once grasped, these ideas can lead recent us to more effective forecasting and decision making. Traditionally, these topics have been the domain of probability and statistics. Although I will assume no prior knowledge of these subjects, for those who *have* had formal training in these subjects, it should take only a few chapters to repair the damage.

My perspective no doubt derives largely from my father, Leonard Jimmie Savage. Although well *below* average on academic scales during his early education, he emerged as a prominent mathematical statistician who collaborated closely with Milton Friedman, among others. One of their students was the founder of modern portfolio theory, Harry Markowitz, who claims that my father "indoctrinated him at point blank range with rational expectation theory." Thus I am a child of the University of Chicago School of Economics.

Early on it was clear I possessed at least one of my father's traits. I, too, was a below-average student, displaying neither athletic nor academic aptitude. The defining moment of my high school education came in an after-class conference with my English teacher in my junior year at the University of Chicago Laboratory School. She explained that I was failing the course, but with a monumental effort might achieve a D by the second semester. Then she helpfully explained the underlying problem: The Lab School was for students who would go on to college, which, quite clearly, I would not. Instead she suggested a technical school where I could get practical training as a mechanic or a plumber.

She therefore presented me with my first serious career decision: to work my butt off for a lousy D in English or play my guitar for immediate gratification. I made the obvious choice, and music has brought me joy and solace ever since. Better yet, I was able to have my cake and eat it too, because I ended up with a D anyway. In retrospect I cannot question this individual teacher's judgment, because all told I received three D's in four years of high school English, each under a different instructor.

My father was in no position to complain, because when *he* graduated from high school in Detroit, he too "was classified by his teachers as 'not college material,' and consequently was refused admission to the University of Michigan."[1] My grandfather, in desperation, called on personal connections to get him admitted on probation to Wayne State University. Allen Wallis, with whom my father later cofounded the University of Chicago Statistics Department, reported what happened next: "In his year [at Wayne] he established a good enough record to be admitted on probation to the University of Michigan. However, he caused a fire in a chemistry laboratory and was expelled."[2]

Once again I followed in my father's footsteps, later flunking out of the University of Michigan myself, although based on academics rather than involuntary arson.

As adolescent misfits, then, neither of us was able to conform to the norms expected by our teachers. Thus nonaverageness itself became a family value, perhaps in some way inspiring this book. After being de-Michiganized, however, our careers diverged. My father fought his way back into Michigan, got his PhD in mathematics, and achieved great academic acclaim. I worked as a mechanic and briefly raced a sports car before ultimately getting a degree in computer science, which is, in deference to my English teacher, just plumbing with bits of information instead of water.

Although *The Flaw of Averages* will discuss concepts from both statistics and economics, I have little formal training in either of these subjects—just the basics picked up at an early age at the dinner table. Therefore, I have written not from the perspective of a statistician or an economist, but from the perspective of a former mechanic and current plumber of information who grew up surrounded by statisticians and economists.

I came up with some of the core ideas and title for this book in 1999, and I started writing. I knew the concept had potential, but somehow the book was not uplifting: The Flaw of Averages asserts that everything is below projection, behind schedule, and beyond budget. Where was the happy ending?

In search of one, I continued to teach, consult, and write articles about various aspects of this problem. Feeling the need to stake out the real estate (in case I ever did finish the book), I wrote an article in October 2000 on the Flaw of Averages for the *San Jose Mercury News*.[3] When it was published, it was, to my surprise, adorned with a drawing by the renowned cartoonist Jeff Danziger depicting a statistician drowning in a river that is on average three feet deep. This is reproduced in Chapter 1 of this book.

Over the years, I have had the good fortune to interact with some exceptional people in academia and industry who were grappling with the Flaw of Averages themselves. As a result of this interaction, an approach that we call Probability Management has recently emerged, offering a potential cure for many variants of this problem. And so at last with a happy ending in hand, I renewed my writing efforts in earnest in 2006. All told, on *average*, I have written 21 words per day since 1999.

When my stepbrother, John Pearce, first heard of this writing project, he assumed that I was working through some sort of psychodrama involving my late father. Wrong. This work has been fueled by a psychodrama involving my high school English teachers.

SAM L. SAVAGE

Palo Alto, California
April 2009

Acknowledgments

I must start by chronologically acknowledging those who were directly involved in the evolution of Probability Management. I am indebted to Ben Ball of MIT, first for infecting me with his interest in portfolios of petroleum exploration projects in the late 1980s, and second for the collaboration that laid the foundations for much that lay ahead. In 1992 Mark Broadie of Columbia University gave me a key (a simple spreadsheet model) that unlocked a world of stochastic modeling. In 2003 I had the pleasure of working with Andy Parker of Bessemer Trust on a retirement planning model that pioneered some important ideas in interactive simulation. In 2004, I began an exciting three-way collaboration with Stefan Scholtes of Cambridge University and Daniel Zweidler, then at Shell. This truly put Probability Management on the map with a large interactive simulation application at Shell and a coauthored article in *ORMS Today*. During this time, Dan Fylstra of Frontline Systems made a breakthrough in interactive simulation, turning my dream of interactive simulation in spreadsheets into reality.

The following group also played critical roles in the development of this book. My father, Leonard Jimmie Savage, and his colleagues Milton Friedman and Allen Wallis served as towering intellectual role models from my earliest memories. Next, I must thank Linus Schrage of the University of Chicago for his collaboration on What's*Best!*, without which I would not have been reborn as a management scientist. By supporting my seminar series on management science in spreadsheets, Jack Gould, then dean of the University of Chicago Graduate School of Business, helped launch the odyssey during which I discovered the Flaw of Averages. Stanford's Department of Management Science and Engineering, with which I have been affiliated since 1990, has been the ideal environment in which to experiment with and teach the ideas underlying the book. I owe special thanks to Peter Bernstein, whose own book, *Capital*

Ideas, assisted me in my own work and who personally helped get this book off the ground. In 1999, Mina Samuels, who was then an editor for John Wiley & Sons, was inspirational in helping me conceive the book and, when I tracked her down in 2007, was even more supportive as a midwife. In the meantime, Bill Falloon, who inherited my nine-year project at John Wiley, deserves the Most Patient Editor of the Century Award: Thanks. Bill Perry of Stanford University has served as both an inspiration and a foundation of support. Marc Van Allen, of the law firm Jenner and Block, realized that the Flaw of Averages underlies the nation's accounting standards and collaborated in researching and publicizing the issue. Several chapters were inspired by discussions with Howard Wainer, and by a prepublication draft of his book, *Picturing the Uncertain World: How to Understand, Communicate and Control Uncertainty Through Graphical Display,* which I highly recommend. Finally, I owe special thanks to David Empey and Ronald Roth for their programming support over the years and in particular for the implementation of the application at Shell and subsequent development of the DIST (Distribution String) data type.

When it takes you nine years to write a book, there is plenty of time to pick up useful ideas from others. So many people provided assistance, contributions, or comments over the years that they won't fit into a paragraph. Therefore I have used the following table. The laws of probability ensure that I have missed a few people who belong here, for which I apologize in advance.

Dick Abraham	Mike Dubis
Bob Ameo	Ken Dueker
Ted Anderson	David Eddy
Matthias Bichsel	Brad Efron
Adam Borison	Martin Farncombe
Jerry Brashear	Roland Frenk
Stewart Buckingham	Chris Geczy
Mike Campbell	Bob Glick
David Cawlfield	Peter Glynn
Kevin Chang	Joe Grundfest
Terri Dial	Deborah Gordon

Kevin Hankins

Ward Hanson

Warren Hausman

Wynship Hillier

Gloria Hom

Ron Howard

John Howell

Doug Hubbard

Darren Johnson

Martin Keane

Gary Klein

Michael Kubica

Paul Kucik

Andrew Levitch

Bob Locw

David Luenberger

Jeff Magill

Harry Markowitz

John Marquis

Michael May

Rick Medress

Robert Merton

Mike Naylor

Abby Ocean

Greg Parnell

John Pearce

Mark Permann

Bill Perry

Tyson Pyles

Matthew Raphaelson

Andrew Reynolds

John Rivlin

Aaron Rosenberg

The late Rick Rosenthal

Mark Rubino

Sanjay Saigal

John Sall

Jim Scanlan

Karl Schmedders

Myron Scholes

Michael Schrage

Randy Schultz

Adam Seiver

William Sharpe

Rob Shearer

John Sterman

Stephen Stigler

Jeff Strnad

Steve Tani

Janet Tavakoli

John Taylor

Carol Weaver

Bill Wecker

Roman Weil

Justin Wolfers

A separate category of appreciation goes to those who contributed to the specifications of the DIST data type, in particular Dave Empey, Dan Fylstra, Harry Markowitz, Ivo Nenov, John Rivlin, Ron Roth, John Sall, Stefan Scholtes, Eric Wainwright, and Whitney Winston.

Special thanks to Aishwarya Vasudevan for her help with the graphics, Debbie Asakawa for her suggestions on the entire manuscript, and Jeff Danziger for his drawings.

In the end, I could not possibly have written this without the guiding light of my wife Daryl, who helped extensively with the editing and who continues to make life so much fun.

S. L. S.

The Flaw
of
Averages

INTRODUCTION

Connecting the Seat of the Intellect to the Seat of the Pants

The only certainty is that nothing is certain.
—Pliny the Elder, Roman scholar, 23–79 CE

As the financial meltdown of 2008 has demonstrated, Pliny is still pretty much on target two millennia later. Despite all its promise, the Information Age is fraught with a dizzying array of technological, economic, and political uncertainties. But on the flip side, the Information Age also offers electronic extensions of our intuition that can provide a new experiential feel for risk and uncertainty. This book shows how.

Let's start off with a simple everyday example in which most people's intellects fail. Imagine that you and your spouse have an invitation to a ritzy reception with a bunch of VIPs. You must leave home by 6 p.m. or risk being late. Although you work in different parts of town, each of your average commute times is 30 minutes. So if you both depart work at 5:30, then you should have at least a 50/50 chance of leaving home together for the reception by 6 o'clock.

This thinking sounds right. But your instinct warns that you will probably be late. Which is correct: your brain or your gut?

Your gut is correct, but not being particularly good with words, it may have difficulty winning the argument intellectually. So here, in terms that even a brain can understand, is why you'll probably be late.

Suppose there really is a 50/50 chance that each of you will make it home by 6:00. Then the trip is like a coin toss in which

1

heads is equivalent to arriving by 6:00 and tails to arriving after 6:00. Four things can happen:

- *Heads/tails*: You are home by 6:00 but your spouse isn't.
- *Tails/heads*: Your spouse is home by 6:00 but you aren't.
- *Tails/tails*: Neither of you is home by 6:00.
- *Heads/heads*: Both of you are home by 6:00.

The only way you can leave by 6:00 is if you flip two heads, for which there is only one chance in four.

Now imagine that your brother, who also works 30 minutes away, is going to join you. The chance of your all leaving on time now drops to one in eight. Or suppose you, your spouse, and five friends and relations all plan to pile into your minivan for the trip to the reception. Assuming that everyone leaves work at 5:30 and has a different 30-minute route to your house, then the chance of leaving on time is the same as flipping 7 heads in a row; that's 0.5 raised to the 7th power, or 1 in 128.

No wonder people are always late!

If you want to teach yourself to get a better grasp on uncertainty and risk, you have to recognize two very different types of learning: intellectual and experiential. To set the stage, let's start with something that everyone has understood since childhood. It may be expressed as follows:

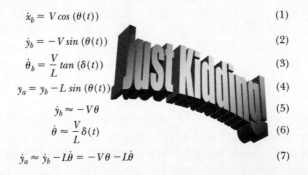

$$\dot{x}_b = V \cos(\theta(t)) \tag{1}$$

$$\dot{y}_b = -V \sin(\theta(t)) \tag{2}$$

$$\dot{\theta}_b = \frac{V}{L} \tan(\delta(t)) \tag{3}$$

$$y_a = y_b - L \sin(\theta(t)) \tag{4}$$

$$\dot{y}_b \approx -V\theta \tag{5}$$

$$\dot{\theta} \approx \frac{V}{L}\delta(t) \tag{6}$$

$$\dot{y}_a \approx \dot{y}_b - L\dot{\theta} = -V\theta - L\dot{\theta} \tag{7}$$

Actually, these are the differential equations of the motion of a bicycle. You have solved them for most of your life, not through the seat of your intellect, but experientially, through the seat of your pants.

The theory of probability and statistics can likewise be presented in terms of mind-numbing equations, and that's the way it's usually taught in school. This is probably why Nobel Prize–winning research in behavioral economics has shown that even people trained in the field consistently make mistakes when faced with day-to-day uncertainties.[1,2]

Steve Jobs, cofounder of Apple, said that "personal computers are bicycles for the mind." Increasingly, through a process called simulation, they are being applied to problems involving uncertainty and risk, allowing us to bypass the equations of the traditional statistics course and to gain an experiential understanding of the subject. In the past few years, I have had the good fortune of collaborating with colleagues in academia and industry in advancing the development of such techniques and applying them in practice. I call our approach Probability Management, and it has been applied to problems as wide-ranging as assessing risks in retirement portfolios, investing in petroleum exploration projects, and designing incentive programs for bankers. It has been an exhilarating and sometimes exhausting ride, and it is far from over.

The book has three sections. The first, Foundations, provides a basis for visualizing risk and uncertainty using simple everyday props such as gameboard spinners and dice. It describes the sorts of consistent errors that occur when uncertain numbers are replaced by single "average" values: the Flaw of Averages. The second part, Applications, describes classic cases of the Flaw of Averages in the real world. The third part describes a potential path toward a cure for the Flaw of Averages: Probability Management.

Foundations

The foundations are intended to help you intuitively grasp and visualize the consequences of uncertainty and risk. If you were learning to ride a bicycle, for example, the foundations phase would end as soon as you no longer required training wheels.

Hey, wait a minute. Didn't I just argue that you can't learn to ride a bike from a book? Yes, I did. Paradoxically, I will attempt to do what I claim is impossible. Here's how. At various stages along the way, you will see this bicycle in the margin.

At that point you will have the option to put the book down and visit FlawOfAverages.com, where you will be able to go for an actual ride. There are plenty of animations, simulations, and other experiential demonstrations to improve your intuition concerning these issues.

Applications

I begin the second section of the book with applications of the concepts of Part 1 to the field of finance, where the Flaw of Averages was first conquered in managing the risk of and return on investments. Although these models are being recalibrated and refined in the light of the economic turmoil of 2008–2009, they provide an excellent foundation for managing uncertainty and risk. Furthermore, they have the potential to be generalized to many other areas of industry and government that are still blind to the Flaw of Averages. I will discuss examples in supply chain management, project portfolios, national defense, health care, climate change, and even sex.

Probability Management

The book concludes with a discussion of the field of Probability Management, an approach toward a general cure for the Flaw of Averages, which is based on recent breakthroughs in technology, coupled to new data structures and management protocols. The approach is being adopted by some large companies today, and your organization can do it too.

In his book *Blink*,[3] Malcolm Gladwell describes the power of snap judgments as thinking "without thinking." He writes that "just as we can teach ourselves to think logically and deliberately, we can also teach ourselves to make better snap judgments," a process I refer to as *connecting the seat of the intellect to the seat of the pants*. The goal of this book is to help you make better judgments involving uncertainty and risk, both when you have the leisure to deliberate and, more importantly, when you don't.

A Note from Your Author

I now interrupt this book to bring you an important announcement. Some of the material is a bit mathematical and may challenge certain readers. Accordingly, to accommodate a wide variety of technical backgrounds, I will occasionally offer opportunities to jump ahead without missing the main thrust of the argument. What you choose to do at these forks in the road will depend on your aptitude, previous knowledge of the subject, and how badly you want to get to the juicy chapters on investments, the war on terror, and sex.

FOUNDATIONS

The foundations are intended to help you intuitively grasp and visualize the consequences of uncertainty and risk. If you were learning to ride a bicycle, for example, the foundations phase would end as soon as you no longer required training wheels.

PART 1

THE BIG PICTURE

In Part 1, I will provide an overview of the Flaw of Averages, how it rose to prominence, and how technology and new business practices have the potential to provide a cure. I will finish with some general thoughts on the use and benefit of analytical management models.

1

The Flaw of Averages

Our culture encodes a strong bias either to neglect or ignore variation. We tend to focus instead on measures of central tendency, and as a result we make some terrible mistakes, often with considerable practical import.
— Stephen Jay Gould, naturalist, 1941–2002

The measure of central tendency that Gould refers to is typically the *average*, also known as the *expected value*, and the mistakes he warns of result from a common fallacy as fundamental as the belief that the earth is flat. It permeates planning activities in business, government, and the military. It helped mask the recent subprime mortgage fiasco until it became a world crisis, and it will plague those trying to clean up the mess. It is even enshrined within our accounting codes. I call it the Flaw of Averages.[1,2] It states, in effect, that:

Plans based on *average* assumptions are wrong on *average.*

An apocryphal example concerns the statistician who drowned while fording a river that was, on average, only three feet deep, as depicted in the sensitive portrayal by cartoonist Jeff Danziger.

In everyday life, the Flaw of Averages ensures that plans based on *average* customer demand, *average* completion time, *average* interest rate, and other uncertainties are below projection, behind schedule, and beyond budget.

So people have been confused in the face of uncertainty for 2,000 years. What else is new? Plenty! What's new are several dramatic advances in software, data structures, and managerial outlook. Together, they form the bases of Probability Management, which brings a new transparency to the communication of risk and uncertainty. It is changing our perception of these concepts as profoundly as the light bulb changed our perception of darkness.

Give Me a Number

To understand how pervasive the Flaw of Averages is, consider the hypothetical case of a marketing manager who has just been asked by his boss to forecast demand for a new-generation microchip.

> *"That's difficult for a new product," responds the manager, "but I'm confident that annual demand will be between 50,000 and 150,000 units."*

> *"Give me a number to take to my production people," barks the boss. "I can't tell them to build a production line with a capacity between 50,000 and 150,000 units!"*

The phrase "Give me a number" is a dependable leading indicator of an encounter with the Flaw of Averages, but the marketing manager dutifully replies: "If you need a single number, I suggest you use the average of 100,000."

The boss plugs the average demand, along with the cost of a 100,000-unit capacity production line, into a spreadsheet model of the business. The bottom line is a healthy $10 million, which he reports as the projected profit. Assuming that demand is the only uncertainty and that 100,000 is the correct average (or expected) demand, then $10 million must be the average (or expected) profit. Right?

Wrong! The Flaw of Averages ensures that on *average*, profit will be less than the profit associated with the *average* demand. Why? If the *actual* demand is only 90,000, the boss won't make the projection of $10 million. If demand is 80,000, the results will be even worse. That's the downside. On the other hand, what if demand is 110,000 or 120,000? Then you exceed your capacity and can still sell only 100,000 units. So profit is capped at $10 million. There is no upside to balance the downside, as shown in Figure 1.1, which helps explain why, on average, everything is below projection.

But why are things behind schedule on average? Remember the chance of making it to the VIP reception on time, as described in the Introduction? When this occurs on an industrial scale, it can

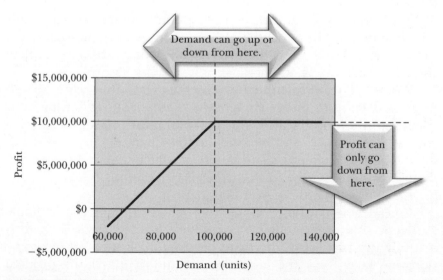

Figure 1.1   Average profit is less than the profit associated with average demand.

be much worse. Consider an idealized software project that will require ten separate subroutines to be developed in parallel. The boss asks the programming manager of the first subroutine how long development will take.

"I'm confident it will take somewhere between three and nine months" replies the programming manager.

"Give me a number," says the boss. "I have to tell the chief operating officer when we'll be operational!"

"Well," says the programming manager, "on average, programs like this take about six months. Use that if you need a single number."

For simplicity of argument, assume that the boss has similar conversations with each of the nine remaining programming managers. The durations of all the subroutines are uncertain and independent, and they are expected to range between three and nine months with an average of six months. Because the ten subroutines are being developed in parallel, the boss now goes to the COO and happily reports that the software is expected to be operational in six months.

Assuming the durations of the ten subroutines are the only uncertainties and that each one has an average of six months, then the average or expected duration of the entire software project should be six months. Right?

Wrong! If you read the Introduction you know why. All ten projects coming in under six months is analogous to having your friends all show up on time. But now you must flip ten heads in a row instead of seven, and the odds are less than one in a thousand. Figure 1.2 displays a possible outcome in which many tasks take less than six months, yet the project takes 10.4 months.

And why is everything over budget on average?

Consider a pharmaceutical firm that distributes a perishable antibiotic. Although demand fluctuates, the long-term average is a steady five cartons of the drug per month. A new VP of operations has taken over the distribution center. He asks the product manager for a forecast of next month's demand. "Demand varies," responds the product manager, "but I can give you an accurate distribution, that is, the probabilities that demand will be 0, 1, 2, and so on." The product manager, who was apprehensive about his new

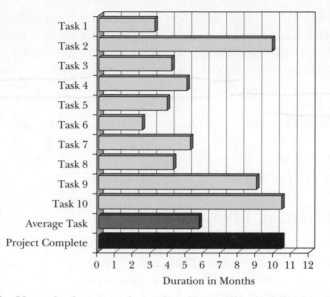

Figure 1.2   Many tasks come in under six months, but the longest is 10.4 months.

boss, is relieved that he could provide such complete information in his first professional interaction.

"If I had wanted a distribution, I would have asked for a distribution," snaps the boss, "give me a *number* so that I can calculate our operating costs." Eventually they settle on the time-honored tradition of representing the uncertainty by its average.

Armed with the accurate average demand of five cartons per month, the boss now proceeds to estimate inventory operating costs, calculated as follows:

- If monthly demand is less than the amount stocked, the firm incurs a spoilage cost of $50 per unsold carton of the perishable drug.
- On the other hand, if demand is greater than the amount stocked, the firm must air freight the extra cartons at an increased cost of $150 each.

A quick calculation indicates that if five cartons are stocked, and the demand happens to come in right at its average of five, then there will be neither spoilage nor air freight costs. Thus, the boss reasons, the average inventory operating cost will be zero. Right?

Wrong! If demand is below average, the firm gets whupped upside the head with spoilage costs, whereas if demand is above average, the firm gets whupped up the other side of the head with air freight costs. No negative costs exist to cancel out the positive ones; so, on *average*, the cost will exceed the cost associated with the *average* demand.

Later in the book I will distinguish between the strong form and weak form of the Flaw of Averages, as well as many subcategories. In the remainder of this chapter, I will present a few actual occurrences in various walks of life.

Statisticians to the Rescue?

Where do all those averages come from that people erroneously plug into their business plans? You guessed it. They come from statisticians and other analysts, whose so-called sophisticated models often perpetuate the Flaw of Averages.

Consider the graph in Figure 1.3 depicting economic growth data. By running regression analysis on the historical data represented by the solid black line, a statistician could estimate the average growth in the future, a single number represented by the slope of

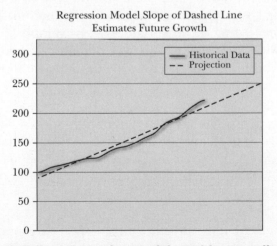

Figure 1.3   A statistical regression model provides an estimate of future growth as a single number, the slope of the dashed line.

the dashed line. Because this was derived from a "mathematical model" developed by an "expert," people are likely to believe it.

This nearly irresistible tendency to fixate on a single number has been well documented by Patrick Leach in a book entitled _Why Can't You Just Give Me the Number?_[3] He points out that "once a value is generated, put down on paper, and incorporated into the business plan, it becomes gospel."

In actuality, the data in Figure 1.3 represents the national growth in housing values from January 2000 to December 2005, taken from the S&P/Case-Shiller Home Price Index.[4] And numerous models analogous to the dashed regression line were used as justification for devastatingly bad investments.

What really happened to housing values is shown in Figure 1.4. Astonishingly, this possibility was not even considered by some of the risk models monitoring the economy. In the December 2008 issue of _Portfolio.com_, Michael Lewis chronicles the disaster in an article entitled "The End." According to Lewis, when someone inquired of Standard & Poor's what falling housing prices would do to default rates, they told him their model for price growth couldn't even accept negative numbers. This is like a model of coin flips that generates only heads!

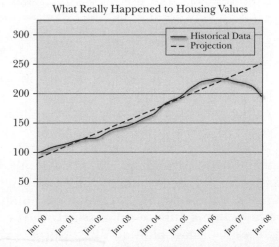

Figure 1.4   Actual data from January 2000 to January 2008.

Red Lobster

Summer 2003: Red Lobster seafood restaurants promote "Endless Crab: a celebration of all the hot, steaming snow crab legs you can eat." Shortly thereafter, the president of Red Lobster was replaced. According to the *St. Petersburg Times*,[5] "The move came after management vastly underestimated how many Alaskan crab legs customers would consume." Furthermore, "The chain was pinched by rising wholesale prices."

I suspect that during the planning of the ill-fated promotion, a high-level manager asked for the average number of customers expected to order crab. Further, the manager might have inquired about the average number of helpings per customer and the estimated price of crab. It would have been tempting to calculate the expected profit of the promotion based on these three numbers, but this approach would have been deeply flawed.

If the number of helpings exceeded expectations, then the chain was poised to lose money on each crab-eating customer. According to the *Times*, "'It wasn't the second helping, it was the third one that hurt,' company chairman Joe R. Lee said in a conference call with analysts." Worse, the uncertainties were linked: If demand exceeded expectations, the promotion itself had the potential to drive up the price of crab.

Thus estimated profit associated with the *average* demand, the *average* number of helpings, and the *average* price was higher than the *average* profit.

Red River

Spring 1997: The U.S. National Weather Service issues a forecast that the Red River is expected to crest at roughly 50 feet. *The New York Times* later quoted experts who said the problem was "that more precision was assigned to the forecast than was warranted."[6] The City of Grand Forks' communications officer, Tom Mulhern, said "[the National Weather Service] came down with this number and people fixated on it." According to *The Times*, "Actually, there was a wider range of probabilities," but the single number "forecast had lulled the town into a false sense of security." The article continued, "It was, they say, a case of what Alfred North Whitehead, the mathematician and philosopher, once termed 'misplaced concreteness.' And whether the problem is climate change, earthquakes, droughts or floods, they say the tendency to <u>overlook uncertainties</u>, <u>margins of error and ranges of probability can lead to damaging misjudgments.</u>"

This was a classic case of the Flaw of Averages. Consider a hypothetical version of the Red River situation. Assume that, at the time of the forecast, the expected crest level is indeed 50 feet, but the actual level is still uncertain. In this version, Mother Nature determines the weather by flipping a coin. Heads creates torrential rains, which result in a 55-foot crest. Tails creates a mere drizzle, leading to a 45-foot crest. Because the dikes are designed to withstand a 50-foot crest, there is no damage when a tail occurs. But don't forget the 50 percent chance of a head, in which case flooding results in $2 billion in damage.

In short, the damage resulting from the average crest of 50 feet (the average of 45 and 55) is zero, whereas the average damage (the average of zero and $2 billion) is $1 billion.

In fact, what occurred in Grand Forks was a disastrous flood, forcing an estimated 50,000 people from their homes. *The New York Times* reported that "[i]t is difficult to know what might have happened had the uncertainty of the forecast been better communicated. But it is possible, said Mr. Mulhern, that the dikes might have been sufficiently enlarged and people might have taken more steps to preserve their possessions. As it was, he said, 'Some people didn't leave till the water was coming down the street.'" Figure 1.5 shows the difference between a flood slightly below and slightly above the average crest.

Now in case you are questioning the value of planning for above-average natural disasters, consider this scenario. If a Richter 7 earthquake hit a modern city with seismic building codes, it might kill a few hundred people, whereas similar quakes in a less developed part of the world regularly kill tens of thousands.

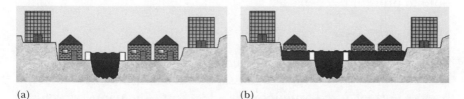

(a)   (b)

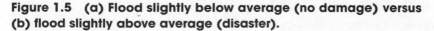

Figure 1.5   (a) Flood slightly below average (no damage) versus (b) flood slightly above average (disaster).

Visit FlawOfAverages.com for animations and simulations of several of the examples in this chapter.

Red Ink in Orange County

Summer 1994: Interest rates are low and are expected to remain so or fall even farther. Orange County, California, has created a financial portfolio to fund the pensions of its teachers and firefighters, based on the expected future behavior of interest rates. For several years, this fund, run by County Treasurer Robert Citron, has yielded much higher returns than comparable funds in similar municipalities. For the sophisticated investor, this is actually a red flag; there is no free lunch, as they say. John Moorlach, who unsuccessfully runs against Citron in 1994, argues in his campaign that "Mr. Citron believes he can accurately anticipate the market all the time, and also outperform everyone. That's impossible."[7] Nonetheless, so many people line up with their money that the county has to turn investors away. In fact, the fund has naively leveraged itself into a very risky position and goes bankrupt in December of 1994.

In 1995, Professor Philippe Jorion of the University of California at Irvine showed that if the county officials had explicitly considered the well documented range of interest rate uncertainties instead of a single *average* interest rate scenario, they would easily have detected the likelihood of the looming train wreck.[8]

There was absolutely no need for such a pension fund to shoot for the moon. Moreover, had the county's government members understood the increased risk they faced as a result, they would no doubt have adopted a more conservative investment strategy in time to prevent the debacle.

The Red Coats

Spring 1775: The colonists are concerned about British plans to raid Lexington and Concord, Massachusetts. Patriots in Boston (my friends in the United Kingdom use a less flattering name) develop a plan that explicitly takes a range of uncertainties into account: The British will come either by land or by sea. These unsung pioneers of modern decision analysis did it just right by explicitly planning for both contingencies. Had Paul Revere and the Minutemen planned for the single average scenario of the British walking up the beach with one foot on the land and one in the sea, the citizens of North America might speak with different accents today.

Why Forecasts Are Always Wrong: A Problem of Dilbertian Proportion

When managers ask for a forecast, they are *really* asking for a number, which involves the Flaw of Averages. For example, the product manager of the new microchip provided the *correct* forecast of average demand to his boss. But the boss turned around and used that single number to *incorrectly* forecast average profit. Each of the ten programming managers gave their boss the *correct* average completion time of six months for their subroutines. But the boss used those single numbers to *incorrectly* forecast the completion of the entire software project. The product manager at the pharmaceutical firm gave the VP of operations the *correct* forecast for average demand. But the VP used that number to *incorrectly* forecast operating costs.

In these cases, the bosses will ultimately claim that they got bad forecasts from their subordinates and will end up punishing them for providing what was in fact the *correct* average. This is indeed a problem of Dilbertian proportion.

In his book, *A Whole New Mind*,[9] author Daniel H. Pink predicts the ascendance in the economy of right-brained, big-picture thinking relative to left-brained analysis. The subjects of statistics and probability have traditionally been the domain of the left. But in fact, the Flaw of Averages often arises due to the left brain's stubborn insistence on a single precise answer. If anything, the right side of brain is better equipped to interpret the patterns inherent in uncertainty.

In subsequent chapters I will discuss new technologies that are making these patterns visible to the naked eye, allowing the right brain to get back in the game.

CHAPTER

2

The Fall of the Algebraic Curtain and Rise of the Flaw of Averages

In 1973 I received a PhD in the application of computers to operations research. OR, as it is also known, grew out of the first widespread use of mathematics in decision making to tackle the unprecedented operational problems of World War II. (It should not be confused with the modern field of opposition research, in which people running political campaigns scour the backgrounds of their adversaries for dirt to discredit them.) After my graduate work I spent a year and a half at General Motors Research Laboratory, working on issues ranging from optimal production to marketing. I was a lot more interested in real-world problems than I had been in school, and had GM acted on my suggestion to relocate the lab to the Italian Riviera, I would probably still be there today.

Becoming a Management Scientist

In 1974, I joined the University of Chicago Graduate School of Business and started teaching management science, which is what they call OR in business schools. This appeared to be the opportunity of a lifetime, but I was soon disappointed to discover that only 10 percent of my students understood what I was talking about and that, of those who did, only 10 percent would go on to apply the stuff.

One of the primary offenders was a resource allocation technique called linear programming (LP). Although in theory it had the potential to optimize profits, in practice it was too cumbersome for all but the largest of applications. The required course in the subject consisted largely of material that looked like the equations of motion of a bicycle.

Abandoning Management Science

There was an algebraic curtain separating the real-life manager from management science, and I abandoned the field as moribund in 1976. While keeping my day job—teaching basic business math and computer science at the business school—I attempted unsuccessfully to become a folk singer in the bars along Chicago's Lincoln Avenue. Two things dissuaded me from a career in music. First, most of the other musicians on the street were much better than I was, and, second, they weren't making it either.

In 1979, still with no desire for a full-time career in academia, I developed and marketed a new variant of jigsaw puzzle based on the tessellation art of the Dutch artist, M. C. Escher. Although the puzzle sold well, we were never able to get the production costs low enough to make money. However, as an aid in running the small company, we purchased a TRS-80 Radio Shack microcomputer, and a half dozen years after getting my PhD in a computer-related field, I developed my first meaningful relationship with a computer.

 Some audio recordings from that period and an interactive electronic version of the puzzle are posted at FlawOfAverages.com.

Being Reborn as a Management Scientist

By 1985, the microcomputer revolution was in full swing. Mike Campbell, a young engineer who had helped program the TRS-80, suggested that we try marketing linear programming software for personal computers. He had studied the subject at Purdue, and was one of the 10 percent who had actually understood it. Having just refused to teach the dreaded required LP course at Chicago, my response was along the lines of "Mike, linear programming is just something they teach in *school*. No one actually *uses* that stuff." But as it turned out, Linus Schrage, a colleague at the University of

Chicago, and his programmer Kevin Cunningham had just created a program that would translate a file saved by VisiCalc, the world's first electronic spreadsheet, and solve it with their LINDO LP software. Mike and I teamed up with them to embed this technology in Lotus 1-2-3, the reigning spreadsheet of the time, and bring it to a broad market. For someone already familiar with spreadsheets, only ten additional function key commands were required to do LP. We called the package What's*Best!*®, and it is alive and well today.

From my new perspective, the required LP course at the University of Chicago had been reduced to . . . one . . . function . . . key . . . per . . . week . . . , a result that did not receive immediate acclaim from academia. In fact, when people with extensive LP experience used What's*Best!*, they would often precisely replicate the set of tedious steps that our program was designed to circumvent—like someone laying a wheel on its side, loading luggage on it, and then dragging it behind a yak. So, although What's*Best!* wasn't an immediate hit with the establishment, it was a breakthrough product and received a *PC Magazine* Technical Excellence Award in 1986.[1] The electronic spreadsheet was bringing down the algebraic curtain, and I was reborn as a management scientist.

As to the others, Linus and Kevin still market What's*Best!* through Lindo Systems.[2] Mike is today chief operating officer of Fair Isaac Corp., a firm that provides analytical business models and is most famous for its personal credit scoring system.

On the Road Again

In 1990, with the support of Jack Gould, who was then dean of the University of Chicago Business School, I launched a series of seminars on management science in spreadsheets, which I delivered around the country for several years. I was now leveraging the human capital picked up playing music in bars a decade earlier. But this time I had a paying audience, and I had transitioned from guitar to keyboard (computer, that is). I covered optimization, simulation, and forecasting, and when attendees had special requests, the interactive environment of the spreadsheet allowed me to improvise.

During this time I met literally thousands of spreadsheet users and discovered an unintended consequence of this seductive new tool. By tempting millions of managers to plug in single numbers to represent uncertainties, it became a contagion vector for the Flaw of Averages. I have been searching for a cure ever since.

From OR to PR and Back

In the early 1990s, as I began my crusade, several technologies already could, in theory, illuminate the Flaw of Averages. The most immediate problem was that people were simply unaware of the issue. In fact, until the last few years, the bulk of my efforts were in area of public relations. PR was not that much of a stretch for me, because you only need to increment the first letter by one to get there from OR, where I began my career.

But PR has its limits. And during a decade of teaching and consulting in the field, I realized that information technology could improve our approach to managing uncertainty in several innovative ways. So these days, I am again focused on the details of how computers can aid our decision making. In short, I am back to doing OR.

CHAPTER

Mitigating the Flaw of Averages

This chapter will provide an overview of some useful technologies in the struggle against the Flaw of Averages. They have evolved significantly since I first began to focus on this problem in the early 1990s, and like most advances they are intertwined with one another and with evolving management practices. I will begin with a comparison to previous advances in information technology and then provide more details using an analogy with the adoption of the lightbulb.

Probability Management

The Microcomputer Revolution can be said to have started in earnest with the word processor in 1976. The tedious tasks of typing, correcting, and editing letters and manuscripts were transformed nearly overnight by the ability to compose electronically before committing ink to paper. Then in 1979, VisiCalc, the first electronic spreadsheet, brought a similar transformation to accounting and business modeling.

By the late 1980s organizations had data management systems in which large central databases could pass numbers back and forth with individual spreadsheets on desktops. Although these systems have many benefits, they are also capable of disseminating the Flaw of Averages on an enterprisewide scale.

Probability Management may be viewed as a data management system in which the entities being managed are not numbers, but uncertainties, that is, probability distributions. The central database is a *Scenario Library* containing thousands of potential future values of uncertain business parameters. The library exchanges information with desktop distribution processors that do for probability distributions what word processors did for words and what spreadsheets did for numbers.

As of this writing, the practice of Probability Management is still in its infancy, but it is already being applied at organizations such as Shell, Merck and Co., and Olin Corporation. At these and other organizations, managers across the enterprise are beginning to coherently visualize, communicate, and interact with risk and uncertainty in ways unimaginable a few years ago. It had its roots in Monte Carlo simulation.

Monte Carlo Simulation

The last thing you do before climbing on a ladder to paint the side of your house is to give it a good shake. By bombarding it with random physical forces, you simulate how stable the ladder will be when you climb on it. You can then adjust it accordingly so as to minimize the risk that it falls down with you on it.

A computational technique similar to the shaking of a ladder can test the stability of uncertain business plans, engineering designs, or military campaigns. Monte Carlo simulation, as it is known, bombards a model of the business, bridge, or battle with thousands of random inputs, while keeping track of the outputs. This allows you to estimate the chance that the business will go bust, the bridge will fall down, or the battle will be lost. The shaking forces you apply to the ladder are known as the *input probability distribution* and correspond to the uncertain demand levels for your product, the magnitudes of potential earthquakes, or the sizes of the enemy forces you will encounter. The subsequent movements of the ladder are known as the *output probability distribution* and correspond to the profit of the business, the deflection of the bridge, or the number of casualties you suffer.

This technique was developed as part of the Manhattan atomic bomb project by a Polish mathematician, Stanislaw Ulam, in 1946. Today, several software packages provide the power of Monte Carlo simulation within the environment of Microsoft Excel.

@RISK, introduced in 1987 by Palisade Corporation of Ithaca, New York, started life as an add-in for Lotus 1-2-3 before migrating to Excel.[1] In the early 1990s it took me an hour using @RISK to replicate an experiment that had taken months of FORTRAN computer programming during my graduate work in the early 1970s. Today, Palisade has a worldwide presence and offers a full range of consulting and training services.

Crystal Ball® was introduced by Decisioneering Inc. on the Macintosh in 1986 to run with Excel, and it soon moved to the Windows environment as well.[2] Crystal Ball has grown to share dominance, along with @RISK, in this burgeoning market. In a sign that Monte Carlo has now become a mainstream approach to risk modeling, Decisioneering was recently acquired by Oracle Corporation, where it has the potential to become more tightly integrated with enterprisewide information systems and impact an even larger audience. Today these software packages have over 100,000 users in industry, government, and the military.

As @RISK and Crystal Ball evolved into ever more powerful industrial packages, I needed something simpler to teach with. In 1998 I developed a package called XLSim® to go along with my text book.[3] This package stresses ease of use and has been successful in teaching the basic concepts of Monte Carlo, as well as in developing small applications.

In 2007, a package called Risk Solver from Frontline Systems ushered in a new era in simulation.[4] It is so fast that simulations are continually being performed as you *interactively* play what-if scenarios in your spreadsheet. *Interactive simulation*, as it is called, allows spreadsheet users to work with probability distributions virtually the way they do with numbers: adding them together, running them through formulas, sharing them with others, and so on. Coincidently, Risk Solver was developed by Dan Fylstra, who was one of the founding fathers of the spreadsheet revolution in the late 1970s.

The most common form of simulation used today is an Excel spreadsheet model using one of the add-on products just described. Uncertain inputs are sequentially replaced with randomly generated numbers, and the outputs of the model are recorded and analyzed. This type of simulation is the most analogous to shaking a ladder.

Other more complex forms of simulation can model processes flowing dynamically through time, such as jobs through a factory, air over a wing, or blood through an artery. These simulations are analogous to releasing a pendulum that hits a billiard ball, causing it to roll into a cascade of dominoes.

Once you have mastered Excel, the ladder-shaking variety of simulation may be accomplished with only a few additional keystrokes. The time-dependent variety takes more skill and effort, and if you haven't done it, ladder shaking is the best place to start.

 Visit FlawOfAverages.com for more on simulation and for a list of simulation software suppliers of both varieties where you can download free trials.

Doing for Probability What Edison Did for Electricity

Simulation does for uncertainty what the lightbulb does for darkness. It doesn't eliminate uncertainty any more than lightbulbs prevent the sun from setting. But simulation can illuminate the Flaw of Averages just as the bulb illuminating your basement stairway reduces the odds that you will break your neck. That's motivation enough for most people to use lightbulbs. In this context, the advance represented by interactive simulation is analogous to that of the modern instant-on incandescent bulb over its predecessor, the carbon arc lamp.

But there are still several nagging problems with simulation.

The Power Grid

To understand the first of these issues, imagine Thomas Edison walking down Madison Avenue with a box full of shiny new lightbulbs in 1880. You would think a great invention like that would be an easy sell, but it was not. Why? There was no electricity. Continuing the analogy, electricity is to lightbulbs as input probability distributions are to simulation. Most people who use lightbulbs have no idea how to generate their own electricity, so they are consumers of electricity generated by experts. Similarly, most managers have no idea how to generate input distributions, so they are potential consumers of distributions. At the other end of the spectrum are statisticians, engineers, and econometricians who are isolated in basement rooms without windows but *do* know how to generate probability distributions; that is, they are suppliers of distributions. So what industry is missing?

Distribution distribution. (Get it? Distributing distributions.)

This is the role of the scenario libraries mentioned earlier. They are the repositories of corporate intelligence on uncertainty and will be discussed in more detail in Part 3 of the book. For now, think of them as the power grid that supports the lightbulbs.

The Power Commissioner

I was discussing these ideas with Kevin Chang, a fellow passenger on a flight from San Francisco to London in 2005. Kevin, who is currently a strategist for Barclays in London, thought for a second. Then he said, "I guess this would be managed by the chief probability officer, the CPO." Thus was born another central concept of Probability Management. If simulation is the lightbulb, and the database of distributions corresponds to the power grid, then the CPO is the power commissioner, responsible for supplying safe standardized electricity. If you receive 20,000 volts when you plug in your hair dryer—whether or not you survive the fireball—the power commissioner loses his or her job. The same should happen to a CPO who fails to deliver realistic probabilities, for example, by using a model for housing prices that does not allow for values to go down.

Simulations Don't Add Up

Can you imagine a large firm assembling its entire financial state-ment using only a single giant spreadsheet? Not only would it take ages for the hundreds of managers to sequentially enter the required data, but the file would be so huge as to be completely unmanageable. That's why corporate financial statements are con-solidated from the statements of divisions, subdivisions, and smaller and smaller organizational units.

Yet until very recently this could not be easily done with simu-lations: Their results could not be added up. I will explain this property of simulations more precisely in later chapters, but for now let's return to the ladder analogy. Consider a firm that has two divisions, each facing its own uncertainties. We will model each divi-sion as its own ladder, and model the entire firm as the two ladders joined by a wooden plank. Now suppose that by shaking either lad-der by itself you would predict a 10 percent chance of its falling over. A reasonable estimate of the chance of both ladders falling over at once is 10 percent times 10 percent, or 1 percent. But when the two ladders are connected by the plank, all bets are off. Now if either ladder falls, the plank may drag the other ladder down with it. Thus, the chance of both falling at once goes from 1 percent to more like 20 percent!

To simulate the entire enterprise, you can't simply shake each ladder individually and add up the results. Instead you need to assemble both ladders and the plank first, *then* shake the whole thing, as shown in Figure 3.1. But, again, as with the single gargan-tuan financial statement spreadsheet, this just isn't practical for a large organization, let alone for a whole industry. In *The Failure of Risk Management: Why It's Broken and How to Fix It* (Wiley, 2009), Doug Hubbard notes this problem as follows: "[T]he lack of collaboration within firms makes another important step of risk management[5] almost impossible—a cooperative initiative to build models of indus-trial, economics and global risks across organizational boundaries."

Figure 3.1   The sum of the simulations of the parts is not the simulation of the whole.

One creditable attempt to measure risk at the enterprise level is known as Value at Risk (VaR), which nonetheless fell flat on its face in predicting the current financial upheaval. I will discuss VaR in more detail later, but it produces a single number (yet again) resulting from either a long chain of calculations done behind the algebraic curtain, or a huge assembly of shaken ladders connected by planks. VaR attempts to estimate the amount of money (or more) that a business unit will lose in a given time period for a given probability. For example, if the 5 percent VaR of an investment is $100,000 for the following business week, it would indicate that there is a 5 percent chance of losing at least $100,000 in the next five days.

The Consolidated Risk Statement

An important contribution of Probability Management is a method of doing simulations that *can* be added up. That is, instead of linking all your ladders together with planks, for a wide variety of simulations you can shake each ladder individually and then consolidate the results, as in a financial statement. And in the event that one business unit changes, you can reshake its ladder alone and merge the results back into the model. This offers a new distributed, collaborative approach to enterprisewide risk modeling that is backward compatible with VaR, if needed, but more general, transparent, and intuitive.

The key is a new computer data type called the *Distribution String* (*DIST*), which encapsulates distributions in a manner that allows them to be added together like numbers. Recently, an industry standards group (which included Oracle Corp., SAS Institute, and Frontline Systems, among other key players) established a standard format for this data type. Think of DISTs as the books in the scenario library. They ensure that distributions can be generated, processed, and consolidated over various applications running on different platforms.

For the past few years Probability Management has been applied to a strategic investment problem at Royal Dutch Shell.[6,7] Numerous petroleum exploration projects were simulated individually, then consolidated into a larger simulation of the entire exploration enterprise, which displayed many dimensions of risk. Recently, Merck and Co. has applied a similar approach to portfolios of pharmaceutical R&D projects. These and other cases will be discussed in more detail in subsequent chapters.

In summary, the methods of Probability Management show great promise in illuminating the Flaw of Averages, but much work remains to be done. Eventually it should be possible for firms to create consolidated, auditable risk statements, which may provide more warning about future financial upheavals of the kind we had in 2008. Ongoing developments in this area may be monitored at www.ProbabilityManagement.org.

The Wright Brothers Versus the Wrong Brothers

The Wright Brothers were always great heroes of mine, but when I learned how to fly gliders in the late 1970s (with considerable difficulty), Orville and Wilbur took on even greater stature. Not only did they build the first plane, they also learned how to fly it *without* the customary benefit of a flight instructor.

So why did their plane fly while so many before them stayed on the ground? In a word, *models.* A critical insight occurred, for example, when Wilbur sat idly twisting a long thin bicycle inner tube box with the ends torn out. Suddenly he realized that the same principle could be applied to warp the wings of an airplane to make it turn right or left. The two brothers immediately built a kite to test this concept, which was one of the cornerstones of their design. Thus the first *model* of the first airplane was a bicycle inner tube box.

Before they achieved their initial flight, they had built many more models, including several unpowered gliders that they flew themselves. Orville stated in a letter at one point that "Wilbur and I could hardly wait for morning to come, to get at something that interested us. *That's* happiness."[1] This remark conjures up images of the famous brothers soaring above the sand dunes of Kitty Hawk, North Carolina, in their glider. But, no, Orville's comment *actually* referred to their pivotal wind tunnel experiments with model wings. They were back in Ohio for the winter, making the breakthrough discoveries that separated their wing geometry from the competition's.

In contrast, consider the approach to developing the first airplane taken by a hypothetical pair of entrepreneurs whom I will call the Wrong brothers. Being venture funded, their overriding goal was to take their company public. To achieve this end, the Wrong brothers realized the need to fly large numbers of passengers great distances. Furthermore, they understood that these passengers would need to relieve themselves during the journey. Therefore, the Wrong brothers' first proud step was the construction of a fully functional outhouse, which they unveiled at an elaborate public relations event.

An ironic lesson in model building is evidenced by the fact that nothing on a modern airliner resembles a bicycle inner tube box. Yet you *will* see something that could easily be mistaken for the Wrong brothers' outhouse. The most important models are like embryos that may not resemble the final product but that nonetheless contain the developmental necessities of the application (DNA).

A Wind Tunnel for Your Business Plan

The surest way I know to detect the Flaw of Averages is to build a small spreadsheet model of your business situation and simulate the uncertainties you face. This is analogous to putting your plan in a wind tunnel. At several points throughout the book, I will present Excel spreadsheet models or animations that you can download or view at FlawOfAverages.com. The first examples were the animations that go with Chapter 1. If you are not experienced with spreadsheets, you can just do a thought experiment in your head. To get you started, I will provide a few general tips from some excellent modelers.

All models are wrong, some models are useful.
—*George Box, industrial statistician*

This quote has also been attributed to W. Edwards Deming, the father of modern quality control. Even very approximate models can help you think about a problem, but no model is exact. Models should not be taken as gospel.

You are allowed to lie a little, but you must never mislead.
—*Paul Halmos, mathematician*

Halmos, a good friend of my father's, was a renowned mathematician and a clear writer of mathematics. I was shocked when I first read his advice to lie a little to get a mathematical point across. But he also insisted that you go back and confess to the truth once your educational goal has been met. So it is with models; they do not represent the entire truth. But think of how much more misleading it is to continue using single *average* inputs.

A successful model tells you things you didn't tell it to tell you.
—*Jerry P. Brashear, Washington, D.C., consultant*

This sound advice should encourage you to model the things you *don't* understand rather than the things you *do*—that is, wings, not privies.

The five stages of model development.
—*Donald Knuth, Stanford computer scientist*

Knuth discovered that computer program development goes through five stages. These steps also apply to building models, and I rigorously adhere to them in my consulting work.

1. Decide what you want the model to do.
2. Decide how to build the model.
3. Build the model.

4. Debug the model.
5. Trash stages 1 through 4 and start again, now that you know what you really wanted in the first place.

Once you realize that step 5 is inevitable, you become more willing to discard bad models early rather than continually to patch them up. In fact, I recommend getting to step 5 many times by building an evolving set of prototypes. This is consistent with an emerging style of system development known as Extreme Programming.[2]

To get a large model to work you must start with a small model that works, not a large model that doesn't work.
> —*Alan Manne, Stanford energy economist*

To demonstrate Manne's principle, I ask you imagine two contrasting models of an actual airplane: One is a beautiful Boeing Dreamliner crafted of Lego blocks that doesn't fly.[3] The other is a simple paper airplane that does fly. From the perspective of this book, the paper model is far more accurate than the Lego block model because it can be made to demonstrate the basic principles of aerodynamics.

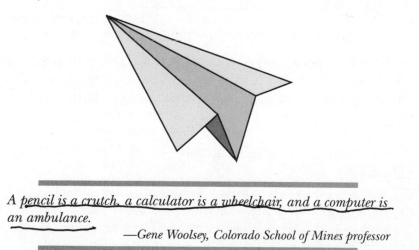

A pencil is a crutch, a calculator is a wheelchair, and a computer is an ambulance.
> —*Gene Woolsey, Colorado School of Mines professor*

A good model improves your intuition by connecting the seat of your intellect to the seat of your pants. Then the next time the situation arises, you may not need a model at all.

Clear and precise seeing becomes as one with clear and precise thinking.
—Edward Tufte, informational designer and author

Tufte has made a career of studying and promoting effective visual display. I can't recall a successful model whose results did not appear in one or more compelling graphs.

Far better an approximate answer to the right question, which is often vague, than the exact answer to the wrong question, which can always be made precise.
—John W. Tukey, chemist, statistician, and inventor
of the Fast Fourier Transform

Tukey was truly a twentieth-century renaissance scientist. He helped pioneer what is known today as visual statistics. His comments summarize how I feel about management science: that it should be applied more toward framing the right question than finding the right answer.

Always look first at what is not being modeled.
—Michael Schrage, MIT researcher and author

Schrage's book, *Serious Play*, describes how and why organizations build and play with models of reality. He stresses that by observing what people are *not* modeling, you will uncover corporate taboos. Ironically, these may be the most important things to model because they can help an organization transform itself. In my experience, something usually *not* modeled explicitly is uncertainty.[4]

[O]ur models—both risk models and econometric models—as complex as they have become, are still too simple to capture the full array of governing variables that drive global economic reality.
— Alan Greenspan, former chairman of the U.S. Federal Reserve

This appeared in Greenspan's article in the *Financial Times* in a March 16, 2008, article, in which he discussed the growing financial crisis. And in response,

> *I disagree—the models in use are not too simple, they are far too complex.*
> —*Stefan Scholtes, professor of management science,*
> *Judge Business School, Cambridge University*

Scholtes argues that the idea that we can apply engineering techniques to modeling risk in the same way that we model airflow through a jet engine is fundamentally flawed.

> *It's dumb to be too smart.*
> —*Sam L. Savage, author of this book*

I side with Scholtes on this. Model builders face a constant temptation to make things more complicated than necessary because this makes them appear more capable than they really are. Remember that a model is not the truth. It is a lie to help you get your point across. And in the case of modeling economic risk, your model is a lie about others, who are probably lying themselves. And what's worse than a simple lie? A complicated lie.

CHAPTER 5

The Most Important Instrument in the Cockpit

Mike Naylor, a vice president at Shell, has compared the oil exploration business to flying a glider. "In both cases you are taking calculated risks in search of energy," says Naylor, and he points out that in either case an academic education is inadequate. "A degree in physics might help you understand how a wing generates lift, but it won't necessarily make you a good pilot," he writes.

I like the analogy between flying a plane and managing a business—and I believe they are pretty close together on seat-of-the-intellect–seat-of-the-pants continuum, as shown in Figure 5.1.

This chapter extends Naylor's analogy to cover analytical business models: They are the instruments of the plane. Many managers are skeptical of analytical business models, and they should be.

To understand why, I will provide a short flying lesson, including time in a flight simulator for those with Internet access.

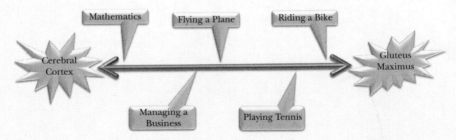

Figure 5.1   The seat-of-the-intellect–seat-of-the-pants continuum.

Learning About Learning

The pilots of small airplanes try to rationalize flying, even if the mission involves burning $50 worth of gas to buy a hamburger at a neighboring airport. Not so with glider pilots. There is no possible rationale for what they do other than the excitement of getting from point A back to point A in the longest time possible. In this particularly pure form of flight, a sleek unpowered aircraft, called a glider or sailplane, is towed up a few thousand feet by a powered tow plane and then released to soar to greater heights on invisible air currents, perhaps for hours.

Naylor has said, "I learned about learning from gliding," and I agree completely. As with scuba diving or mountain climbing, it can be thrilling if you are careful, but it is unforgiving for those who doze off in class.

Having built and flown model planes as a kid, I expected flying to come naturally to me. It didn't. The seat of my intellect and the seat of my pants were often at odds with each other, and they had to reestablish mutual trust a few thousand feet above the world in which they had teamed up to teach me to crawl, walk, run, swim, and ride a bike.

An important lesson that translates from flying to management involves making decisions based on lagged information. Here I will describe it in terms of controlling the speed of a sailplane. It sounds simple enough. Push forward on the stick, and the nose goes down, increasing the speed; pull back, and the nose comes up, slowing the plane down. You are creating your own on-demand roller coaster in midair. If you go too slowly, however, the plane will stall with a sudden loss of altitude. If, on the other hand, you go too fast, the wings will rip off. These two considerations weigh heavily on the minds of novice pilots, who reasonably focus their attention on the airspeed indicator. Unfortunately, the needle on the instrument lags the movements of the stick, resulting in unintended consequences.

Suppose you are trying to maintain 50 miles per hour, but the speed has decreased to 45 mph; the controls have become less effective, and the wind noise has dropped. You push forward on the stick and monitor the airspeed indicator until it reaches the desired 50 mph. Proud of having avoided a stall; you look back out the windshield. The entire time you were pushing forward on the stick, however, the downward pitch was increasing, so by the time you reach

50 mph, the nose is pointed dangerously toward the ground and the roller coaster is really picking up speed. Suddenly you are aware of the howling wind and look at the instruments again to see that you are now going 65. You pull back hard on the stick and watch the airspeed indicator, waiting for it to drop back to 50. By the time you reach 50 again, the nose is already pointed too high and you are destined to slow to 40, whereupon the cycle repeats with greater and greater deviations from the desired speed.

This results in the well-known phenomenon of pilot-induced oscillation (PIO), which can be violent enough to destroy the aircraft. Ironically, the short-term fix is to let go of the stick altogether until the plane settles down. But a more proactive solution is to focus on the pitch (nose-up or nose-down) attitude instead of playing catch-up with the airspeed indicator. This is done by using the seat of your intellect to create imaginary lines on the windshield corresponding to the position of the horizon at various speeds, as shown in Figure 5.2. Eventually this results in calibrating the seat of the pants, whereupon the speed is controlled by adjusting the position of the horizon in the windshield. The airspeed indicator is barely needed anymore.

A simple pitch control flight simulator is available at FlawOfAverages.com, along with links to videos of actual planes undergoing PIO.

So what is the most important instrument in the cockpit? The windshield! In fact, it is customary for flight instructors to cover up the dashboard at some point in the curriculum to force their students to "get their heads out of the cockpit," in other words, look outside and learn to fly by the seat of the pants.

Correspondingly, what is the most important source of information in business, government, or the military? It's not the display on your computer monitor, but rather the view out the window. Your customers, constituents, and adversaries are all out there waiting to be observed.

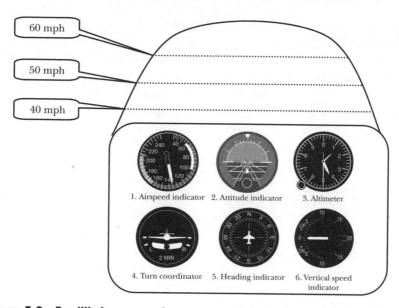

60 mph

50 mph

40 mph

1. Airspeed indicator 2. Attitude indicator   3. Altimeter

4. Turn coordinator   5. Heading indicator   6. Vertical speed
                                                  indicator

Figure 5.2   Equilibrium speeds are associated with positions of the horizon in the windshield.

And when it comes to analytical models, the most important ones, like the airspeed indicator, are for calibration. They change your thought process to the point that you may not need the models themselves any more. This is what Gene Woolsey meant by "a pencil is a crutch, a calculator is a wheelchair, and a computer is an ambulance."

Flying on Instruments: When Gut Instinct Isn't Enough

Flying through clouds is much more difficult than under visual flight conditions. Even birds avoid it. Under instrument flight rule (IFR) conditions, your intuition can misinterpret a death spiral for climbing flight. Because you cannot trust your gut in these situations, you must rely much more on your intellect and use more sophisticated instruments. Fred Abrams, a seasoned flight instructor, describes an experience from his own instrument training. He had been flying on instruments in clouds for over an hour when he started experiencing serious vertigo. His inner ear had lost all confidence in the artificial horizon on his instrument panel, and he literally no longer knew which way was up. His instructor, sensing Fred's confusion, told him to make a few small but sudden pushes and pulls on the controls while keeping his eyes on the artificial horizon. The sharp but low-level G forces had the effect of reconnecting the seat of his intellect to the seat of his pants for the remainder of the flight.

When you expect an analytical model to give you the right answer, as opposed to the right question, you are flying on instruments, and you better know exactly what you are doing. Organizations spend millions on large analytical models that they never use because no one figured out how to connect it to the seat of the CEO's pants. What is needed is some sort of interactive input that lets the user shake the controls the way Fred did when flying in the clouds. When a model builder says "This model will give you the right answer, trust me," that's the last thing the CEO should do. Too bad the financial industry was not more skeptical of the VaR models on their instrument panels in 2006 and 2007.

The best pilots do not fixate on their instruments during good visibility. However, no pilot would survive without them for more than a minute or two in the clouds. If managing a business is like flying a plane, then analytical models are analogous to the instruments. Use them to calibrate your intuition while visibility is good. Then use them with caution if you are suddenly socked in by the fog of uncertainty.

2

FIVE BASIC MINDLES
FOR UNCERTAINTY

The single biggest problem in communication is the illusion that it has taken place.
—George Bernard Shaw, Irish playwright, 1856–1950

And so it is with the typical course in probability and statistics. The subject is usually presented using classical theories, which like the steam locomotive are powerful and elegant, were developed around the same time, and are just as obsolete. This section attempts a different approach.

Just as a handle helps you grasp something with your hand, I define a Mindle (first syllable rhymes with "mind") as the analogous concept for the mind. In this section I will present five fundamental Mindles for grasping various aspects of uncertainty.

Although you may have been exposed to these concepts in the past, they were likely cloaked in Steam Era anachronisms such as VARIANCE or STANDARD DEVIATION. I refer to such technical terms as *Red Words*, and they appear in their own DISTINCTIVE FONT.

I discourage their use but will refer to them occasionally nonetheless to connect something I write in plain English (Green Words) to something you might have heard in a distant class.

If you achieve a seat of the pants understanding of this section, people will no longer be able to threaten you by blowing smoke with Red Words. To assist you further in this regard, there is a summary of the basic Mindles in Table P2.1 and a Red Word glossary at the back of the book.

TABLE P2.1 Five Basic Mindles for Grasping Uncertainty

Green Words Things you know already	Mindles Things to improve your grasp	Things to Remember	Things to Forget
Uncertainty vs. Risk	Risk is in the eye of the beholder.	Risk Attitude	UTILITY THEORY
Uncertain Number	SHAPE	Distribution Histogram Cumulative Distribution Percentiles	RANDOM VARIABLE
Combinations of Uncertain Numbers	S^{H}A^P_E	Diversification Flaw of Averages (weak form)	SIGMA, VARIANCE, STANDARD DEVIATION, CENTRAL LIMIT THEOREM
Plans Based on Uncertain Numbers	The state of the drunk at his AVERAGE position is ALIVE. But the AVERAGE state of the drunk is DEAD	Flaw of Averages (strong form)	FUNCTIONS OF RANDOM VARIABLES, JENSEN'S INEQUALITY
Interrelated Uncertainties		Scatter Plot	STATISTICAL DEPENDENCE, CORRELATION, COVARIANCE

6

MINDles Are to MINDs What HANDles Are to HANDs

O ver the years I have tested thousands of university students and midlevel executives on the basic principles of modeling uncertainty and risk. I have found that teaching probability and statistics is easy. The hard part is getting people to learn the stuff. It helps to bring one's audience to a common level of understanding; so toward that end I will start with a brief history of civilization.

1. *Humans learn to read and write.* Knowledge is preserved from generation to generation.
2. *Humans invent machines.* This culminated in the Industrial Revolution, which involved harnessing the power of physics. At the pinnacle of this era is the field of either physics or mathematics (depending on whether you ask a physicist or mathematician), followed by engineering. Below engineering is the often ignored field of industrial design, which is devoted to the development of *Handles* that allow us to grasp the power of physics with our hands.

The industrial designers are not Nobel Prize winners, but ultimately they are the enablers of the Industrial Revolution.

   3. *Machines learn to read and write.* During World War II machines began to both read *and* write information using electrical impulses, and the theoretical foundations of computer science were laid. I would call this the start of the Informational Revolution, and by all accounts we are still just witnessing its dawn.

DANZIGER

We are not harnessing physics this time. You can't grasp it with your hand. You grasp it with your mind. Thus the field of informational design,[1] which parallels that of industrial design, does not develop handles, but rather what I call *Mindles* (first syllable rhymes with "mind"), which allow us to better grasp information with both halves of our *minds*.

In his famous 1976 book, *The Selfish Gene*, Richard Dawkins defined the *meme* (rhymes with dream), as a societal analog of the gene.[2] Examples of memes include such concepts as the alphabet, farming techniques, and the wheel.

Whereas genes travel across the generations from body to body, memes take a parallel journey from mind to mind. The success of both is measured by their ability to replicate widely, yet evolve to meet changing environments without losing their essential characteristics. Most memes have evolved naturally. In contrast a Mindle is the result of intentional informational design, that is, it is a *designer meme.*

Steam Era Statistics: Things to Forget

In *Ten Rules for Strategic Innovators: From Idea to Execution*, Vijay Govindarajan and Chris Trimble observe that an important part of innovation involves forgetting the old way of thinking about something.[3] In what follows I will both introduce new Mindles for grasping uncertainty and encourage you to forget old ones.

Did you ever take a statistics course? If so, was it the high point of your week? Probably not. Now don't get me wrong, some of my best relatives were statisticians: my father and uncle, for example. But although people no longer teach steam locomotion, they do still teach *Steam Era Statistics*, whose precomputer Mindles look like bicycle equations to most of us and are better off forgotten.

Brad Efron, a Stanford University statistics professor who by his own admission is pretty good at Steam Era Statistics, is one of the founding fathers of its replacement, the modern school of Computational Statistics. But according to Efron, "As far as what we are teaching new students, statistics stopped dead in 1950."[4]

Mindle 1: Uncertainty Versus Risk

Do you skydive? Or perhaps, instead, you check your morning oatmeal for razor blades that slipped in at the factory? You probably don't do both. The branch of economics known as **UTILITY THEORY** (our first Red Word), describes an individual's willingness to incur risk in the quest for reward. I will use the name *"risk attitude"* instead and define it no further than to point out that we all have one and that it ranges from going for broke at one extreme, to covering our butts at the other.

The tension introduced during the popular TV game show, *Deal or No Deal*, is based on the contrasts between the risk attitudes of members of the audience and that of the live contestant. Imagine that you are the contestant. An idealized event on the show might go as follows. You are presented with two closed briefcases, each attended by an attractive model in a brief outfit. One case is known to contain $100, and the other is empty, but you don't know which is which. You must choose a briefcase to remove from the game, thereby keeping the contents of the other. This provides a 50/50 chance of zero or $100, for an average outcome of $50.

Before you choose, the host makes you an offer: $30 in cash to walk away and leave both briefcases behind. Is it a deal or no deal? I expect many readers would go for the gamble and incur the risk of coming home emptyhanded for the 50/50 chance of winning $100. But suppose you were a penniless wino on skid row. Given the choice between being assured of getting drunk for three days with $30 and only a 50/50 chance of getting drunk for ten days or of staying sober, the wino might well go for the guaranteed three-day binge.

Now suppose instead of $100, the amount of money is $1 million. The average this time is $500,000, and the host offers you $300,000. I expect most readers could not tolerate the risk of explaining to their wife or significant other for the rest of their lives, why they didn't just take the money and buy a new house. But if you were Bill Gates, you might say to yourself, "Three hundred grand is chump change. If I had an extra million, my foundation could fund a science lab for a year and perhaps cure a new disease."

The audience members watching this at home are all saying to themselves either, "Take the cash, you fool" or, "Go for the gamble," depending on their own risk attitudes.

Risk Is in the Eye of the Beholder

The terms "uncertainty" and "risk" are often used interchangeably, but they shouldn't be. For example, a wino and Bill Gates might attach very different risks to the same uncertainty. I consider uncertainty to be an objective feature of the universe, whereas risk is in the eye of the beholder.

Merriam-Webster's Collegiate Dictionary, 11th Edition, defines uncertainty as "the quality or state of being uncertain: doubt."

When you flip a coin, roll dice, or anticipate tomorrow's weather, you cannot predict the outcome in advance. In fact, according to Heisenberg's Uncertainty Principle, even physicists admit that the behavior of fundamental particles is ultimately uncertain. Einstein found it hard to accept that God "played dice" with the universe, but even he had to admit that God could do things that were not visible to man. I myself believe that uncertainty is an inevitable consequence of what a friend calls the Grand Overall Design, which I abbreviate as GOD. Regardless of where you believe uncertainty comes from, it is indeed an objective feature of the universe. Not so for risk.

Merriam-Webster's Collegiate Dictionary, 11th Edition, defines risk as "possibility of loss or injury."

Is there a risk that XYZ Corporation stock will go down tomorrow? Not for me. I've sold XYZ short. That is, I have engaged in a transaction that makes money only if XYZ loses value. I will suffer a loss only if it goes up.

The uncertainty is the volatility of XYZ stock; the risk depends on whether an individual is long or short. Risk is in the eye of the beholder. This is the first of the five basic Mindles of dealing with uncertainty.

You have no doubt heard the expression, "I'd bet my bottom dollar." People uttering this saying are so confident that they would stake their entire net worth on the outcome. It's a lot more convincing than "I'd bet my millionth dollar." Although a single dollar is at risk in each case, they indicate vastly different risk attitudes.

So if a tree with a coin sitting on a branch falls in the forest and no one is there to bet on the outcome, is there still risk? No. There is uncertainty as to whether the coin ends up heads or tails, but, because nobody knows or cares, there is no risk.

Things to remember:

- Risk is in the eye of the beholder (Mindle 1).
- Risk reflects how uncertain outcomes cause loss or injury to a particular individual or group.
- Risk attitude measures the willingness to incur risk in the quest of reward.

Things to forget:

- UTILITY THEORY—Use "risk attitude" instead.

Mindle 2: An Uncertain Number Is a Shape

Next month's sales, tomorrow's price of your favorite stock, or the time it will take you to get to the airport are typical of the uncertain *numbers* we face daily. And as discussed earlier, risk is often associated with uncertainty, but risk is subjective. If the sales are your own, the risk is that they will go down, whereas if they are your competitor's, the risk is that they will go up. If you own the stock, the risk is that it will go down, but if you have shorted the stock, the risk is that it will go up. If traffic on the way to the airport is worse than expected, you risk missing a flight to Europe for which you have a nonrefundable ticket. If traffic is lighter than expected, the airline risks not being able to keep your money, while reselling your seat to that standby passenger with the backpack.

This chapter presents a widely used Mindle for visualizing and communicating uncertain numbers. It is a shape with its own distinctive patterns, easily viewed from the right side of the brain.

New Brunswick Hold 'Em

"Invest $500 million to acquire a company; if it performs true to its acquisition scenario, the investment yields $1 billion in net present value. Do you want to bet?" This is how Bob Ameo began his internal executive training sessions on new business evaluation when he was director of business development for the Medical Devices & Diagnostics Group of Johnson & Johnson in New Brunswick, New Jersey. The give-me-a-number mentality can hide the obvious fact that starting any new venture is a gamble. Next Bob answered his own question, "Whether you bet or not depends on the chances of winning, that is, the odds."

Bob, who has a PhD in psychology, has always liked statistics. In his first career, however, he was a practicing psychologist helping individuals, couples, and families make constructive and needed changes in their lives. "Organizations, like people, need to overcome their behavioral inertia—the tendency to keep doing what they have been doing," says Bob. "The long-term benefits of analyzing and managing risk and uncertainty, like the long-term benefits of healthy eating or exercise, are competing with immediate reinforcers (ice cream sundaes, or the excitement of closing a high profile acquisition)," he continues. Bob views the management of uncertainty as a discipline, requiring a commitment to trade short-term rewards for long-term gains. He teaches that a new venture is a gamble, that a gamble has odds, and that odds must be at least estimated. What a concept.

"Whether you are playing a friendly game of Texas Hold 'Em or evaluating a major investment for Johnson & Johnson (New Brunswick Hold 'Em) you need to know the odds."

Uncertain Numbers: The Shape of Things to Come

Statisticians often describe a numerical uncertainty using the Red Words, RANDOM VARIABLE, but I will stick with "*uncertain number*."

Think of it as a shape, the shape of things to come. Statisticians call it the *probability distribution*, or just *distribution* for short, and so do I. This is the second basic Mindle for grasping uncertainty.

Consider, for example, an R&D program for an experimental drug. The long-term economic value of the program (an uncertain number if there ever was one) might look something like Figure 8.1, in which the heights of the bars represent the relative likelihood of the various outcomes. Note that the sum of the heights must be 100 percent, because there is a 100 percent chance that *something* will happen.

You might have expected "distribution" to be a Red Word, and you may not have used it yourself in casual conversation. If that's the case, don't worry, this is the only formerly Red Word in the whole book that I will urge you to adopt, because it is essential to replace numbers with distributions to cure the Flaw of Averages. Here, I'll use it in plain English to show you how easy it is. The distribution of economic value in Figure 8.1 has three bumps:

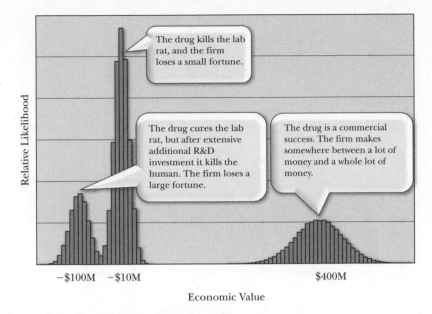

Figure 8.1   **Uncertain economic value.**

1. A short fat bump on the right indicates a wide range of possible profits centered around $400 million.
2. A tall skinny bump in the middle indicates a good chance of losing pretty close to $10 million.
3. A short skinny bump on the left indicates an uncomfortably large probability of losing around $100 million.

Although statisticians view distributions in other ways as well, some of which will make your head spin, I like to start with this bar graph representation, which is called a *histogram*.

So suppose you are managing the R&D program pictured in Figure 8.1, and the head bean counter asks you what value it should have on the books. When you tell him that the "R" in R&D stands for research, and that it's highly uncertain, he gives you a cold look and says, "Give me a number." Now what number would *you* use to characterize this shape? It is common to use the *average*, also known as the *mean*, or *expected value*, but most people don't even know what these terms really refer to. This being a book on averages, I will define the word "average."

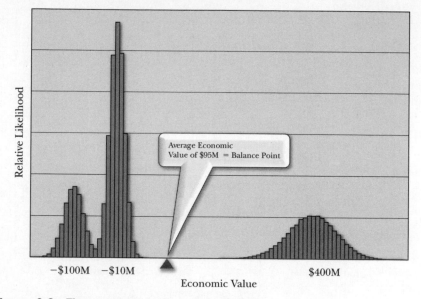

Figure 8.2 The average is the balance point.

The *average* of a bunch of numbers is the sum of the numbers divided by the size of the bunch. For example, the average of 3 and 7 is $(3 + 7) \div 2 = 5$.

But averages also apply to uncertain numbers. For the average value of the R&D project, imagine that you could repeat the project a million times in a million parallel universes. If you added up the economic outcomes of each one and divided by a million, you would get the *average* value of the project, which is a single number.

Here is a Mindle that relates the average of an uncertain number to its shape. Imagine that the bar graph were sawed out of wood. Then it turns out that the average is where the thing would balance. In the case of the R&D project, this is $95 million, as shown in Figure 8.2.

But give me a break,

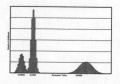 is not equal to 95.

The Weak Form of the Flaw of Averages

So what's really wrong with representing an uncertain number by its average? I call this the *Weak Form of the Flaw of Averages*, and here is an extreme example. If you hijack an airliner, ask for $1 billion, and have one chance in 1,000 of getting away with it, your average take is $1 million. But no one would characterize a hijacking as making a million dollars. As we will see in a future chapter, the Strong Form of the Flaw of Averages is worse, in that you don't even get the average right. The only way to avoid these problems is to stop thinking of uncertainties as single numbers and begin thinking of them as shapes, or distributions.

"So," you say, "I can see how a single number doesn't give the whole picture, but how the heck would you even come up with a shape like the one shown in Figure 8.1?" Maybe you never would come up with it on your own and would instead receive it from the chief probability officer. But it's important for you to understand the concept well enough to interpret the results; so here's some practice with a much simpler investment opportunity.

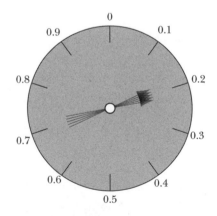

Someone gives the game board spinner, shown here, a good whack. The pointer will come to rest somewhere between 0 and 0.999999999, whereupon you receive that amount multiplied by $1 million. Thus a spin of 0.65213947 returns $652,139.47.

Oops, I forgot to tell you about your risk. A return of $200,000 or less will result in financial ruin, you will lose your house and car, and your love interest will run off with the hairdresser.

The uncertainty underlying the investment is the number indicated by the pointer. The risk is that the value comes in at 0.2 or less. Now test your intuition on the following questions:

- What is the average return of this investment?
- What is the chance of ruin?
- Which shape in Figure 8.3 represents the bar graph (histogram) of the spinner?

You could answer all these questions by spinning a spinner thousands of times while tediously writing down each resulting number on a clipboard, but can you simulate it in your head? I suggest that you take a shot at each of these questions now, before continuing.

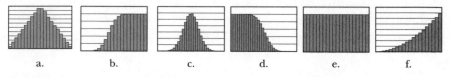

a.   b.   c.   d.   e.   f.

Figure 8.3   Sample histograms.

Are you ready for a bike ride? This is one of those times when a picture is worth a thousand words, and a simulation is worth a thousand pictures. So if you're near a computer, I suggest a visit to FlawOfAverages.com.

The latest simulation software can perform 10,000 spins nearly instantaneously, but at Chapter 8 on the web site you will be able to run a slow-motion simulation of the spinner to see how a histogram is generated, and answer these questions.

If you ran the simulation on the web, you will have seen that each time the spinner is spun, the bar in the graph corresponding to that number is raised by one notch. That is, if the spin is between 0 and 0.2, the first bar is raised; if it is between 0.2 and 0.4, the second bar is raised, and so on. Figure 8.4 shows a possible histogram

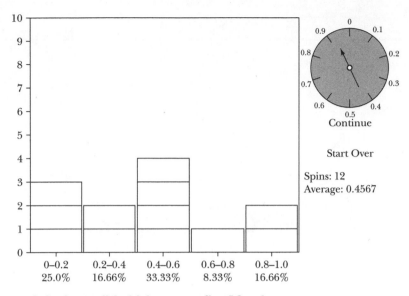

Figure 8.4   A possible histogram after 12 spins.

after 12 spins. Because the numbers are generated randomly, the exact results are different each time you run the simulation.

But after 1 million spins, regardless of how things looked near the beginning, the histogram will have converged to that of Figure 8.5. This answers the questions regarding average return, chance of ruin, and the histogram's shape.

The average return is roughly $500,000. The chance of falling into the ruinous first bin of the histogram is 20 percent, and the correct shape is Figure 8.3(e).

Although this flat shape is simple enough to work out from first principles, many graduates of statistics courses get it wrong. Of the thousands of subjects I have tested on these questions, roughly a third draw something like histogram (c) in Figure 8.3.[1,2,3] This would mean that some numbers are more likely than others, which isn't possible given the symmetry of the spinner. In the words of Mark Twain, such students have let their schooling interfere with their education.

Bob Ameo distributed a spreadsheet histogram template to J&J managers to help them grasp the shapes of various ventures (Figure 8.6). Playing what-if with the parameters of a deal and clicking the calculate button caused the histogram and other risk

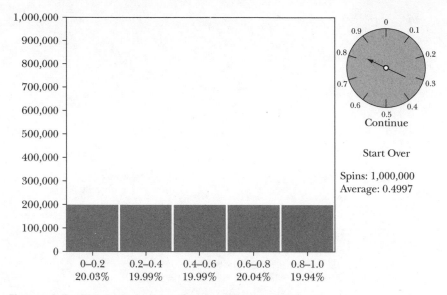

Figure 8.5   The histogram after 1 million spins.

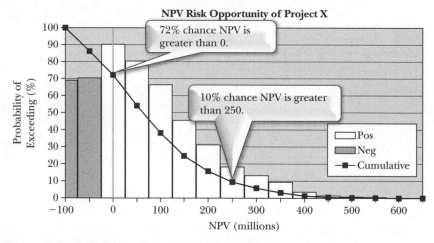

Figure 8.6   Bob Ameo's investment risk graph.

Source: Graph courtesy of Johnson & Johnson.

indicators to change immediately. The white bars in Ameo's histogram display positive outcomes, and the shaded ones reflect negative outcomes. Interactive displays of this type can help management visualize the risk implications of their decisions far better than single numbers.

The smooth line on this graph, known as the *cumulative distribution,* displays a different representation of the same information. This curve indicates the chance of exceeding any given NPV. Thus, according to the graph, there is a 72 percent chance of making at least *some* money, and a 10 percent chance of making *more* than $250 million. People typically use histograms to eyeball the relative odds of various outcomes, while the cumulative graph is for reading off more accurate probabilities of achieving different levels of success.

Ameo, now a private consultant, continues to model decisions made under uncertainty as gambles. "I like to be the 'handicapper' or odds setter when asked to create uncertainty analyses of potential investments," he jokes.

Give Me a Distribution

If we are ever to conquer the Flaw of Averages, bosses must begin to ask for distributions rather than numbers. But you can't just give your boss a picture of a histogram. How would you plug such a thing into your business plan?

This is where Probability Management comes in. The Distribution String (DIST), introduced in Chapter 3, is a way of storing a probability distribution in a single data element. In terms of the spinner, think of the DIST as consisting of the outcomes of one thousand spins, stuffed, like a genie in a bottle, into a single cell in your spreadsheet. This concept will be discussed in more detail in the last section of the book.

Black Swans

So once you have the histogram of an uncertain number, you know all there is to know about the distribution of outcomes. Right?

Of course not.

Take the spinner, for example. What if you spin the pointer so hard, that it flies off and hits you in the eye, or what if the friction of rotation sets the cardboard on fire, burning down your house? You won't find those outcomes in the typical histogram of a spinner, and if I hadn't suggested them, you would never have imagined them. But they could happen.

The philosopher, Karl Popper, referred to such events as Black Swans, because for hundreds of years the residents of Europe could not conceive of a swan that wasn't white. When a seventeenth-century explorer discovered a black swan in Australia, it made quite a stir.

Nassim Nicholas Taleb has refined this concept in his recent book, *The Black Swan: The Impact of the Highly Improbable*.[4] His definition of a Black Swan is an event that (1) has never occurred before, (2) would have an extreme impact if it did occur, and (3) is easy to explain after the fact. Examples include the rise of Google, the 9/11 attack, or the pointer flying off a game board spinner and hitting you in the eye. I would not call the financial meltdown of 2008 a black swan because there were far more warnings than for 9/11, and indeed a number of people saw it coming and got rich as a result.

So although a histogram is a great way to start visualizing uncertainty, don't forget that extreme events can and do occur and that they are difficult to account for in advance. The best defense against Black Swans is the right half of your brain. Psychologist Gary Klein has developed an exercise he calls the *Pre Mortem*[5] that helps in this regard. The idea is to vividly all imagine your plans in shambles, and then creatively explain how it all went bad.

Things to remember:

- An *uncertain number* is a SHAPE known as its *distribution*. (Mindle 2).
- A common way to display the distribution is in a bar graph, known as a *histogram*. The heights of the bars indicate the relative likelihood that the number takes on various values, and they must sum to 100 percent.
- Another important shape is the *cumulative distribution*, which shows the probability that the number is less than a given value.
- The *average*, also known as the *mean* or *expected value*, of the uncertain number is the balance point of the distribution.
- Creatively imagine Black Swans not included in the distribution.

Things to forget:

- RANDOM VARIABLES—Use "uncertain numbers" instead.

A Word from Your Author

If this stuff is too technical for you, feel free to jump to the next chapter; otherwise, read on.

Some More Stuff on Distributions

Continuous Distributions

In Steam Era Statistics, distributions were often represented as smooth curves instead of bar graphs. This just gives statistics professors an excuse to slip CALCULUS into their courses, as if you weren't bored and confused enough already. But technically speaking, smooth curves disappeared the day a computer scientist discovered that the smallest positive number was 2^{-32} (that was a joke for mathematicians, because really there isn't a smallest positive number). If your left brain is obsessed with perfectly smooth curved distributions, just make a histogram with a whole lot of really narrow bars. This is the perfect place for me to take Paul Halmos's advice to lie a little. If you think of an uncertain number as a bar graph, you will not be seriously misled.

Median and Mode

Two concepts related to the average are the *median* and the *mode*.

The *median* is the quantity that the uncertain number has a 50/50 chance of being greater than or less than. That is, it is the point at which the bars add up to exactly 50 percent. If the histogram is symmetric in shape around its middle, the median is the same as the average, but this is not always the case. For example, suppose you have ten people in a room, whose average income is $80,000. The median income is also likely to be about $80,000, with half earning more and half less. If you now replace one of those people with Warren Buffet, the median income in the room stays about the same, because half still earn less than $80,000. But on average, they are now all multimillionaires.

The *mode* is the place at which the histogram has its highest peak: –$10 million in Figure 8.1. The mode is also called the most likely, but from the figure you can see how misleading this description is. In any event, the median and the mode are again single numbers, which fail to capture the shape.

The Law of Averages and Where It Fails

The longer you run the simulation of the spinner, the closer the average will tend toward 0.5000. Run the simulation at the web site a few times if you don't believe me. This is an example of the *Law*

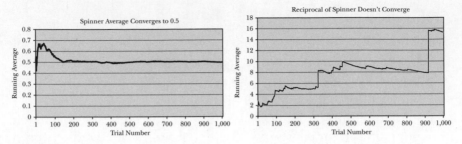

Figure 8.7   Running averages of the spinner and its reciprocal.

of Averages, which states that if you repeatedly take samples of the same type of uncertain number, the average of the samples will converge to a single result: the true average of the uncertain number.

This law is widely misinterpreted by people who think it justifies plugging in averages everywhere in place of uncertainties, and by now you know where that leads. But the Law of Averages sometimes fails all on its own. Because the Law of Averages is true for most uncertain numbers, it has served as a challenge to contrarian mathematicians over the years to invent pathological distributions that don't even *have* averages.

Don't worry, these sorts of uncertainties rarely appear in daily life, but here is an example. Consider the number 1 divided by the outcome of the spinner (that is, take the reciprocal of the spinner). Figure 8.7 shows the running average of 1,000 spins of the spinner on the left and its reciprocal (1/the number on the spinner) on the right.

In the left-hand graph, by the time 150 trials have been run, the average has reached 0.5, and it barely moves from then on. In the right-hand graph, the average looks like it has converged to 8 by trial 900. But shortly afterward, a single spin came so close to zero, that its reciprocal was huge, dragging the average from 8 to 16 in one shot. In theory, this graph would never converge, and the uncertain number would have no average, thereby kicking the law of averages in the teeth.

CHAPTER

9

Mindle 3: Combinations of Uncertain Numbers

On a June morning in 2000, Rick Medress, the president of Cineval LLC, and I sat on the veranda of the Georgian Hotel in Santa Monica, California, looking out across Ocean Avenue to the Pacific. In front of us, Medress's laptop computer displayed the distribution of the profits of a set of films (Figure 9.1).

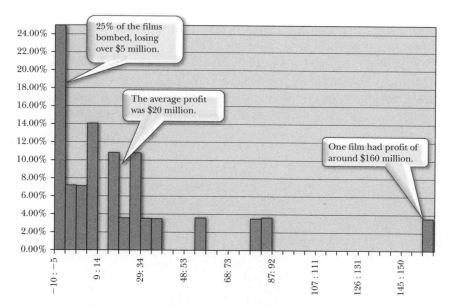

Figure 9.1 **Distribution of film revenues in millions.**

Source: Courtesy of Cineval LLC.

Medress had received a degree in Near Eastern languages from Berkeley, did a stint in the Peace Corps, worked overseas, and then got an MBA from UCLA before ending up at a large New York bank. One of his assignments at the bank was to establish a line of credit for the film company that had produced the 1987 hit *Dirty Dancing* and several less successful films. From this and similar projects, Medress gained expertise in valuing theatrical and television property rights. After working as an entertainment banker for several years, he founded his own valuation firm, Cineval LLC, in the mid-1990s.

In early 2000, Medress attended a simulation seminar of mine in Palo Alto. During lunch he described how he was putting together an investment in film properties and wondered whether it made sense to simulate the uncertainty of the portfolio for the investors. I told him it would be dereliction of fiduciary duty if he did *not* run a simulation, and a few weeks later we had our meeting at the Georgian in Santa Monica near his office to explore the idea.

A Portfolio of Spinners

Before addressing how a portfolio of films would behave, let's start with a much simpler investment: a portfolio of spinners.

Recall the investment in the last chapter, in which the outcome of a spinner was multiplied by $1 million. Also remember that a spin of less than 0.2 resulted in ruin. The average return of the investment was $500,000, with a 20 percent chance of disaster.

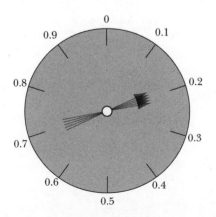

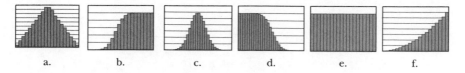

Figure 9.2   Sample histograms.

Now imagine that you're about to take the plunge on the spinner investment, when another opportunity arises. In the prospectus for the new investment it states that *two* spinners will be spun. The results will be averaged and then multiplied by $1 million. That is,

Return = $1 million × [(Spin 1 + Spin 2) ÷ 2]

Again you will be ruined if the return is less than $200,000. How does this second investment compare to the first? The average return is still $500,000.

What is the shape of the average of two spinners? (See Figure 9.2.) Go ahead, make a guess before continuing.

If you're ready for another bike ride, visit FlawOfAverages. com and click on Chapter 9 to simulate the two-spinner investment. If you've already had enough exercise today, read on.

To understand what happens when you spin two spinners, I find it useful to think about what happens when you roll dice. If you roll a single die, you can get the numbers 1 through 6 with equal likelihood, as displayed in Figure 9.3.

When you roll *two* dice, you can get any of the numbers from 2 through 12. If you think these occur with equal likelihood, meet me at the craps game behind Joe's Bar and Grill tonight—and don't forget your wallet.

Figure 9.3   The outcomes of rolling one die.

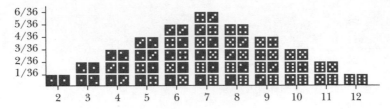

Figure 9.4   Combinations of two dice.

There are more combinations for getting numbers at the center of the distribution than at the ends; so the shape goes up in the middle, as shown in Figure 9.4.

Similarly, two spins of the spinner can average 0.5 in many more ways than either 0 or 1; so this distribution also goes up in the middle, as shown in Figure 9.5. Congratulations if you chose shape (a) in Figure 9.2, but I will give you full credit for shape (c) as well. Only about half the graduates of statistics courses that I test get *this* one right.

So what happens when you combine more than two spinners or dice? Figures 9.6a and 9.6b display these results.

 At FlawOfAverages.com, you can simulate other numbers of spinners as well.

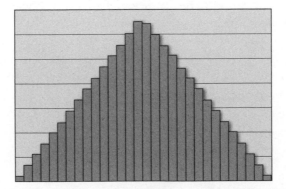

Figure 9.5   The histogram of the average of two spinners.

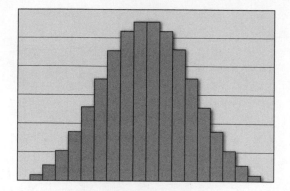

Figure 9.6 (a)   The histogram of three spinners.

Figure 9.6 (b)   The histogram of three dice.

So What?

You've been patiently reading this chapter in hopes of learning something practical about uncertainty and risk, and all I've told you is that one spinner is flat and that a combination of spins goes up in the middle. What does that have to do with risk?

Everything. That's why this is the third Mindle for grasping uncertainty. If the distribution goes up in the middle, it must go down on the ends; so in the case of the spinner investment, there's

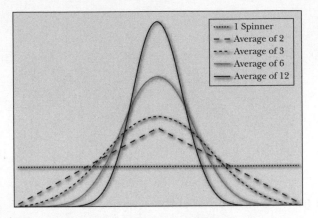

Figure 9.7   The effects of the central limit theorem.

less chance of ruin. In fact, the chance of ruin with two spins is only 8 percent as compared to 20 percent with the single spin. This is proportionally a greater risk reduction than going from two bullets to one bullet in a game of Russian roulette!

This phenomenon is described by something you saw in your probability or statistics class: the **CENTRAL LIMIT THEOREM**. It implies that, as you add up or average more and more independent uncertain numbers, the shape of the histogram approaches the famous *bell-shaped,* or **NORMAL** distribution, as shown in Figure 9.7.

By the time you have averaged 12 spinners, the shape is so close to the **NORMAL DISTRIBUTION** that even their own mothers couldn't tell them apart. Note that I have used smooth curves here instead of histograms, because five overlaid histograms on a single graph would cover each other up.

Diversification: A Green Word for the
CENTRAL LIMIT THEOREM

Let's rest our horses here for a bit because we've been riding through Red Word territory, and I want to give the stragglers time to catch up. As to the **NORMAL DISTRIBUTION**, most people will get through life just fine substituting the term "bell-shaped." However, the **CENTRAL LIMIT THEOREM** is a bit trickier. It is far too red to mention in, say, a singles bar, but far too important to ignore. Luckily there is a Green Word that comes sufficiently close.

What is a Green Word for why the distribution of two spins or two dice goes up in the middle? *Diversification*.

Hey, I didn't say the word would help you score in a singles bar, but at least it won't get you kicked out. Although it doesn't mean exactly the same thing as **CENTRAL LIMIT THEOREM**, diversification does describe its most important effect on daily life, which is captured in the old adage about not putting all your eggs in one basket. Diversifying your investment across two dice or two spinners increases the chance of an average outcome and reduces the chance of extreme outcomes.

As explained in the last chapter, spinners—and dice for that matter—are a great way to think about uncertainty and risk. In fact, Harry Markowitz's seminal book on Portfolio Theory begins with a discussion of spinners.[1] However, diversification has similar effects with almost any type of distribution, such as that of movie profits.

You Don't Need to Know

Take a look at Figure 9.8, which is the same as Figure 9.1, showing 28 live-action films of a particular genre, which had been selected

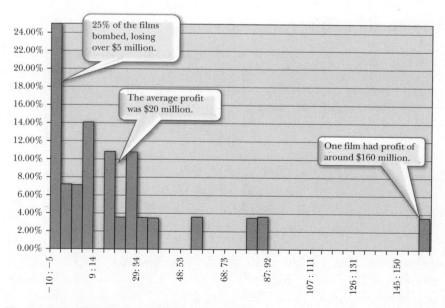

Figure 9.8   Distribution of film revenues.

so as not to overrepresent any single theme or star. The average profit was $20 million, but 25 percent of the films bombed badly, losing over $5 million each. One of the films was something of a *Titanic* (the movie, not the ship) that racked up $160 million.

Medress and I took just a few minutes to build a model in Excel and to simulate the outcomes of portfolios of various numbers of films on the computer. Conceptually, it worked like this. Imagine painting each of the 28 movie profits on ping-pong balls and throwing them into a lottery basket. Now if you crank the lottery basket and pull out a ball, you will get an uncertain number. How is that number distributed? You don't need to know. It is simply the distribution of the original numbers on the ping-pong balls.

Technically, this approach is known as *resampling*, because all you do is resample the ping-pong balls over and over, throwing them back into the basket after each draw. It is a basic building block of computational statistics that will be covered in a later chapter. Of course, a computer can simulate hundreds of thousands of cranks of a lottery basket per second, so it goes a lot faster than it did when the founding fathers of Steam Era Statistics compelled their graduate students to perform such drudgery with dice and real numbered balls to confirm their theories.

The Power of Diversification

If you invest in a single film chosen at random from this genre, Figure 9.8 provides a reasonable estimate for the shape of your profit, with an average of $20 million and a 25 percent chance of losing your shirt. Medress and I simulated what would happen if you diversified your investment over two or more films drawn independently from this distribution. The simulation shows that the average profit does not change as you diversify. However, because the losers and blockbusters tend to balance each other out, the shapes of resulting histograms and hence the risk of loss differ greatly, as shown in Figure 9.9. Note how rapidly the chance of losing your shirt (defined here as losing $5 million or more) drops as the portfolio is diversified.

After viewing these results, I observed that only a fool would invest in a slate of less than four films. Medress responded, "It takes some people decades to learn that." Although it might not be practical to create a portfolio of a really large number of films, it is instructive to see how bell-shaped the distribution would become

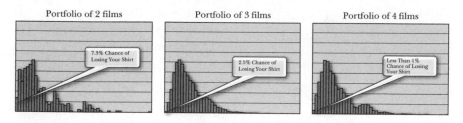

Figure 9.9 The effects of diversifying across films.

Source: Courtesy of Cineval LLC.

FlawOfAverages.com has an animation of the diversification of film portfolios.

if you could invest in 10 or 100 films, as shown in Figure 9.10. This clearly shows that, as you increase your diversification, you reduce both the upside potential and downside risk of your investment.

Poster Child for the CENTRAL LIMIT THEOREM

A few months after we had performed this simulation, Medress phoned me up. "It works with the animated feature film database as well!" he reported excitedly. "What works?" I inquired. "When you simulate diversified portfolios based on historical animation revenues, the outcomes become bell-shaped just as they did with live-action films," he explained.

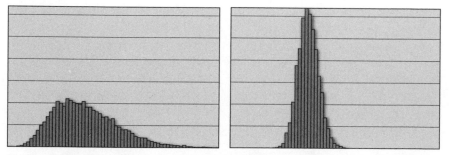

Figure 9.10 The effects of further diversification: Portfolio of 10 films (left) versus a portfolio of 100 films (right).

I grabbed my probability textbook off the shelf and looked it up. Sure enough, he was right; the CENTRAL LIMIT THEOREM *does* apply to animated features as well as to live-action films! (OK, I'm pulling your leg on the textbook part, but some statisticians find this bit hysterical. I hope this is of benefit to nonstatisticians who are nonetheless interested in statistician humor.)

Of course, the CENTRAL LIMIT THEOREM applies to animations. It's like gravity; it applies to basically *everything*. Medress first used simulation while assisting a domestic television distributor who was raising funds for TV movies and miniseries. The distributor was able to provide him with representative historical data to resample, as described earlier. But Medress warns that this is not always easy to come by.

"Most studios are reluctant to release revenue on a by-title basis for competitive reasons," he says, "making it difficult to accurately forecast the range of outcomes of a new film." He points out that when he started using Monte Carlo simulation in 2000, its application to film investments was pretty limited. "But in recent years," Medress continues, "its use has expanded greatly, as hedge funds and private equity firms have invested in theatrical film funds." And without actual data, a number of advisers have used their own estimates to drive their simulations. According to Medress, "In some cases, investors have been lulled into a false sense of comfort by receiving sophisticated statistical analyses which support their required equity returns, but the output was based on hypothetical rather than actual data, with disastrous results."

Here is how Medress worked around the data problem in modeling a recent fund to produce a slate of independent films: "I reviewed a list of all films that this group of producers had made over the years and compared the budget to domestic box office receipts as a performance metric." Both of these numbers were available in publicly available databases. Medress then excluded films that were not comparable to those planned for the fund. "The films they planned to put into their film fund," he says, "have lower budgets than blockbuster films that the same producers had made at large studios. Furthermore," he continues, "some actors were not expected to participate in films of the planned genre." This left him with approximately 50 films that he believed to be statistically similar to those in the fund. "I then ran a Monte Carlo simulation of the films they planned to make in the fund based on the historical ratios of budget to domestic box office receipts," he goes on. "I was able to provide management, investors, and lenders with insight into the optimum capital structure, levels of risk at different performance results, and expected returns to the various stakeholders."

Only about a quarter of my graduate students correctly draw both the single- and double-spin histograms, yet almost all have seen the CENTRAL LIMIT THEOREM in a statistics course. After drawing a flat histogram for the average of two spinners, a PhD student told me sheepishly that he thought it would take more than two spinners before the shape started going up in the middle. Actually the step from one spinner to two is the most dramatic in this regard. Hopefully, like Rick Medress, you will internalize the lessons of diversification and apply them often.

Things to remember:

- A combination of uncertain numbers is a $_SH^AP_E$ that goes up in the middle (Mindle 3).
- This effect arises from *diversification*.
- When enough independent uncertain numbers are added together, the resulting distribution becomes bell-shaped.

Things to forget:

- CENTRAL LIMIT THEOREM—Use "diversification" instead.
- NORMAL DISTRIBUTION—Use "bell-shaped distribution" instead.

CHAPTER

10

I Come to Bury SIGMA,
Not to Praise it

We have seen that representing an uncertain number by a single point provides no indication of risk or uncertainty. So, long ago, even before the Steam Era, mathematicians came up with a yardstick for measuring the degree of uncertainty that has become the gold standard. Unfortunately, it is a Red Word: SIGMA (the Greek letter σ), also known as the STANDARD DEVIATION. People also often refer to the square of SIGMA, which is known as the VARIANCE or σ^2. One Red Word is confusing enough, let alone three of them and a Greek letter that all mean pretty much the same thing. Basically, they all measure how wide the distribution of an uncertain number is. This is usually obvious from looking at the shape (see Figure 10.1). The wider the distribution is, the greater is the possible variation and the higher the value of SIGMA and the VARIANCE.

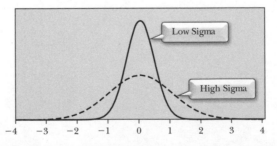

Figure 10.1 Distributions with the same average but different degrees of variation.

I have asked thousands graduate students and managers over the years to indicate by a show of hands whether they could write the formula for SIGMA. Although virtually all have heard the term, only a small fraction can actually define it. What kind of gold standard is that?

You may have heard of SIX SIGMA, a set of practices for improving the quality of manufactured goods or services, originally developed by Motorola. In the hands of technically competent managers, this can reduce the variability of a product or service, yielding more consistent quality. However, I was shocked recently when I found that even a group of managers in an executive education class, who had prior SIX SIGMA training, still couldn't define SIGMA!

For comparison, I also ask people which pedal would they step on if a kid suddenly ran out in front of their car chasing a soccer ball. For this question, the entire class responds immediately. Now *that's* a standard for you. And to their credit, even the few misanthropes who claim they would step on the gas pedal instead of the brake respond quickly and decisively.

Ah, some readers are thinking, the solution to this problem is a better way of teaching people what SIGMA really means. Wrong. Not only is it hard to understand, but in my book it's pretty much obsolete (and this *is* my book).

Before providing a formal definition of SIGMA, an analogy will be useful. Imagine that learning the value of a particular uncertain number corresponded to apprehending a criminal. Then the average and SIGMA are comparable to the height and weight of the suspect, and they provide little detail. This may be important in a Sherlock Holmes mystery, but today we use security cameras, mug shots, and DNA samples to nail the bad guy. These high-tech forensic tools are analogous to the outputs of simulations as described next and as seen earlier in Bob Ameo's deal-visualizing simulation template at Johnson & Johnson.

Outputs of Simulations

In Figure 10.2, the histogram (at the top right) was introduced in Chapter 8. This is the shape of the uncertain number (perhaps the

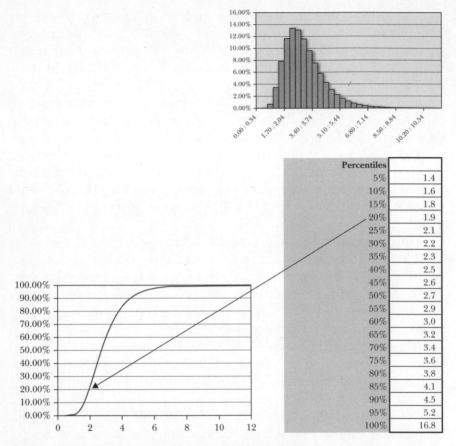

Figure 10.2   The Primary Outputs of Simulation.

facial features of your suspect) showing the relative likelihoods of its possible outcomes. The balance point of this graph is the average.

The cumulative graph displays the chance that the uncertain number is less than any particular value. The same information is carried in the percentiles, shown on the right. For example, the 20th percentile is 1.9, meaning that there is a 20 percent chance that this uncertain number will be less than or equal to 1.9. Note that the 5 percent Value at Risk (VaR), introduced in Chapter 1, is basically a fancy name for the 5th percentile of the distribution. The acronym VaR is good, though, from the standpoint of Mindle management, because it reminds us that it plays a somewhat similar role to that of the obsolete concept of VARIANCE.

One additional Mindle is required to understand *groups* of uncertainties: the interrelationships between them, as discussed shortly. This might correspond to the gang affiliation of our suspect. But when uncertain numbers travel *alone*, the graphs and percentiles of Figure 10.2 contain all there is to know about them. In the special case that the uncertain number has a perfect bell-shaped distribution, the average and SIGMA, taken together, provide a shorthand notation for the *same* information. But for all other distributions, they provide *less* information. I am now ready to provide a working definition of SIGMA.

Definition of SIGMA

SIGMA is an anachronism of the Steam Era whose primary function is to discourage people from trying to understand probability and statistics.

SIGMA did play an important historical role in the development of theoretical probability and statistics, and it is still used today in many areas of science and in quality control. But for most of us, it is irrelevant and becoming increasingly so with the spread of Computational Statistics. I suggest using the word "*variation*" instead, because it sounds sort of like VARIANCE, has a similar meaning, and is not Red. I would have liked to have included a bit more on this subject in the book, but did not want to risk making some of my readers lose their lunch. The beauty of the Internet is that I can put such material on the web for those who want it.

 At FlawOfAverages.com I provide a brief history of SIGMA, *discuss confidence intervals, and present a more mathematical but still far from traditional definition of* SIGMA.

Things to remember:

- Histogram
- Cumulative graph
- Percentiles
- Variation

Things to forget:

- STANDARD DEVIATION, SIGMA, VARIANCE, and σ—Use the phrase "degree of variation" instead of any of these, but then back it up with the "percentiles of the distribution."

Mindle 4: Terri Dial and the Drunk in the Road

"Consider a drunk staggering down the middle of a busy highway," I told a group of Wells Fargo bank executives in 1995, "and assume that his average position is the centerline. Then the state of the drunk at his *average* position is alive, but on *average* he's dead."[1]

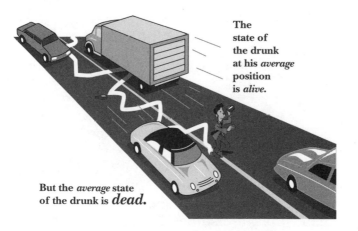

The state of the drunk at his *average* position is *alive*.

But the *average* state of the drunk is *dead*.

Practically before the words were out of my mouth, one of the bankers exclaimed: "Why that's the reason we always blow the budget on our incentive plan!"

I wasn't yet sure what she meant by this, but I knew that Terri Dial had just detected a case of the Strong Form of the Flaw of Averages. Terri had started her banking career as a teller in the 1970s, had worked her way up to executive vice president, and was two years away from being the chief executive of the retail banking division of Wells Fargo. The bank had difficulty in forecasting the total paid out in incentive bonuses, and Terri was looking for new perspectives on the problem.

She explained her insight with a simplified example, as follows. Suppose the number of checking accounts sold per year by employees varied widely but averaged 200. To increase performance, you decide to reward everyone with above-average sales (201 or more), with a $1,000 bonus, while everyone else gets zero. I have heard some in the industry refer to such a hurdle as a "champagne moment." On *average* how much do you need to pay each employee? Well, the bonus of the *average* employee is zero because they don't make the hurdle of 201 sales. So zero must be the *average* bonus. Right? Think again.

Roughly half of your employees will be drinking champagne, so the *average* bonus paid is around $500. Of course, the real problem is more complex, but it should be clear that designing an incentive plan around an average employee is futile.

The Strong Form Versus the Weak Form

As explained earlier, there are two flavors of the Flaw of Averages. Recall that as Rick Medress diversified across multiple films, the risk changed, but the *average* profit remained $20 million. In representing the profit of each film by its average, you are blind to the risk implications, but at least you get the *average* profit of the portfolio right. That's the Weak Form.

The Strong Form is worse; you don't even get the *average* right. The bonus of the *average* employee is *not* the *average* bonus. This is the fourth Mindle for grasping uncertainty. Recall the following examples of the strong form from Chapter 1.

- The average (or expected) profit from microchip production was less than the profit associated with the average demand.
- The average (or expected) duration of the software project was greater than that implied by the average duration of its subroutines.
- The average (or expected) monthly cost of managing the perishable antibiotic was greater than the cost associated with average demand.

It's Too Hard to Change the Way People Do Business

I am always thrilled when someone like Terri grasps a new concept such as the Flaw of Averages. Like a successful first date, one is left with a sense of anticipation. But frankly, the most common result of such an encounter is deafening silence. Even if some manager sees the light, it's "too hard to change the way people do business." So when Wells Fargo didn't call, write, or send flowers, I wasn't surprised.

But that was before I knew what to expect from Terri Dial. I'm sure the rest of the people in the room knew it would not be the last they would hear of the drunk in the road. As it turned out, Wells Fargo was then in the process of acquiring another bank, which consumed their attention for the next couple of years. But with that behind them in 1997, I got a call from Matthew Raphaelson, a former student and my primary contact at Wells. They wanted me to visit again.

When I arrived at Matthew's office, I was amazed. Wells was using Crystal Ball simulation software to model bonus incentive plans and several other activities involving uncertainty. When the light-bulb had gone on for Terri Dial two years earlier, it stayed on. The expression "too hard to change the way people do business" is not in the Dial vocabulary, which helped earn her the nickname of the Human Cyclone at Wells. Since then the bank has maintained a culture of analytical thinking and Flaw-of-Averages awareness through continued executive education programs.

Tugging at the Distribution

Today, Wells Fargo's incentive program is headed up by Tyson Pyles, senior vice president of sales measurement and reporting for the retail bank. He has made presentations on this blend of applied psychology and statistics in my management science course at Stanford's Engineering School. From the relaxed and interactive manner in which Pyles engaged my class, it was clear he had coached Little League baseball. He is a people person, and he'd better be. In his day job, he manages and advises 45,000 bank employees and has to deal with complaints, questions, and suggestions on an individual level. With a group of that size, again like a baseball coach, he must also deal with the statistics.

"We have made huge strides over the years in recognizing the distribution of sales performance," says Pyles. "At first we thought of it as a bell-shaped curve," he continues, "but then we realized that an incentive program could tug at various parts of the distribution in different ways."

Figure 11.1 shows how the distribution of performance can change as a hurdle is moved. According to Pyles, "The reaction to incentives from your top performers may be very different from

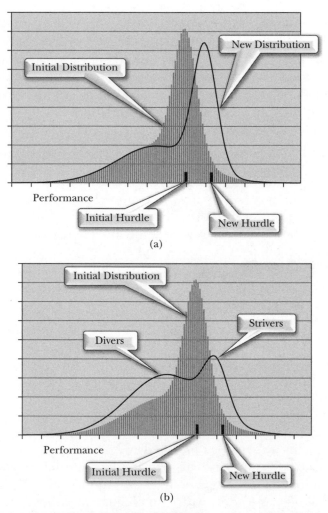

(a)

(b)

Figure 11.1 (a) A performance distribution being tugged by the change in a hurdle; (b) strivers and divers.

those at the bottom." Mark Rubino, a former student of mine who works with Pyles, has discovered situations in which increasing a hurdle raises the performance of some but actually causes others to give up and slack off. Mark calls these two groups the "Strivers" and the "Divers." Compare Figure 11.1a to Figure 11.1b, in which the incentive plan pulls the distribution in two directions at once.

"And of course the incentive program is a multidimensional problem," says Pyles. "You may need different types of incentives for selling different products. You need specialists for filling in holes in the product space." Needless to say, he does not try to manage the nonexistent average employee.

Evaluation of a Gas Well

I will now present an example of the Strong Form of the Flaw of Averages with a distinctly different flavor. Suppose your firm is planning to purchase a natural gas reservoir known to contain a million units of gas. Currently the market price of gas is $10. But it costs $9.50 to pump it through a pipeline to the market, so the profit per unit is only $0.50. Unfortunately, if you decide to purchase the reservoir, the transaction will take a month to complete, and the price of gas may have changed before you have the opportunity to pump it.

Your boss asks you to estimate the price of gas in one month so that he can calculate the value of the property. "It's highly uncertain," you respond, "and could go either up or down by several dollars from today's price." This is not what the boss wanted to hear. "Give me a *number* so I know how to value the reservoir," he demands. "Well," you say, "I guess on average it will stay where it is now." The boss, finally satisfied, calculates the expected value of the property based on the average price of $10 per unit. That is, he takes the $0.50 profit per unit times the million units, to arrive at a value of $500,000.

Here is a Mindle for thinking about the average or expected value of the reservoir given the uncertain future price of gas. Imagine that instead of purchasing a single reservoir, you were purchasing one-thousandth of a share in 1,000 reservoirs, each on its own planet. There is no future uncertainty in gas price. However, the price is different on each planet, and it averages $10 per unit. I probably don't need to remind you that there is no interplanetary gas transport. The average or expected value of your investment is then just the sum of the values of the 1,000 properties divided by 1,000.

Now back to the boss's approach of just plugging in the average gas price. This ignores the uncertainty in gas price, and if you've learned anything by now, you know that the average value of the 1,000 reservoirs must be less than the value based on average gas price. Right?

Nope.

On average it's worth *more*. If the gas price goes up, the value goes up. "But what if the price goes down?" you say. "You could lose a lot of money in that case." No, you couldn't. If gas drops below $9.50, you won't pump. You have the option *not* to pump, and this limits the downside to zero, as displayed in Figure 11.2. Those planets on which the gas price was less than $9.50 would just shut in their wells, so when you added up the results of all 1,000 investments, although some might not make any profit, none would actually lose money.

Consider, for example, a world in which today's gas price is $10 and the future price will either go up or down by exactly $2.50 with equal likelihood. The average price is still $10. If the price goes up

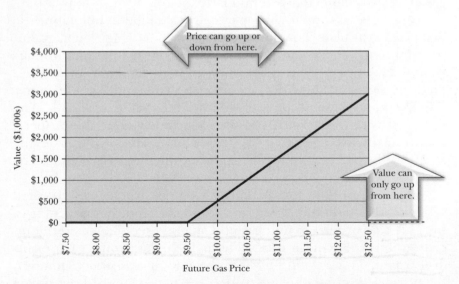

Figure 11.2   Value of the gas property given possible future gas prices.

by \$2.50, the profit per unit is \$12.50 – \$9.50 = \$3.00. Multiplied by the million units, this is \$3 million. If the price drops by \$2.50, you would lose money on each unit pumped, so you will just shut the property down and settle for a profit of zero. The average of \$3 million and zero is \$1.5 million, three times the profit associated with the average gas price! (See Figure 11.2.) Notice that if your contract forces you to pump, the average value drops back to \$500,000.

Now what you choose to pay for such a property is your business, but if you do not recognize that its average value is way over the value based on average gas prices, then you will be outbid by people who recognize the option opportunity.

The last example shows that the Flaw of Averages cuts both ways. Sometimes when you plug averages of uncertain values into your plans, it *overestimates* the average outcome, and sometimes it *underestimates* the average outcome.

The Cyclone Hits London

And what ever happened to Terri Dial? In 2005, she became CEO of Lloyds TSB Retail Bank in London. Yes, a brash blond American woman running a stodgy British bank sounds like the basis of a Monty Python sketch, and it could have turned out that way. But instead in 2007 she was listed as one of the 50 most influential Americans in the United Kingdom and has earned the admiration of the British business press, who rather enjoy having a Human Cyclone in London.[2]

One of her early decisions at Lloyds was to establish an analytical culture similar to the one she had fostered at Wells Fargo. In 2006, Stefan Scholtes, a colleague at the Judge Business School at Cambridge University, and I assisted in this effort by initiating a series of courses for Lloyds executives. Whereas top managers may pay lip service to executive education and will even fund a course for their middle managers, they rarely take the time to internalize the sobering lesson of the drunk in the road. Terri's approach was a little more hands-on. She came up to Cambridge from London herself for two and a half days, bringing 16 of her managing directors with her. Stefan and I delivered a prototype version of the course to this group, which left its imprimatur on it for the many classes of Lloyds executives that followed.

The Human Cyclone Meets the Financial Tsunami

Recently Terri was recruited away from London to New York, where she was appointed CEO of North America Consumer Banking and Global Head of Consumer Strategy of Citigroup. Terri had already left by the time Stefan and I taught our last course for Lloyds. Because she was no longer there, I felt freer to gather opinions about her performance from the attendees. To a woman (and man), they expressed admiration and amazement at what she had accomplished in such a short time. As I write this, the Cyclone is doing battle with the Tsunami in New York. I hope she comes out on top.

Things to remember:

- The Strong Form of the Flaw of Averages states that average or expected inputs don't always result in average or expected outputs (Mindle 4).
- The drunk in the road

Things to forget:

- That it is too hard to change how people do business.

CHAPTER

Who Was Jensen and Why Wasn't He Equal?

THE NUTS AND BOLTS OF THE STRONG FORM OF THE FLAW OF AVERAGES

The Strong Form of the Flaw of Averages, which is known to mathematicians as Jensen's Inequality, masks both risks and opportunities. Familiarity with the concept will help you avoid the former and seize the latter. In the last chapter we saw that the Flaw of Averages cuts both ways. When you plug averages of uncertain values into your plans, they sometimes *overestimate* the average outcome and sometimes *underestimate* the average outcome. What follows are some general rules that characterize these two situations.

Spreadsheets with Uncertain Inputs

The prevalence of the Flaw of Averages is due to the fact that millions of spreadsheet users plug their best guesses of uncertain numbers into their models, naively believing that they are getting the best outputs. However, the Strong Form of the Flaw of Averages isn't news to mathematicians. They have known it for over a century as JENSEN's INEQUALITY. Of course, with a name like that, no wonder no one else has heard of it.

A mathematician, by the way, would refer to a typical spreadsheet model with inputs, outputs, and formulas connecting them as a FUNCTION. And if some of the inputs were uncertain numbers, a mathematician would call it a FUNCTION OF RANDOM VARIABLES.

Therefore, the millions of spreadsheet models in the world with uncertain inputs are actually **FUNCTIONS OF RANDOM VARIABLES**. So if you use spreadsheets, you had better run to the web and find a definition for a **FUNCTION OF RANDOM VARIABLES**. On second thought, you would probably gag on the Red Words. You had better go with my explanation.

Mathematicians use the term "inequality" not to indicate social injustice, but rather to describe situations in which one number is guaranteed *not* to equal another number. Johan Ludwig William Valdemar Jensen was a Danish telephone engineer in the late 1800s, practically before there were telephones in Denmark.[1] He was also an amateur mathematician (this is a derogatory term applied by mathematicians to other mathematicians who also have real jobs). Jensen proved some important theorems, the best-known of which is his famous 1906 inequality.

A Note from Your Author

The paragraphs coming up may be challenging for some readers. They are also some of the most important for developing intuition into the Strong Form of the Flaw of Averages. I suggest that you at least glance at the figures, and read the part about smiles and frowns.

Jensen's Inequality describes four cases of formulas that depend on uncertain inputs (see also Figure 12.1).

Here is **JENSEN's INEQUALITY** in a nutshell. There are four cases.

1. The graph of the formula is a *straight line* (**LINEAR**). The *average value* of the formula *equals* the formula evaluated at the *average input*.
2. The graph of the formula *curves up* (**CONVEX**). The *average value* of the formula *is greater than* the formula evaluated at the *average input*.
3. The graph of the formula *curves down* (**CONCAVE**). The *average value* of the formula *is less than* the formula evaluated at the *average input*.
4. The graph of the formula is none of the above. **JENSEN's INEQUALITY** keeps its mouth shut.

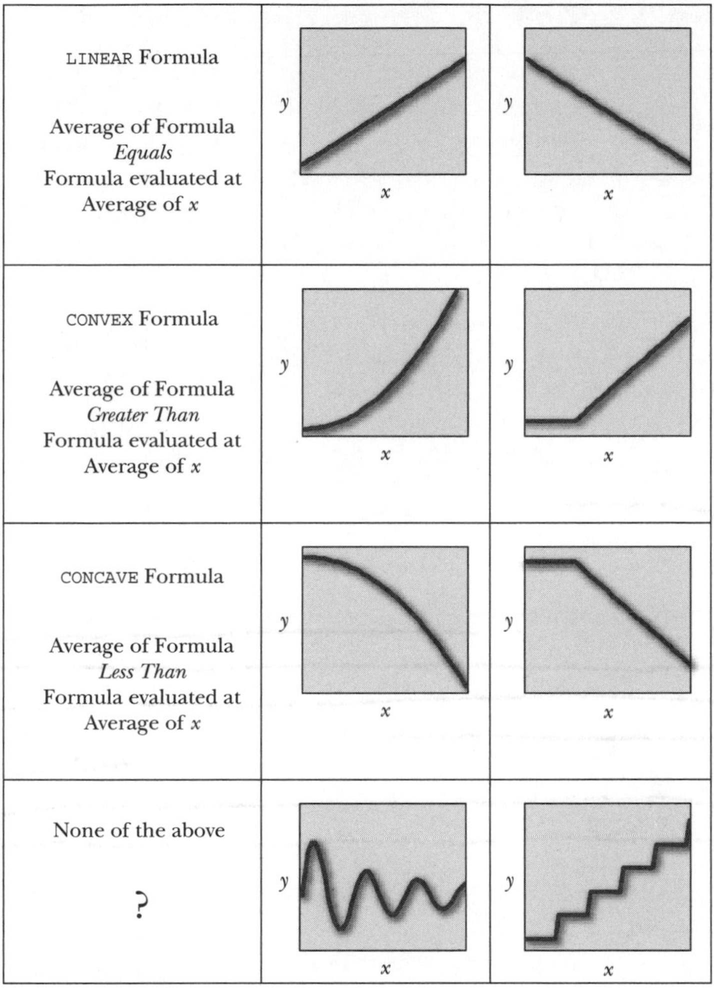

Figure 12.1   Summary of JENSEN's INEQUALITY.

Now for a spreadsheet model to be LINEAR, it must pretty much use only addition, subtraction, and in some instances multiplication. All it takes is one instance of an IF statement, MAX, MIN, LOOKUP, or indeed the majority of spreadsheet formulas, and the model is *not* LINEAR, leading to the Strong Form of the Flaw of Averages. In such cases, running a simulation is usually the only practical way to estimate the true average output of your model.

Options, Restrictions, Smiles, and Frowns

Stefan Scholtes was born and raised in a small farming village in Germany and was one of a handful of students who went on to high school in the nearest town. There his teachers had difficulty understanding his dialect, and if trouble with his native German wasn't enough, foreign languages were worse. English was his downfall, forcing him to be held back a year (making us brothers in English teacher psycho drama). Some 16 years later, he was a professor at Cambridge University in England, where we developed the courses for Lloyds TSB bank described in the last chapter.

In teaching the Flaw of Averages to his MBA students, Scholtes describes two common characteristics of business plans that lead inexorably to the Strong Form of the Flaw of Averages: options and restrictions.[2]

Options

If your business plan allows you the *option* to take remedial action after an uncertainty has been resolved, then the average outcome of your plan will be better than the outcome of the plan based on the average value of the uncertainty. The gas reservoir described earlier in this chapter demonstrates this principle. The average value of the property was more than the value associated with the average gas price because you had the option not to pump if the price fell (see Figure 11.2).

Scholtes describes this graphically. "Plot a graph of the value of your business plan vs. the possible values of an uncertain number. If it *smiles* at you, this is good news.[3] The average value will be greater than the value based on the average of the uncertain number," as in row 2 of Figure 12.1.

Restrictions

If some outcomes of an uncertainty lead to *restrictions* in your future actions, then the *average* outcome of your plan will be worse than the outcome of the plan based on the average value of the uncertainty. This problem is demonstrated by the microchip production case (see Figure 1.1, chapter 1), in which sales were restricted by the capacity of the plant, regardless of demand. The average profit was less than the profit associated with average demand, or, as described by Scholtes: "If, on the other hand the value graph frowns—bad news—the average value will be less than the value based on the average of the uncertain number," as in row 3 of Figure 12.1.

Note: If you plotted costs rather than value against the uncertain number, then a curve upward or downward becomes a devil's smile or frown, and things work in reverse.

A classic case of the Strong Form of the Flaw of Averages is related to the 2008 subprime mortgage fiasco. It involves the relationship between mortgage default rates and housing prices. In times or locations where property values fall, defaults tend to go up with profits going down. In times or locations where property values rise, defaults tend to go down with profits going up. It is tempting for analysts to base the profits of their mortgage portfolios on average property values, but this overestimates the average profit.

Here's why. Consider a diversified portfolio of mortgages spread across various housing markets. Suppose that property values are expected to rise in some of these markets but fall in others, remaining the same on average. What do you suppose the profit graph looks like with respect to property values? In locations where values increase, defaults drop slightly, increasing profit slightly. But where values fall, defaults go up. In some cases values will fall to the extent that the equity in the houses drops below the amount owed. At that point defaults increase dramatically, with owners just dropping off the house keys at the bank and moving into Motel 6.

This is reflected in Figure 12.2, which, although based on hypothetical numbers, is qualitatively correct: a frown if there ever was one. It doesn't matter whether it is a right frown as in row three of Figure 12.1 or a left one as in Figure 12.2; it's the same bad news. In this example, an 8 percent increase in value in one location improves profit by less than 5 percent, whereas an 8 percent devaluation in another location decreases profit by a whopping 40 percent. Thus the profit of a mortgage portfolio based on what are expected to be average property values will overestimate average profit.

Stuart Buckingham of Lloyds TSB was financial planning director of the retail bank reporting to Terri Dial before she returned to the United States. He summarizes the bank's approach to internalizing the Flaw of Averages through executive education. "We now

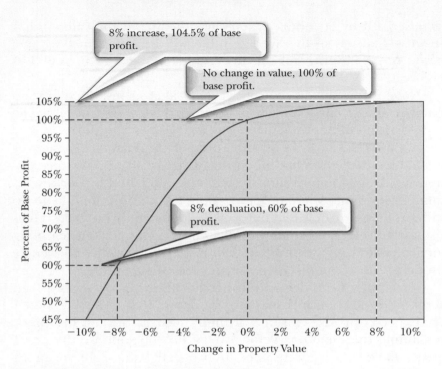

Figure 12.2   Profit versus property value.

have a body of graduates who speak a 'common modeling language' throughout the business," says Buckingham, "They know to look for non-linear relationships and recognize that uncertainty gives rise to a range of possible outcomes rather than one single, flawed estimate." He relates how Lloyds avoided a common pitfall that occurs in promoting new technical perspectives. "It was important to train the bosses as well as the modelers to make sure they could leverage the new skills acquired by those reporting to them."

So has this changed how the bank does its planning? "You bet," says Buckingham, "our plans are more thought through in terms of cause and effect relationships, uncertainties are recognized for what they are, and we simulate ranges of outcomes. I could cite tactical examples that we have used in the business, but this is confidential stuff, right?"

Things to remember:

- Options
- Restrictions
- Smiles
- Frowns

Things to forget:

- ~~FUNCTIONS OF RANDOM VARIABLES~~—Use "plans with uncertain inputs" instead.
- ~~JENSEN'S INEQUALITY~~—I recommend the "Flaw of Averages (Strong Form)" instead, although Jensen is probably turning over in his grave.
- ~~CONVEX~~—Use "curves up (smiles)" instead.
- ~~CONCAVE~~—Use "curves down (frowns)" instead.

Mindle 5: Interrelated Uncertainties

Michael Kubica had boxed himself into a corner. Because he was math-phobic, he had put off taking any quantitative courses in college as long as possible. In his last term, with a perfect 4.0 grade point average that he wanted to keep, the only way out was to learn math. The converted make the best proselytizers, and today Michael is president of Applied Quantitative Sciences, Inc., a consultancy he founded to help firms model risk and uncertainty for a number of business problems.[1]

Recently Michael had a client that manufactured a line of surgical instruments, with several product development teams working on new product lines. The problem was to value the portfolio of existing and new products over an uncertain future. Historically, each new product team was responsible for developing their own forecasts of future demand, whereas the marketing department created the demand forecast for all currently commercialized products.

To their credit, some of these teams were not blindly churning out single average estimates of demand but were actually running simulations to produce distributions. This is one of those cases where each team was shaking its own ladder. But the full portfolio of current and future products was like a bunch of ladders connected by planks, which meant that they could not be simply added up.

Consider, for example, just one *new* product, as forecast by its development team, and one *existing* product, which might be replaced by the new one, as forecast by the marketing team. Suppose that each team models future demand as having a 50/50 chance of being high or low, as shown in Figure 13.1.

Figure 13.1   Demand outcomes as modeled by the two teams.

Up to this point everything is valid. However, if the corporation consolidated these results, it would come up with the four outcomes shown in Figure 13.2 with equal probabilities of 25 percent.

Figure 13.2   Erroneous consolidation showing a chance of both products going up.

But the only way to keep high demand on the existing product is for the replacement product to fail, and the only way to get high demand on the new product is to cannibalize the existing product. So outcomes 1 and 4 are both impossible, and the correct distribution of outcomes looks more like Figure 13.3.

By running the simulations separately, the product and marketing teams had not taken into account the interrelationships between the demands of the existing and new products. "Had this dependency not been addressed, there would have been significant overstatement of upside demand, which in turn would have translated into unnecessary capital expenditures and shortfalls of expected revenues," says Kubica, who helped them create a model that took the interrelationships into account. The fifth Mindle for grasping uncertainty is the notion of interrelationships like this one.

Figure 13.3   The actual possible outcomes.

COVARIANCE and CORRELATION are Red Words

In Steam Era Statistics, the words "COVARIANCE" and "CORRELATION" are used to describe uncertain numbers that are interrelated in a LINEAR manner. People also use the term "STATISTICAL DEPENDENCE" when discussing interrelated uncertainties, but this phrase implies that one uncertainty depends on another, when in fact the relationship may be mutual. So I will stick to *interrelated uncertainties* instead. It is not only more general but also does not require Red Words.

As another example of interrelated uncertainties, consider the stock prices of two oil companies. When petroleum prices go up or down, they drag both companies' stock prices along with them. But since oil price is not the only influence, it is also possible for the stocks to move in opposite directions, perhaps due to new taxation or environmental regulation that affect the firms differently.

Interrelated uncertainties are at the heart of managing investments, as first described in the Nobel Prize–winning Portfolio Theory of Harry Markowitz in 1952.[2] Later chapters will discuss Markowitz and his protégé William Sharpe in more detail. Here I will explain some Mindles underlying their Nobel Prize–winning work.

Three Idealized Investments

For purposes of introducing interrelated uncertainties, I will present three hypothetical investment opportunities.

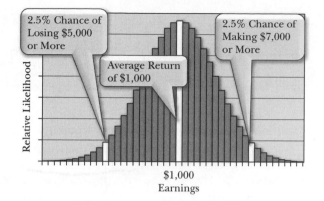

Figure 13.4 The petroleum investment.

1. *Petroleum:* Petroleum is expected to earn $1,000. However, there is great uncertainty, as shown in Figure 13.4. On the downside, for example, an experimental engine that runs on seawater might reduce petroleum demand. In this case you will lose more than $5,000. On the upside, the Chinese might develop a taste for large sport utility vehicles, and you will earn $7,000. If you are comfortable with Red Words, think of this as a NORMAL DISTRIBUTION with an average of $1,000 and SIGMA of $3,000.

2. *Airline stock:* The second investment is airline stock. Imagine that the uncertainty here is exactly the same as that of petroleum. That is, expected earnings are $1,000 with a 95 percent chance of having between a $5,000 loss and a $7,000 gain.

3. *Licorice:* The final investment is in licorice, the black rubbery confection. Again expected earnings are $1,000, with a big upside (licorice is discovered to cure cancer) and a big downside (licorice is discovered to *cause* cancer). As with the other investments, there is 95 percent chance of having between a $5,000 loss and a $7,000 gain.

For comparison, the three uncertainties are displayed in Figure 13.5.

Suppose you had to put every last penny in one of these three investments. Where would you put it? Hint: There is only one correct answer, and it's a trick question.

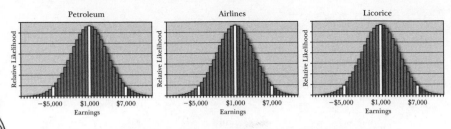

Figure 13.5 Comparative uncertainties of the three investments.

The only correct answer is that it doesn't matter (I told you it was a trick question). An investment in any of these investments is equivalent to any of the others.

Now some people are saying, "But there must be some sort of interrelationship between these investments because the title of the chapter is 'Interrelated Uncertainties.'" You're right, that is the title of the chapter, and they probably are interrelated, but if you invest all your money in a single one of them, interrelatedness is irrelevant. They are all the same shape, and that's that.

Portfolios

Of course, in the real world, no one ever has every last penny invested in a single asset. When you have money in more than one uncertain investment, it is called a *portfolio*, and two kinds of effects come into play. The first of these *portfolio effects* is the straight diversification that we observed in the film investments. The second effect arises from *interrelations* among the assets. Neither of these effects can change the *average return* of a portfolio, but they both can change the degree of uncertainty, which ties to *risk*.

Recall that people have different attitudes toward risk, ranging from those who go for broke to those who cover their butts. For purposes of the following discussion, let's assume that you are a butt coverer.

Three Idealized Portfolios

Consider three idealized portfolios:

- Portfolio 1 splits your investment equally between petroleum and airlines.
- Portfolio 2 splits your investment equally between airlines and licorice.

- Portfolio 3 splits your investment equally between licorice and petroleum.

The average return of each individual investment is $1,000, so the average of each portfolio is also $1,000. Note: The Strong Form of the Flaw of Averages does not apply here because we are just adding up averages, which is **LINEAR**. But from a risk perspective, they are not all the same due to the interrelationships among the constituent assets.

What are the primary interrelationships? The cost of fuel is a large fraction of the overall operating expense of an airline. So when petroleum prices go up, they cut into the bottom line, and you would expect airline stock to be driven down. Conversely, when petroleum goes down, you would expect airline stocks to rise due to lower fuel prices. The real world is more complicated than this, especially because the airlines already know what I am talking about, and they use derivative financial instruments to reduce their risk in this regard. But for this chapter I will assume that the only significant interrelationship among the investments is between petroleum and airlines.

A Mindle for Interrelated Uncertainties: The Scatter Plot

Imagine that over the years, you had kept a record of the changes in both petroleum and airline stock prices (and people have). If these changes were graphed in a scatter plot, they might look like the left side of Figure 13.6. Each point corresponds to one year, with the x coordinate representing the change in petroleum price, and the y coordinate representing the change in airline stock. Each uncertainty on its own is bell-shaped, but a high value of one tends to lead to a low value of the other, and vice versa.

On the other hand, assuming that there is no interrelationship between petroleum and licorice (although I'll bet there are trace amounts of petroleum in the coloring and flavoring), a similar scatter plot would display no particular pattern, as shown in the right-hand graph in Figure 13.6.

Now as a butt coverer, you are about to invest all your money in one of these three portfolios. Where would you put it? To force yourself to make an intellectual commitment, scribble your choice on a piece of paper before going on.

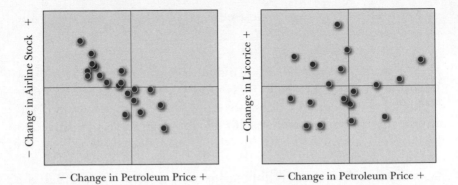

Figure 13.6   Scatter plot of changes in airlines and licorice versus petroleum.

If I just gave you the answer, it would be too easy and you might not learn anything. As they say, give a man a fish and you will feed him for a day; teach him to fish and he will sit in a boat all day and drink beer. So I will help you discover it on your own.

We will start with licorice and petroleum because we are assuming they are not interrelated. I like to think of each investment as rolling a die. Then the licorice and petroleum portfolio is like rolling two dice, resulting in the shape in Figure 13.7.

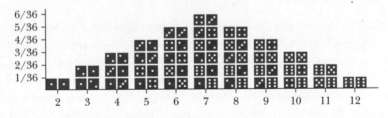

Figure 13.7   The outcomes for two dice.

What part of this shape do you hate as a butt coverer? If you answered the extremes then, again, your schooling has interfered with your education. Even butt coverers love to get rich. What they hate is rolling a two on the far left.

So suppose your broker comes to you with the bad news that the new Seawater Engine has made petroleum worthless. What does this do to the chances that licorice causes cancer? Nothing, they are independent. As a result, even with your petroleum investment in the toilet, there is still only one chance in six of the dreaded double dots known as snake eyes.

Exactly the same behavior is exhibited by airlines and licorice because these two assets are also assumed to be independent. But now suppose you owned petroleum and airlines. Again, news about the Seawater Engine will cause your petroleum investment to tank, but what does this do to the chance that your airline stock dives as well? Petroleum is now so cheap they're practically giving jet fuel away, and thus the probability of snake eyes is greatly reduced.

Although all three portfolios earn $1,000 on average, petroleum and airlines does so at a significantly lower risk. The actual distributions would look more like those shown in Figure 13.8.

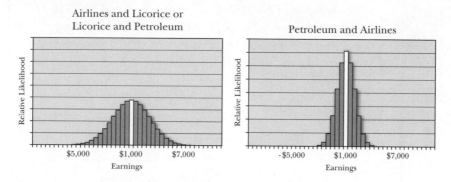

Figure 13.8   Comparative distributions of the portfolios.

When I present this example to my university and executive classes, a common knee-jerk reaction is to reject petroleum and airlines because the elements are interrelated. The correct knee-jerk reaction is to reject portfolios whose interrelations are *direct* (or *positive*); for example, a portfolio consisting only of two airline stocks might appear as shown in Figure 13.9.

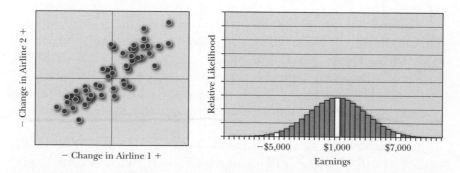

Figure 13.9   A portfolio of two assets with a positive interrelationship.

Inverse (or *negative*) interactions reduce uncertainty, and the name for an investment added to a portfolio for this purpose is a *hedge*.

CORRELATE This!

People wonder what I have against **CORRELATION**. They argue that it was good enough for the Steam Era, and even if its derivation would leave you cross-eyed, you can use the CORREL function in Microsoft Excel to calculate it easily.

 *Try using the CORREL function on the Excel XY Data for this chapter at FlawOfAverages.com. The resulting value of 0.0075 (as shown in Figure 13.10) is negligible, leading the casual analyst to believe that X and Y are not interrelated.*

	D2			f_x	=CORREL(A3:A1002,B3:B1002)		
	A	B	C	D	E	F	
1	Data			Correlation			
2	X	Y		0.0075			
3	0.305747	0.447602					
4	0.041731	0.999129					
5	0.249475	-0.96838					
6	0.300301	0.38903					
7	-0.30335	0.363549					
8	0.13844	-0.78793					
9	-0.30055	0.414816					
10	0.857529	-0.51444					

Figure 13.10   The CORREL function in Microsoft Excel.

However, an astute observer who created a scatter plot from the data might perceive a nonlinear relationship between the variables, as shown in Figure 13.11. The Steam Era concept of **CORRELATION** does not adequately describe this situation, whereas the methods of Probability Management do, as described in a future chapter. Scatter plots are my favorite way to grasp the interrelationships between uncertain numbers.

For my attempt at an intuitive explanation of what **COVARIANCE** and its cousin **CORRELATION** mean, visit FlawOfAverages.com.

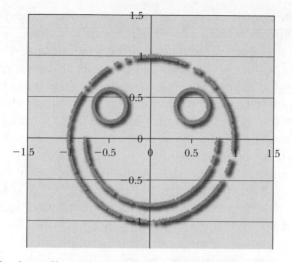

Figure 13.11 A scatter plot with a clear interrelationship, but no correlation.

   While we are on the topic of interrelationships, we must not forget how uncertain numbers may be related to themselves over time. The Red Word for this is AUTOCORRELATION. As an example, if a stock price goes up today, it has almost no bearing on whether it will go up or down tomorrow. On the other hand, historically, if interest rates get very high over some time period, they are more likely to go down in the future, whereas, if they are very low, they are more likely to go up.

   There are also uncertainties that change dynamically over time, for which using a single number is even more misleading. Take housing prices, for example. What would happen if prices fell in some location to the point that a few homeowners now owed more to the bank than their houses were worth? They would either walk away or be foreclosed on. How would future housing prices relate to this? Well, the banks who now owned the houses would try to unload them quickly in an already depressed market, and the increased supply of houses would further drive down prices. Uh-oh. These new lower prices would force even more homeowners under-water on their mortgages, and guess what? There would now be even more abandoned houses to drive the prices even lower. There is an obvious mechanism from your basic economics class that can get us into such a death spiral, so there is no way it can be described as a black swan. In fact, it is called a bubble burst, and it can have very scary effects on the economy, as you may have noticed. The problem is that even if you know a bubble is going to burst, it is very hard to predict when it will happen and how loud the bang will be. These situations are governed by what is known as chaos theory. They don't simulate well, in that very slight changes in the assumptions will produce drastic changes in the results. But the risk is clear even if it can't be perfectly quantified, and any prudent investor would want to be cognizant of it.

So how exactly *was* the risk of the housing bubble monitored? According to Felix Salmon in a February 2009 article in Wired Magazine[3], the huge market in mortgage backed securities that crashed and burned in 2008 was largely based on a formula called the *Gaussian copula function,* derived by mathematician David X. Li. Salmon writes that investors adopted this calculation widely "as a quick–and fatally flawed–way to assess risk." This approach reduced the complex interrelationships between various real estate investments to a "(F)inal correlation number–one clean, simple all-sufficient figure that sums up everything." No scatter plots, no shapes, no recognition of the potentially chaotic behavior described above. Again, according to Salmon, "(T)he outputs came from 'black box' computer models and were hard to subject to a commonsense smell test." Here we had people trying to fly an airplane with a single instrument and no windshield.

Things to remember:
- Interrelationships between uncertainties (Mindle 5).
- The difference between positive and negative interrelationships.
- Scatter plots.

Things to forget:
- CORRELATION
- COVARIANCE—Use scatter plots instead of either of these.

PART 3

DECISIONS AND INFORMATION

Information reduces uncertainty. As such, it must be worth something. In fact, most people agree that we now have an information economy. So what's a fair price for a piece of information? Here's a clue. If it cannot impact a decision, it's worthless.

Part 3 formalizes the connection between decisions and information.

Decision Trees

My introduction to what is known today as *decision analysis* occurred in Paris. It was the winter of 1951, when at age 6, I asked my father what he was working on. He had received a Guggenheim fellowship to write his book, *The Foundations of Statistics*,[1] and was on sabbatical from the University of Chicago. He told me that he was thinking about how people made decisions, and he gave me the following example of how they *don't*.

A man in a restaurant is trying to decide between the fried chicken and the roast beef. He is inclined toward the chicken, but asks the waiter one more question: "Do you also have duck today?" "Yes we do," responds the waiter. "Oh, in that case," says the man, "I'll have the beef." My father eventually arrived at a set of rules that proposed to describe how rational people would make decisions in the face of uncertainty. The preceding restaurant decision would be deemed irrational, because whether the restaurant had duck was irrelevant to the choice between chicken and beef.

My father stayed in this line of work for the rest of his life, collaborating with Milton Friedman and others on what came to be known as the THEORY OF RATIONAL EXPECTATION. He put it this way on page 16 of *The Foundations of Statistics*:

> The point of view under discussion may be symbolized by the proverb "Look before you leap," and the one to which it is opposed by the proverb, "You can cross that bridge when you come to it."

The theory is based on the principle that people will correctly assess the uncertainties facing them (look) and make rational decisions (leaps) so as to maximize their expected gain. But my father understood that life was so complicated that this could *not* easily be adhered to in practice. A few sentences later he writes:

> It is even utterly beyond our power to plan a picnic or to play a game of chess according to this principle.

But he believed it was at least a good starting place for a theory of decision making. In point of fact, he has been proven wrong in the particular case of chess; today, computer programs are the reigning champions. So score one for rationality. But when it comes to decision making under uncertainty by humans using their bare brains, experiments show that even sophisticated people often behave irrationally. For example, when subjects are presented with a hypothetical medical decision between one procedure that has a 90 percent chance of saving a patient's life and another procedure that has a 10 percent chance of letting the patient die, they generally prefer the first, even though they are mathematically equivalent.[2]

I myself don't believe that all decisions can or even should be made rationally. Creating art, for example, requires at least tacit decision making, yet art that springs from rationality instead of emotion is contrived. My position is that decisions are made using the seat of the intellect at one extreme and the seat of the pants at the other and that the best decisions are those upon which both extremities agree.

Because of his early work on decision making in the face of uncertainty, my father is often considered also to be one of the founding fathers of decision analysis.[3] (Does that make me its brother?) However, the field was not formally defined until the mid-1960s by Professor Ronald A. Howard of Stanford University.[4] I no doubt picked up a good deal of my knowledge of the subject at the family dinner table over the years, but my formal exposure to decision analysis came from auditing Howard's class at Stanford in the mid-1990s after I had started teaching there. Just as you can actually see the minute hand move on a very large clock, you could sense yourself getting smarter in his class. I have heard many others describe their eye-opening experiences in this course on rational thinking; ironically, in quite emotional terms.

Decision Trees

One of the great Mindles of decision analysis is the *decision tree*. I will introduce this concept with a simple example that can be done in the head, freeing the mind to more quickly absorb the mechanics of the process.

Suppose you must choose between a *Good Time* and a *Stick in the Eye.*

Imagine that you would pay up to $200 for the pleasure associated with the Good Time. The Stick in the Eye, on the other hand, is not very sharp and will not blind you, but to submit to it voluntarily would require a payment of at least $300, that is, it is worth –$300. This situation can be displayed in a *decision branch*, as shown in Figure 14.1.

The value displayed under the square decision node on the left is $200 because you would obviously choose the Good Time over the negative $300 associated with the Stick in the Eye. The basic idea is that, given multiple alternatives, you should pick the best one, which is displayed by the solid line. So far, this is hardly rocket science.

We cross the line into decision analysis, however, when we introduce uncertainty. If you go for the Good Time, there is a chance you will *Get Caught*, and that's really bad. Whereas if you would put up with a Stick in the Eye for $300, you would not willingly suffer the embarrassment, humiliation, and other repercussions of getting caught, for less than $1,000. This situation is displayed in Figure 14.2. Following common convention: the uncertainty nodes are circular. This tree has no value at this point because we haven't quantified the uncertainty of getting caught yet.

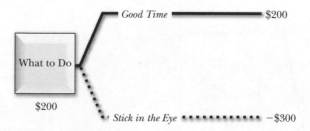

Figure 14.1   A decision branch.

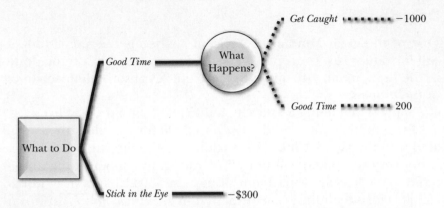

Figure 14.2   A tree with one decision branch and one uncertainty branch.

If you believe there is a 10 percent chance of getting caught, then the *average* value of going for the Good Time is calculated as a 10 percent chance of –$1,000 (–$100), plus a 90 percent chance of $200 ($180), for a net of $80, as shown in Figure 14.3. Although not as enticing as the risk-free $200, this is nonetheless better than a Stick in the Eye, so you would still go for the Good Time. Note: In true decision analysis, this formula would be modified to account for risk attitude, as discussed in Chapter 7.

But where does that 10 percent chance of getting caught come from? At this stage, the naive decision analyst is in danger of getting laughed off the stage by trying to justify a precise probability. A better

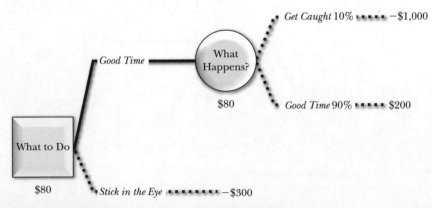

Figure 14.3   Full decision tree with probabilities.

thing to do is turn the question around, and ask, "What chance of the uncertain event would make you change your decision?" This is so important that I will repeat it: *Turn the question around, and ask, "What chance of the uncertain event would make you change your decision?"*

This is easy to do with decision tree software. The add-in used to create these examples in Excel was XLTree®, which comes with my textbook.[5] If you have Microsoft Excel, you may wish to play with the model at FlawOfAverages.com.

If you experimented with the model at FlawOfAverages.com, you would have discovered that when the chance of getting caught reaches 42 percent you should just take the Stick in the Eye and be done with it (see Figure 14.4).

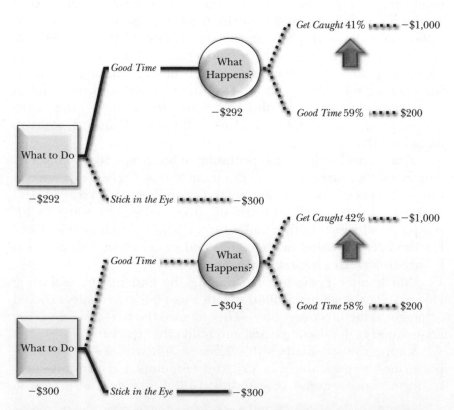

Figure 14.4   A 42% chance of getting caught changes the decision.

Asking the Right Question

Management science has long attempted to build complex models that provide the right answer. As John Tukey reminded us in Chapter 4, these answers are often to the wrong question. On the other hand, simple models can sometimes quickly provide the right question.

In this case, the original question was whether to go for the Good Time. The right question was whether the chance of getting caught is 42 percent or greater. A committee of several people might never agree on the actual probability of getting caught, but they might easily agree on whether it was greater or less than 42 percent, and that ices the decision.

Giving Back

Howard continues to teach his course and direct several doctoral theses in decision analysis each year at Stanford. He is also a founding director and chairman of the Strategic Decisions Group (SDG), a respected consulting firm established in 1981. By the late 1990s, Howard and his colleagues had had long lucrative consulting careers. "A feeling began to emerge among us that it was time to start giving back," Howard recently told me. This is eloquently expressed by Bob Loew, who, after a stint in the Peace Corps, an engineering job, and an MBA from Stanford, went to work for SDG.

"During my 20 plus years consulting to business leaders, I became convinced that there was another clientele that needed exposure to the principles of good decision-making: adolescents," recalls Loew. So he made an almost unheard-of career change, trading in his passport and frequent flyer miles for a teaching credential in 1999. He has been teaching mathematics and decision analysis at a San Francisco Bay Area high school ever since.

Shortly after Loew began teaching, he and others, including Howard, came together around the idea that decision analysis should be taught at the precollege level. They formed the Decision Education Foundation to develop curricula and train other teachers.[6]

Among the self-analyses that Loew's high school students have performed is the case of a girl who contemplated running away from an abusive home (she didn't). Or the student athlete who weighed the prospects for a risky knee operation in an attempt to qualify for a college scholarship (he had it, it worked, and he got in). Or the student who wrote a perfectly lucid analysis of whether to commit suicide (he didn't).

Things to remember:

- Decision trees.
- That people aren't rational.

Things to forget:

- The **THEORY OF RATIONAL EXPECTATION**.

CHAPTER

15

The Value of Information

BECAUSE THERE ISN'T ANYTHING ELSE

Several years ago I gave a workshop for about 50 government intelligence analysts. Before beginning, I asked whether any of them were working specific problems. One of the analysts raised his hand and said that he was exploring ways to optimize the allocation of resources used to gather information. Because information was their primary product, this seemed like a central issue. I asked how many in the audience had heard of decision trees, and all the hands went up. I then asked how many had heard of the value of information and was surprised to count only about five. The analyst who had brought the subject up made an important observation that will be born out in the following discussion: Information has no value at all unless it has the potential to change a decision.

The Complement of Uncertainty

Information is the complement of uncertainty, that is, for every uncertainty, there is information that would reduce or remove it. Sometimes such information is cheap, and sometimes it is unavailable at any price. My father put it this way in his book: "One must indeed look before he leaps, in so far as looking is not unreasonably time-consuming and otherwise expensive."

The Information Age is devoted to supplying information, but what defines whether the information is unreasonably expensive? The answer is the economic worth, or the value, of the information.

Severn Darden, the great comedian and original member of The Second City comedy troupe, did a routine involving a professor of metaphysics that began as follows: "Why—you will ask me—have I chosen to talk about the Universe, rather than some other topic? It's very simple: there isn't anything else!"[1]

In the Information Age, the same could be said of the value of information. Yet few people are aware of the simple and elegant theory devoted to this concept.

Can you imagine any of the following?

- A manufacturing company is introducing a new product but is uncertain about demand and is not sure how many to produce. A market research firm claims that for a million dollars they can cut the uncertainty in half. Is it worth it?
- A pharmaceutical firm is developing a new compound. It must choose between two costly clinical trial procedures that will resolve different sets of questions concerning its efficacy. Which one should it pick?
- A military campaign is being organized against an enemy whose capabilities are poorly known. A covert mission is considered to collect information. How many lives should be risked to determine the enemy's true strength?

These are the sorts of issues addressed by the value of information.

In 1966 Stanford's Howard published a short paper on "Information Value Theory," which today is known as the *value of information.*[2] This extension of decision analysis has deep implications for the Information Age. It fits hand in glove with the concept of decision trees, yet is not nearly as widely understood. Here is how it applies to the choice between a Good Time and a Stick in the Eye.

What's It Worth to You?

Imagine that the person who would catch you (if you got caught) is the night watchman. He is known to patrol one of ten buildings each night. Since you have no knowledge of his actual schedule, there is a one in ten (10 percent) chance of a patrol at the building housing the Good Time. Notice that we now have justification for picking this probability, but as in the earlier discussion of the decision tree we could have left it a variable to play with. Suppose further that you have an acquaintance who knows the night watch-man's schedule.

Your acquaintance has information that will completely remove the uncertainty surrounding the building to be patrolled. So just before you embark on the risky Good Time, you call your con-tact and ask for that night's security details. He gives you a classic response: "What's it worth to you?"

Virtually no one gets this correct unless they are already familiar with the value of information, which is to say that virtually no one gets it. Here is the key.

Without the information, you decide what to do and then find out what happens.

With the information you find out what will happen and then decide what to do.

This just means that the tree is rearranged, or _flipped,_ as some people call it, as shown in Figure 15.1.

Because we assume that your acquaintance always tells the truth, you will get one of two possible messages from him. There is a 10 percent chance the watchman will be present, in which case you receive a warning to stay away. Unfortunately, the only other choice

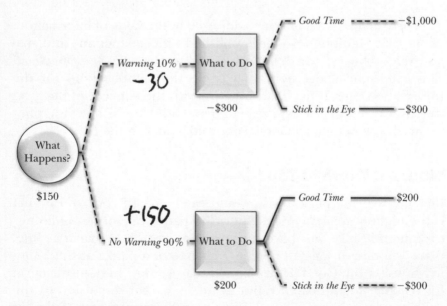

Figure15.1   The flipped tree.

in that case is to take the Stick in the Eye. There is a 90 percent chance he will tell you that the coast is clear, in which case you go for the Good Time. This means that the average outcome is now a 10 percent chance of −$300 (−$30), plus a 90 percent chance of $200 ($180) or $150, as shown in Figure 15.1. The big change is that there is now no chance of getting caught.

Your contact's information took you from a situation with an average value of $80, to one with an average value of $150; so it is worth $70. If he demands $100, you should tell him to buzz off and just take your chances.

As in the example in the last chapter, you do not need to know the probability up front, and could use the analysis to determine what the probability of getting caught would have to be for the information to actually be worth $100. Furthermore, the concept is easily extended to the case in which your contact does *not* always tell the truth. In that case it is called the *value of imperfect information*.

A Military Example

Consider a military example in which the good guys (the Blue team) have a tank that must cross a river at either one of two bridges. The bad guys (the Red team) have soldiers defending both bridges and are also known to have one tank. Because of a smoke screen, Blue doesn't know which bridge the Red tank is guarding.

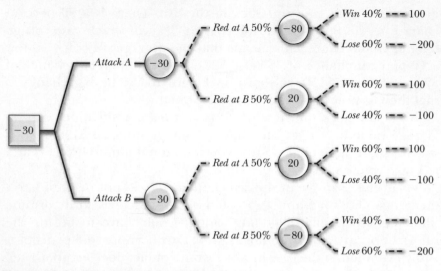

Figure 15.2   Blue's decision tree.

The various outcomes are displayed in the tree in Figure 15.2. The numbers in the far right represent the difference between Red's casualties and Blue's casualties, positive numbers being good for Blue and negative ones bad. Clearly it is better for Blue if the bridge they attack is not defended by another tank, but due to the symmetry of the situation, Blue has an expected score of 30 more casualties than Red regardless of the decision.

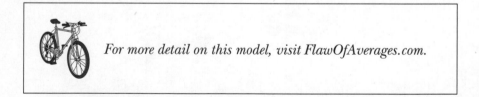

For more detail on this model, visit FlawOfAverages.com.

Blue's commander is reluctant to carry out this mission as planned and is weighing a life-or-death decision to send out a team of scouts to locate Red's tank. He knows they can find it, but they are expected to take five casualties as a result. Is it worth it? Figure 15.3 shows the flipped tree, in which Blue learns Red's location in advance and attacks the opposite bridge.

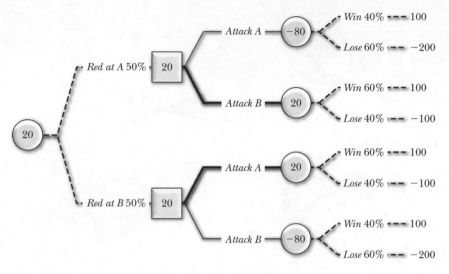

Figure 15.3   The flipped tree: Blue learns Red's location in advance.

With the knowledge of Red's location, the expected value goes from 30 *more* casualties than Red to 20 *fewer*. Thus the information is worth a relative reduction of 50 casualties. There is no need for soul-searching about the value of human life to know that five casualties is a small price to pay to pick up a 50-casualty advantage.

The Value of Obfuscation

Now let's switch Blue to defense and, to make things more interesting, remove the smoke screen. Red can see the Blue tank's location through binoculars and will attack the other bridge, for an expected score of 20 in favor of Red. Blue's commander knows that Red will attack only if he expects to end up ahead in the casualty score. Blue realizes that a perfect decoy tank at the other bridge will reduce Red's chance of attacking the correct bridge to 50 percent. This in turn reduces Red's expected score to –30 and removes the incentive to attack. Unfortunately, headquarters can't deliver a perfect decoy but are able drop an inflatable rubber tank by parachute. Once it is installed at the other bridge, Blue reckons that the chances are two out of three Red will know it is phony. Will Red attack?

Using the decision tree in Excel, it is easy to calculate Red's incentive to attack. Figure 15.4 shows this graphically, based on the probability that Red thinks the real tank is at Bridge A.

Let's start without the rubber tank. Then, because there is no smoke screen, Red knows exactly where Blue's tank is. If Blue is at bridge B, it takes us to the left end of the graph; that is, Red knows there is a 0 percent chance that Blue's tank is at bridge A. Red has an incentive of 20 to attack, and Blue is in trouble. If Blue is at Bridge A, then we are at the other end of the graph, and Red's incentive to attack is still 20.

Now suppose Blue's tank is at B, with the rubber tank at A. If Red thinks there is only one chance in three that the rubber one is the real one, it puts us one-third of the way across the graph, and Red has a serious disincentive (–13) to attack. In fact, if all Blue had at B was a big picture of a tank, which Red thought had only a one in five chance of being real, it would reduce B's incentive to zero and might still serve as a deterrent.

During World War II, the Allies had an entire army of rubber tanks. (If you search the web, you will find a photograph of four soldiers lifting one of these realistic looking tanks off the ground.[3,4]) They were used to confuse the Germans both before and after the 1944 Normandy invasion.

The value of information should always be considered in military planning. One must not forget that keeping one's true defense

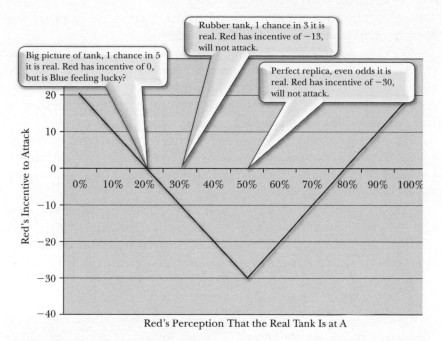

Figure 15.4   Red's incentive to attack by perceived probability that the real Blue tank is at A.

capabilities uncertain serves as a powerful deterrent. For this reason, war should be intentionally waged only when a short decisive victory is assured. Otherwise, the value of the information provided to the enemy may be great. This is especially true in the Internet age, in which that information, in the form of videos of people blowing up your previously considered invincible tanks, are posted for all to see. The large bully at the bar who picks a fight with a much smaller opponent, but who still hasn't knocked him out after an hour's effort, of has increased the incentive for throngs of people to take him on the following night.

Prototyping

Recall Donald Knuth's five steps of model building, in which the fifth step is to trash steps 1 through 4 once you know what you really wanted in the first place. Prototypes often tell us something that we didn't tell them to tell us, thereby providing us with information. And what is that information worth? Plenty, according to Michael Schrage, whose book, *Serious Play*, describes how the spreadsheet "launched the largest and most significant experiment in rapid prototyping and simulation in the history of business."

Schrage advises organizations on how to invest in models and prototypes to manage innovation risk. In this context he says that the concept of the value of information was a revelation in "helping to assess what it was 'worth' to do one more experiment, one more iteration, one more simulation, one more tweak of a prototype."[5] Schrage explains that "A few of my clients have even brought their own customers into the VOI debate. Why? Because the customer's perception of what's valuable from an experiment or a prototype is worth knowing."

An inexpensive prototype, such as a paper airplane, can provide more informational bang for the buck than some purposeful information-gathering activities, as will be presented shortly. No one describes the value of information better than Ron Howard himself, who has generously contributed the close of this chapter.

The Value of Information

BY RONALD A. HOWARD

When you really think about it, the three elements of any decision are alternatives, information, and preferences. I like to think of a three-legged stool because, if any one of these is missing, you really don't have a decision. If you don't have any alternatives, you don't have a decision. If you don't see a connection between what you do and what's going to happen—that's the information—you don't have a decision. And if you don't care what happens, you can do anything and it doesn't make any difference. So you need all three.

It is right to emphasize the value of information when considering information-gathering activities. Our experience with organizations who have gathered information using surveys, pilot plants, test drilling, controlled trials, etc. shows that they often spent ten times the value of information in these pursuits, a huge waste of resources. An information-gathering activity must produce a result that is observable, relevant to the uncertainty of interest, material in that it has the possibility of changing the alternative selected, and, finally, economic in the sense that finding the result does not cost more than it could possibly be worth.

PART 4

THE SEVEN DEADLY SINS OF AVERAGING

Part 4 lists some important variants of the Flaw of Averages. Many of these are based on the Mindles presented earlier but a few require further explanation.

The Seven Deadly Sins of Averaging

Stefan Scholtes and I began corresponding in 1999 when he started using my textbook and spreadsheet software with his MBA students at the Judge Business School at Cambridge University. We then worked together on executive education programs for several clients at Cambridge. This ultimately led to collaboration on an approach to managing uncertainty we now call Probability Management.[1]

Before teaching together, Stefan and I had individually taught the Flaw of Averages to thousands of students and had done it in very similar ways. Compared to explaining something like calculus, it's like shooting fish in a barrel. The students walk into class, and you ask a few simple questions about average outcomes, which they all get wrong. Then you explain how the statistician drowned in the river and the drunk got killed on the highway, and a hundred faces light up with comprehension. A few days later the students are running simulations and explaining the stuff to others.

During one of our early executive courses together, we had just gone over a simple example of the Flaw of Averages when suddenly one of the participants got up and excused himself. During the next break, a colleague of the executive who had left explained that our example had exposed the folly of a deal the fellow had gotten into the day before, and he was now on his cell phone trying to get out of it.

After class, Stefan and I went off for our customary postclass discussion at a local pub. We felt a bit like faith healers who had just witnessed a blind man toss his white cane into the trash and run out of a sermon into the sunlight. We knew there were many more managers in need of salvation.

"Why not come up with a list of the Seven Deadly Sins of Averaging," I suggested. "Great idea," said Stefan, and by the time we had finished our second pints, we had our seven. Of course, from the beginning, we knew the list was potentially endless, so we added an eighth deadly sin: "assuming that there are only seven." As of this writing the eleventh deadly sin is assuming there are only ten. (Oops, make that twelve.) I plan to go on calling them the Seven Deadly Sins regardless of how long the list becomes. Be sure to check in at FlawOfAverages.com to see where it stands today.

The List

Much of this list first appeared in an article in *ORMS Today* and is used here with permission. You will recognize some of these sins from previous chapters.[2] Others are covered in more detail in later ones.

1. *The family with 1½ children.* Often the average scenario, like the average family with 1½ children, is nonexistent. For example, a bank may have two main groups of young customers: students with an average income of $10,000 and young professionals with an average income of $70,000. Would it make sense for the bank to design products or services for customers with the average income of $40,000?

2. *Why everything is behind schedule.* Recall the problem of getting you and your spouse to the VIP reception on time or the software project with ten parallel tasks that each averaged six months. Setting each task at its average results in project completion in six months, but the chance that all ten come in at their average or sooner is the same a flipping ten heads in a row, so the chance of finishing by six months is less than one in a thousand.

3. *The egg basket.* Consider putting ten eggs in the same basket, versus one each in separate baskets. If there is a 10 percent chance of dropping any particular basket, then either strategy results in an average of nine unbroken eggs. However, the first strategy has a 10 percent chance of losing

all the eggs, whereas the second has only one chance in 10,000,000,000 of losing all the eggs (in case you still question the wisdom of diversification).

4. *The risk of ranking.* When choosing a portfolio of capital investment projects, it is common to rank them from best to worst, then start at the top of the list and go down until the budget has been exhausted. This flies in the face of modern portfolio theory, which is based on the interdependence of investments. According to the ranking rule, fire insurance is a ridiculous investment because on average it loses money. But insurance doesn't look so bad if you have a house in your portfolio to go along with it.

5. *Ignoring restrictions.* Recall the microchip example involving an investment in infrastructure sufficient to provide capacity equal to the average of uncertain future demand. If actual demand is less than average, profit will drop. But if demand is greater than average, the sales are restricted by capacity. Thus there is a downside without an associated upside, and the average profit is less than the profit associated with the average demand.

6. *Ignoring optionality.* This is exemplified by the natural gas property, with known marginal production costs but an uncertain future gas price. It is common to value such a property based on the average gas price. If gas price is above average, the property is worth a good deal more. But if you have the option to halt production if the price drops below the marginal cost, then there is an upside without an associated downside, and the average value is greater than the value associated with the average gas price.

7. *The double whammy.* Consider the earlier example of the perishable antibiotic with uncertain demand, in which the quantity stocked was the average demand. If demand exactly equals its average, then no costs are associated with managing the inventory. However, if demand is less than average, then there will be spoilage costs; if demand is greater than average, there will be air freight costs. So the cost associated with average demand is zero, but average cost is positive.

8. *The Flaw of Extremes.* In bottom-up budgeting, reporting the 90th percentile of cash needs leads to ever thicker layers of unnecessary cash as the figures are rolled up to higher levels.

Even more harmful things result from focusing on above- or below-average results, such as test scores or health-related statistics. A full explanation appears in Chapter 17.

9. *Simpson's Paradox.* Can you imagine a nutritional supplement that on average causes people to lose weight? The only exceptions are people who are either male or female, in which case, on average, they gain weight. In Chapter 18 I will explain how this bizarre statistical situation can occur.

10. *The Scholtes Revenue Fallacy.* Suppose you sell different quantities of various types of products, each with its own profit per unit. You might make a nice profit on your average product and yet lose money overall, as discussed in Chapter 19.

11. *Taking credit for chance occurrences.* We all like to take credit for our hard work, but some successes may be due to dumb luck. Chapter 20 can help you tell the difference.

12. *Believing there are only eleven deadly sins.* The twelfth of the Seven Deadly Sins is being lulled into a sense of complacency, thinking you now know all of the insidious effects of averaging.

A Note from Your Author

The next four chapters present sins 8 through 11 in no particular order. You should not feel guilty about jumping ahead to the Applications section of the book, if you like, and reading these chapters later.

CHAPTER

The Flaw of Extremes

Did you know that localities whose residents have the largest average earlobe size tend to be small towns? More amazingly, if this seeming bit of trivia were more widely understood, it could save millions of dollars per year. To explain why, I will start with a problem familiar to anyone who has worked in a large organization: bottom-up budgeting.

Sandbagging

Consider a firm in which each of ten divisional vice presidents submits a budget to the CEO. The VPs are not completely certain of their cash requirements, but suppose for argument's sake that each is 95 percent confident of requiring between $800,000 and $1.2 million with an average of $1 million. Further, their needs are not interrelated. If any one of them requires more or less than average, it won't affect the needs of the others.

If each VP requests the average requirement of $1 million, then the CEO can add the ten estimates together to arrive at the correct average of $10 million. The Strong Form of the Flaw of Averages does not apply because summing is a straight line calculation.

But what kind of VP submits a budget that has a 50 percent chance of being blown? Instead of submitting their averages, the VPs will probably provide numbers they are pretty sure they won't exceed—let's say 90 percent sure. This is the widely practiced budgeting technique known as sandbagging.

Assuming the uncertainties are bell-shaped and based on the preceding ranges of uncertainty, then the cash required to make

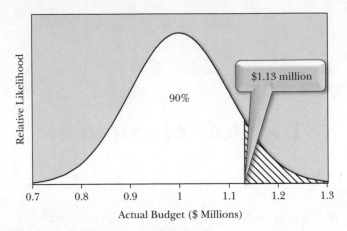

Figure 17.1   Uncertain cash requirement.

them 90 percent confident (the 90th percentile) would be roughly $1.13 million. Figure 17.1 displays the relative likelihood of the various actual cash requirements, and Figure 17.2 displays the same information in a cumulative graph.

Suppose there were only two divisions with two VPs, each of whom submitted a budget of $1.13 million for a total of $2.26 million. Then the CEO is 90 percent sure to stay within his own budget. Right? I'm afraid not.

When independent uncertainties are added together, diversification causes the distribution to get relatively narrower, as

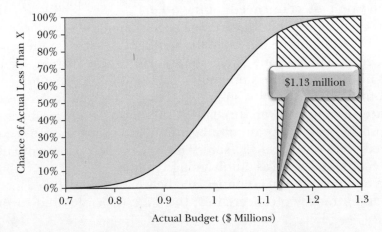

Figure 17.2   Cumulative distribution of cash requirement.

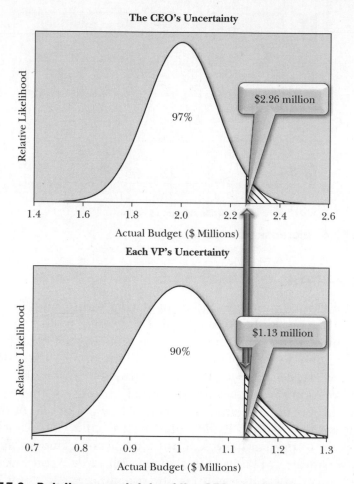

Figure 17.3 **Relative uncertainty of the CEO and the VPs.**

demonstrated with the dice and film portfolio. The effect is shown in Figure 17.3, in which the *x* axis has been scaled to show the perspective from both the CEO's and the VP's positions.

If each of the two VPs is 90 percent sure of not blowing a budget of $1.13 million, then the CEO will be 97 percent sure of not blowing a budget of $2.26 million. What happens when there are ten divisions? The total budget is now 10 times $1.13 million, or $11.3 million. And the increased diversification across ten divisions assures that the CEO is now 99.998 percent sure of not blowing the total budget, as shown in Figure 17.4.

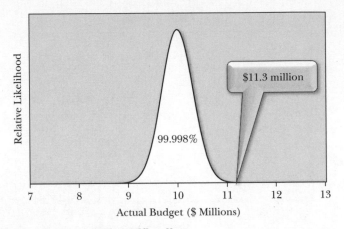

Figure 17.4   Increased diversification.

Layers of Fat

So if the CEO is more confident of staying within budget than his VPs, that's good. Right? Wrong again.

If you do the math, it turns out that the CEO needs only $10.4 million to be 90 percent confident of not exceeding his budget. With $11.3, the CEO has an extra $900,000 gathering dust instead of being used as working capital. Intuitively, the reason he needs a proportionally smaller reserve is that at the end of the year, if Paul is short of cash while Peter is flush, the CEO can borrow from Peter to pay Paul and still not blow his own budget. Ignoring this diversification results in a budget with layer upon layer of fat as the budget works its way up in the organization. If you still don't appreciate the importance of this phenomenon, try going out and raising an extra $900,000 sometime.

Wells Fargo's Matthew Raphaelson is well aware of this problem. At one point he asked the managers reporting to him to estimate the 50th percentiles of their anticipated budgets to avoid sandbagging. Most of the managers understood the request and appreciated that their boss was acknowledging the uncertainty. But old habits die hard, and one manager reported a number that seemed out of line. "So what is the chance your cash needs will be below this number?" Matthew asked. "Fifty percent," responded the manager. "And what is the chance they will be greater than this number?" Matthew continued. "Oh, I am completely confident I won't go above it," responded the manager. Some people will do anything not to violate their budgets, even violate the laws of probability.

Howard Wainer's Most Dangerous Equation

Enough about budgets, which is where I first encountered the Flaw of Extremes. I know my inquiring readers are wondering what all this has to do with earlobes.

A few months ago, I phoned an old friend, Howard Wainer, just to chat. I told him that I was heavy with book; he responded that he was likewise, and we emailed our incomplete manuscripts to one another. Wainer is a distinguished research scientist at the National Board of Medical Examiners and spent 20 years as a statistician at the Educational Testing Service (the people who design the College Board exams).

In Chapter 1 of *Picturing the Uncertain World: How to Understand, Communicate, and Control Uncertainty Through Graphical Display*,[1] Wainer focuses on the same universal diversification effects that cause the layers of fat in budgets. He points out that this was perfectly explained by De Moivre in 1730. Applied to the problem of average earlobe size, it may be understood as follows. Consider the smallest possible town size, that is, one inhabited by a single individual. In the event that this person has huge earlobes, then the average size of the earlobes in that town will be huge. And how about the average earlobe of New York? Because you are averaging over so many New Yorkers, it will be very close to the average of the whole United States.

By the way, did I mention where one would find the smallest average earlobes? Small towns, of course. The sizes of towns and earlobes have nothing to do with each other; it's just that averages with small samples have more variability than averages over large samples.

Why are earlobes so important? They're not. Beyond budgets, this also applies to the prevalence of specific diseases, crime rates, educational test scores, and anything else you might care to average. Wainer describes how billions of dollars were wasted, breaking large school districts into smaller ones because some well meaning but boneheaded group of do-gooders had noticed that high average test scores occur more often in small districts than in large ones. If the same group had looked at low average test scores instead, they would have noticed that low scores also occur more often in small districts, and the billions of dollars would have been wasted on consolidating smaller districts into larger ones instead of the other way around.

Wainer refers to the basic law of diversification as the "Most Dangerous Equation" because being oblivious of it has led to a series of misguided, costly, inept, foolhardy, and counterproductive decisions spanning nearly 1,000 years. I refer you to Wainer's book for the fascinating details.

To summarize, the flaw of extremes results from focusing on abnormal outcomes such as 90th percentiles, worse than average cancer rates, or above average test scores. Combining or comparing such extreme outcomes can yield misleading results.

Things to remember:

- The smaller the sample size, the greater the variability of the average of that sample.

Things to forget:

- De Moivre.

Simpson's Paradox

Simpson's Paradox is an insidious example of the Flaw of Averages that has tripped up sophisticated researchers for years. It is most easily understood in terms of a graph in which a straight line (known as a REGRESSION line) is fit to data so as to indicate the average change in one variable given a change in the other variable. Consider a fictitious dietary supplement based on rutabaga juice that appears to cause rapid weight loss. Figure 18.1 displays the results of 48 test subjects who have been on various doses of the supplement.

The *x* axis displays the daily intake of the stuff for each of the 48 subjects, and the *y* axis shows the pounds of weight gained or lost over the one-week test. The downward-sloping line indicates an

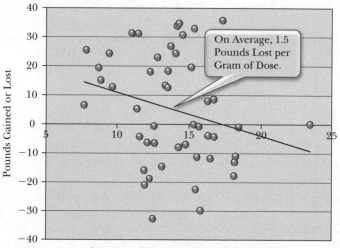

Figure 18.1   Weight change versus daily intake.

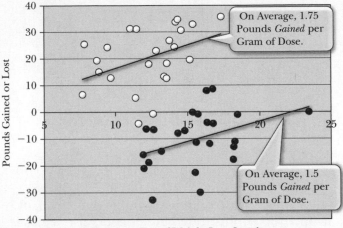

Figure 18.2   Weight change versus daily intake by sex (male denoted by dark, female by light).

incredible average of 1½ pounds of weight lost per week per gram of the supplement. This looks great so far, but before jumping to conclusions, we need to know more about the data.

As it turns out, another variable was not accounted for in the data: the sex of the subjects. Figure 18.2 displays the data separated into males (dark dots) and females (light dots), whereupon it becomes obvious that although on average people *lose* weight by taking rutabaga juice, it makes you *gain* weight if you're either a man or a woman.

What the . . . ?

How could such a thing happen? Imagine that the test period was just after basketball season, and most of the men in the study had just stopped sitting in front of the TV all day while consuming vast quantities of beer. This would explain the greater weight loss in men, which had nothing to do with rutabagas. Because the men were also given larger doses of the supplement on average, weight loss appears to be associated with dose size in the population as a whole.

Kidney Stones

A study of kidney stones provides a real-world example of Simpson's Paradox. An article in a British Medical journal reported on the relative effectiveness of two treatments for kidney stones.[1] For the entire population, treatment B had a higher success rate than treatment A. However, when the patients were classified by the size of their kidney stones, then treatment A was more successful with patients with stones smaller than 2 cm in diameter *and* with patients whose stones were greater than 2 cm.

What the . . . ?

Baseball

Ken Ross, a math professor at the University of Oregon has written a book, *A Mathematician at the Ballpark*, in which he presents the following example of Simpson's Paradox in batting averages.[2] For three years running (1995, 1996, and 1997), David Justice had a higher batting average than Derek Jeter (see Table 18.1). Yet for the combined three-year period, Jeter had a higher average than Justice.

What the . . . ?

The Explanation

Simpson's Paradox occurs when the variables depend on hidden dimensions in the data. In the preceding examples, the fact that men took a higher dose of the supplement and also lost more weight during the time period made us think that the weight loss was due to the supplement. But in fact, their weight loss was due to their reduced beer consumption, which is completely hidden in the data. In the kidney stone example, the hidden dimension was the size of the stones, which, if ignored, reversed the results. I believe the baseball example can be explained by accounting for the total number of at-bats for each player, which is ignored by batting average alone. Unfortunately, every time I try to work it out, my head hurts. Maybe one of my readers will provide a clear explanation that I can post at FlawOfAverages.com.

TABLE 18.1 Jeter and Justice Batting Averages

	1995		1996		1997		Combined	
Derek Jeter	12/48	0.250	183/582	0.314	190/654	0.291	385/1,284	**0.300**
David Justice	104/411	**0.253**	45/140	**0.321**	163/495	**0.329**	312/1,046	0.298

CHAPTER

19

The Scholtes Revenue Fallacy

One of the ways a bank makes money is to borrow the stuff at a low interest rate (which it can do because it has excellent credit) and loan it to you and me at a higher interest rate (which we have to pay because our credit is not as good as a bank's). The difference between the interest a bank pays and the interest it charges is called the *margin*. Suppose the bank pays 4 percent per year for its money and loans it to its best customers at 6 percent. The margin on those accounts is 2 percent. If the bank is also willing to loan money to less creditworthy customers for 14 percent, then those accounts would have a margin of 10 percent. In reality, banks lend money at a whole range of margins depending on the borrower's credit score, age, income, and other considerations.

The bank's amount of net revenue depends not only on the margin, but also on the balance, that is, the amount of money owed. For example, an account with a 6 percent margin and a $600 balance would yield annual net revenue of 6 percent times $600, or $36. Of course, there is an overhead cost associated with maintaining the loan, let's say $25 per account per year. So the profit would be $36 − $25 = $11 for that account. Now imagine that 6 percent and $600 turn out to be the average balance and margin of all accounts. Then the bank makes an average profit of $11 per account. Right? You wish.

This is a subtle but insidious example of the Strong Form of the Flaw of Averages, described to me by Stefan Scholtes of Cambridge. If there were no statistical relationship between balance and margin, then $11 *would* be the correct average profit. But actually the larger the balance is, the better the customer is, and the lower the margin will be.

So before you put that $11-per-customer profit projection in your annual report, consider this. What would happen if the average margin and balance reflect exactly two types of accounts? Half your customers are well-to-do, with margins of 2 percent and balances of $1,000, for an average annual net revenue of $20. The other half are relative deadbeats, with margins of 10 percent and balances of $200, again for an average annual net revenue of $20. But don't forget that dratted overhead of $25 per account, leaving you with a loss of $5 for each of your accounts, as reflected in Table 19.1. The profit associated with the average customer is $11, yet the bank loses $5 on every account.

"Of course, banks aren't that stupid at calculating the revenue from their current loans," says Scholtes. "Otherwise they would be out of business. But when they go on to project future growth in revenue," he goes on, "they do often assume average balance growth. This results in the same flaw—unless the growth across the population of accounts maintains the exact proportions."

Note that, had larger balances been associated with the larger margins instead of the other way around, the average profit would have been greater than the profit associated with the average margin and balance.

TABLE 19.1   Profit of Average Account is $11, but on Average You Lose $5

	Balance	Margin	Net Revenue	Profit After Overhead
❑ High balance	❑ $1,000	❑ 2%	❑ $20	❑ −$5
❑ Low balance	❑ $200	❑ 10%	❑ $20	❑ −$5
❑ Average	❑ $600	❑ 6%	❑ $20	❑ −$5

❑ **Flawed Average Calculation Based on Average Margin and Balance**

	Balance	Margin	Net Revenue	Profit After Overhead
❑	❑ $600	❑ 6%	❑ $36	❑ $11

Economics 101

The revenue derived by selling a quantity of items at a given price is simply the price times the quantity. And the most basic idea in economics is that, as the price goes up, fewer people will want to buy, and more will want to sell. This results in the famous supply and demand curves seen in every economics book (Figure 19.1).

So what happens if supply and demand are uncertain? We will consider two special cases: pure supply uncertainty and pure demand uncertainty.[1]

Pure Supply Uncertainty

Consider a commodity for which the demand curve is known with certainty, such as a microchip for a specific application. But suppose the cost of production and therefore the supply curve for this chip are uncertain, as shown in Figure 19.2.

The *average* price and quantity have not changed from Figure 19.1, but because the equilibrium may be in a region either of high price and low quantity or of low price and high quantity, the average revenue is now *less* than the average price times the average quantity. The key here is that, as you move from the northwest to the

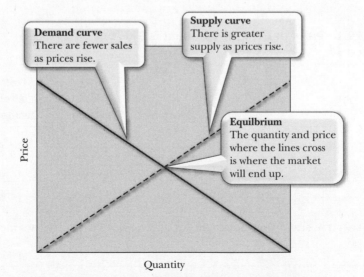

Figure 19.1   Supply, demand, and market equilibrium.

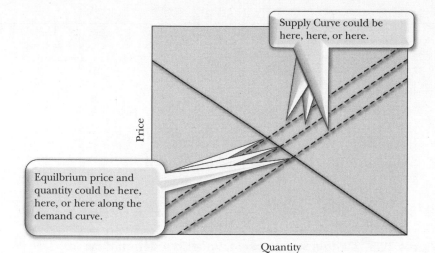

Figure 19.2   Certain demand curve, uncertain supply curve.

southeast on the demand curve in Figure 19.2, price times quantity is a frowning function, extending into a third dimension coming out of the page.

Pure Demand Uncertainty

Now consider a style-driven product such as apparel, with uncertain demand but for which the cost of production and therefore the supply curve are certain (cloth is cloth, regardless of the exact style of the garment). This situation is shown in Figure 19.3. Again, the *average* price and quantity have not changed, but because the equilibrium may be in a region either of high price and high quantity or of low price and low quantity, the average revenue is now *greater* than the average price times the average quantity. Now as you move from the southwest to the northeast on the supply curve in Figure 19.3, price times quantity is a smiling function coming out of the page.

To my knowledge this asymmetry in the behavior of average revenue has not been described explicitly, so I will call it the *Scholtes Revenue Fallacy*. Be sure to check FlawOfAverages.com to see whether I get a bunch of incensed letters from economists, claiming that this was their idea years ago or that Adam Smith had nailed this down in the eighteenth century.

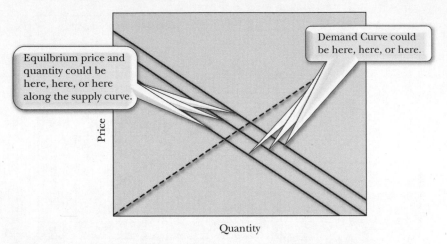

Figure 19.3 Certain supply curve, uncertain demand curve.

In summary, the Scholtes Revenue Fallacy occurs when revenue is the result of multiplying two uncertain numbers, such as margin and balance or price and quantity.

- If the two uncertain numbers are inversely (negatively) inter-related, the average revenue is less than the revenue associated with the average uncertainties.
- If the two uncertain numbers are directly (positively) interrelated, the average revenue is greater than the revenue associated with the average uncertainties.

CHAPTER

20

Taking Credit for Chance Occurrences

You have probably heard the one about the marketing director who knew that half of her advertising dollars were effective; she just never knew which half. It's hard enough to manage a business when you can directly measure the results of your actions. But when the things under your control are combined with numerous things beyond your control, such as market conditions, competition, and the weather, running a business is like shooting in the dark.

Advertising Results

Suppose, for example, that the sales figures have just come in from your marketing test. Of your 30 sales regions, you ran ads in ten, while the other 20 received no ads. The results consist of the percentage change in sales from the previous month for each market, as displayed in Table 20.1.[1]

The ten markets in which you advertised saw sales increase by 7.35 percent on average, while the 20 markets without ads had sales grow on average by 3.93 percent. The difference in averages is 3.42 percent, so the ads obviously worked.

Or could the average difference of 3.42 percent have happened by chance? The eleventh deadly sin is taking credit for something that was in fact just the luck of the draw. This is the realm of the Red concept of HYPOTHESIS TESTING, which consists of things like the F-TEST and T-TEST. But the operable question is, "Did it happen by chance?"

TABLE 20.1 Percentage Change in Sales from Previous Month by Market

Markets with Ads		Markets Without Ads		
Market 1	6.6%	Market 11	−2.8%	
Market 2	9.8%	Market 12	1.9%	
Market 3	8.6%	Market 13	−7.9%	
Market 4	−1.3%	Market 14	8.5%	
Market 5	4.9%	Market 15	4.1%	
Market 6	14.1%	Market 16	3.0%	
Market 7	11.4%	Market 17	3.3%	
Market 8	13.9%	Market 18	1.7%	
Market 9	6.6%	Market 19	6.6%	
Market 10	−1.1%	Market 20	7.0%	
		Market 21	3.4%	
		Market 22	5.0%	
		Market 23	8.2%	
		Market 24	6.6%	
		Market 25	4.1%	
		Market 26	10.1%	
		Market 27	−3.5%	
		Market 28	−1.2%	
		Market 29	10.6%	
		Market 30	9.9%	
Average	**7.35%**	**Average**	**3.93%**	**Difference of averages is 3.42%**

A simple example involves coin tosses. Suppose I walk into the room and claim that I can call coin tosses. Someone takes up my challenge and flips a coin, which I correctly call *heads*. "See?" I say, "I told you I could call tosses." This is hardly convincing, because there is a 50 percent probability that my correct guess was just a chance occurrence. The Red Word for this probability is the P-VALUE, and no one gets very excited about numbers like 50 percent. If, on the other hand, I call ten tosses in a row, people will sit up and take notice. Could that have happened by chance? Yes, but the probability is 0.5 raised to the tenth power, or only 1 chance in 1,024, so it lends credence to my special coin-predicting powers. But remember, if a few thousand people were all calling coin tosses, it would be amazing if *no* one called ten in a row.

So how would we apply this logic to the data of Table 20.1? There are numerous Steam Era techniques to do this, but I far prefer the following computational approach. Start by taking the position of the devil's advocate. We will assume the 3.42 percent difference *did* happen by chance, that is, it had nothing to do with the advertising. The Red Word for this is the NULL HYPOTHESIS, and it is equivalent to saying that all 30 sales figures in Table 20.1 came from the *same* distribution. So how unlikely is it that 30 numbers picked from this distribution and placed in one column of ten and another column of 20, would display an average difference of 3.42 percent?

This can be estimated through the resampling technique discussed in connection with Rick Medress's movie portfolio. We start by painting the 30 sales figures on ping-pong balls and throwing them into a lottery basket. Then we repeatedly draw the balls randomly from the basket (tossing them back in after each sample) and write the numbers into a column of ten on the left and a column of 20 on the right. After we have filled both columns, we check to see whether the left column average is at least 3.42 percent greater than the right column average. The whole procedure is repeated thousands of times, all the while counting the number of times the difference was as large as the one observed in the actual data. This can be simulated in seconds on a computer. It turns out that a difference of 3.42 percent or larger occurs in less than 5 percent of the randomly generated cases. This bolsters your case that the ads were indeed the cause of the increased average sales.

Pharmaceutical Effectiveness

Similar tests are also used for determining the efficacy of new pharmaceuticals. Here the benefit may be measured in increased years of life or in the reduction of the duration or severity of symptoms.

A P-VALUE of 5 percent or less is generally considered to be statistically significant. That is, the probability is only one in 20 that the improvement was due to chance. But there is a trap here. Like having thousands of people predicting coin tosses, if a large pharmaceutical firm tested sugar pills on enough diseases, 5 percent of the tests would appear statistically significant just due to chance. When it comes to life or death matters, I suggest consulting a trained statistician.

An Age-Old Scam

An age-old scam starts out when you receive a phone call from an anonymous stranger, who tells you that he works for the XYZ company and has inside information that can make you rich on the stock market. It would be strictly illegal for him to trade the stock because of his high position in the company, but if you, a complete stranger, make money on his information and provide him a share of your earnings in unmarked bills, it will be untraceable. He doesn't expect you to believe him until he proves that he has the information, but he tells you that XYZ stock will go up the following day and that he will call back after the markets close.

Sure enough, XYZ goes up the next day, but you figure there was a 50 percent probability that it happened by chance. The stranger calls back at the appointed time and tells you that XYZ will drop the following day, and it does. In fact, he calls for five straight days with correct predications, which you now take as a strong confirmation of his insider status. You reason that there is only one chance in 32 (0.5 raised to the fifth power) that he could have been right five days in a row by chance.

He now advises you to start investing your money in stock options based on his information, and after five more days you have made a tidy profit. Your mysterious contact reminds you that he has been right ten days in a row and says that if you want to keep the information coming, you must take 75 percent of what you have earned in unmarked bills, place it in a plain paper bag, and leave it at a specified park bench, which you do. That's the last you hear from him.

How did the stranger do it? Easy. He started with thousands of people and told half of them that XYZ would go up and half that XYZ would go down. The next day, half of the original group still believed him, so he again divided them in half. You were the lucky one for whom all his random predictions were correct. This illegal practice is even easier to carry out using email. No doubt some of you have received unsolicited predictions of stock movements or outcomes of sporting events based on this idea. Don't fall for it, and above all don't engage in it or you might go to jail.

Things to remember:

- Be sure to test to determine whether things could have happened by chance.

Things to forget:

- HYPOTHESIS TESTING—Use "Did it happen by chance?" instead.
- P-VALUE—Use "The probability that it could have happened by chance" instead.
- F-TESTS AND T-TESTS—Use "simulation" instead. See www.FlawOfAverages.com for examples and references.
- NULL HYPOTHESIS—Use "The assumption that something happened by chance" instead.

APPLICATIONS

The foundations discussed up to this point include the basic Mindles for managing uncertainty and risk. To fully understand them, you need to apply them. Ironically, understanding may not happen when you are concentrating on an application, but rather when your mind is wandering and you suddenly make a connection.

In this section, I will present some important areas of application that may serve as catalysts for those connections.

I will begin with Part 5 on modern finance, an area in which Nobel Prizes were won for conquering the Flaw of Averages. I will then discuss other areas in which the Flaw is still prevalent.

THE FLAW OF AVERAGES
IN FINANCE

In the early 1950s the Portfolio Theory of Harry Markowitz revolutionized the field of finance by explicitly recognizing what I refer to as the Weak Form of the Flaw of Averages. Specifically, the *average* return is not enough to describe an investment; you also need to know its *risk*. This work was extended and brought into widespread practice by William Sharpe in the 1960s. Soon modern portfolio theory was broadly acknowledged in the investment community, and Markowitz and Sharpe received the Nobel Prize in 1990.

The option pricing models of Fischer Black, Myron Scholes, and Robert Merton, introduced in the early 1970s, illuminated a special case of the Strong Form of the Flaw of Averages. Specifically, the *average* payoff of a stock option is not the payoff given the *average* value of the underlying stock. Their improved modeling of this situation led to tremendous growth in the area of financial derivatives, and option theory resulted in its own Nobel Prize in 1997.

These modern-day pioneers began to make the field of finance compliant with the Flaw of Averages. By understanding their work, we may attempt to generalize these principles to other areas of business, government, and military planning that are still average-centric.

CHAPTER

Your Retirement Portfolio

Nearly all of us share a problem that lies deep in Flaw of Averages territory: investing for retirement.

In *Die Broke*, Stephen Pollan and Mark Levine argue that wealth is of no value once you're dead, so make sure your family is taken care of while you are still alive and aim to die with nothing beyond your personal possessions.[1] This sounds about right to me, but whether or not you agree with this philosophy, it is a useful starting point for retirement planning. If, instead, you want to die with a specific sum in the bank, the following discussion requires only slight modification.

So suppose your retirement fund has $200,000 and you expect to live another 20 years. In fact, to simplify the analysis, let's assume that through some arrangement with the devil you know that you will die in *exactly* 20 years. How much money can you withdraw per year to achieve that perfect penniless state upon your demise? We will assume the money is invested in a mutual fund that has decades of history and that is expected to behave in the future much as it has in the past. Recent events have shown what a bad assumption this can be, but it is still much better than using averages alone and will be useful here for exposition. The annual return has fluctuated, year by year, with an average year returning 8 percent. Traditionally, financial planners have put this sort of information into a retirement calculator that starts with your $200,000, and then subtracts annual withdrawals year by year, while growing the remainder at 8 percent. By adjusting the amount withdrawn, you can quickly arrive at the expenditure level that exhausts your funds in exactly 20 years. For this example, $21,000 per year does the trick and results in balances over time, as shown in Figure 21.1.

You may wish to visit FlawOfAverages.com to see animations for this section or, if you have Microsoft Excel, to play along with the downloadable model there.

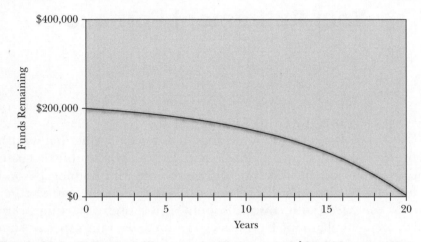

Figure 21.1   Balance with annual withdrawal of $21,000, assuming 8 percent return every year.

What's wrong with this picture? Plenty. The assumption that every year will yield the average return of 8 percent is terribly misleading. To avoid the Flaw of Averages, you must also model the year-by-year fluctuations of the fund. Assuming that past fluctuations are representative of future fluctuations, your wealth could equally likely follow a myriad of other trajectories. Figure 21.2 depicts a dozen potential wealth paths simulated at random by a computer, along with the flawed average projection of Figure 21.1 (dotted line).

Now if you run out of money two or three years early, you can just move in with your kids or hitch a ride to San Francisco and hang out with the other bums in Golden Gate Park. But going belly-up five years or more ahead of schedule (depicted by the bold scenario paths in Figure 21.2) would be ruinous and has roughly a 50/50 chance of occurring.

Thus the Flaw of Averages applied to this example states that, given the *average* return of 8 percent every year, there is *no* chance of ruin. But if you *average* over all the things the market could do, there is a *50 percent* chance of ruin. And this assumes that the future is like the past, which it probably isn't!

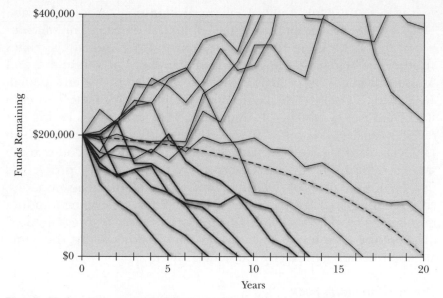

Figure 21.2   A dozen potential wealth path scenarios.

Simulation for the Masses

Financial Engines, a firm founded by Nobel Laureate Bill Sharpe, pioneered the use of Monte Carlo simulation of retirement accounts in 1996.[2] In 1997, Sharpe told me that at first he expected competition at the technical level, with different firms fighting it out over who had the most accurate simulation. But to his surprise, he found that most financial advisory companies at the time were still using averages; that is, their analyses were based on the approach of Figure 21.1. Sharpe wrote a humorous essay at the time, entitled "Financial Planning in Fantasyland," that is available online.[3]

In a sense Financial Engines is the prototypical Probability Management company. At its core is a database of distributions on the returns of more than 25,000 investments. Initially, all they provided was access to their simulations online, mostly to large organizations, whose employees used the service to monitor their retirement accounts. But as time went on, their clients have asked them for investment management services as well.

Once Financial Engines had broken the simulation ice, many smaller firms followed suit, creating their own models with @Risk or Crystal Ball or by developing their own stand-alone simulation software.

But Michael Dubis, a Certified Financial Planner in Madison, Wisconsin, has this warning: "Many financial planners use Monte Carlo as if it were the Holy Grail of Financial Planning success," he says. "This is dangerous if they don't have a solid understanding of statistics or the assumptions that go into simulations." And Dubis relates another problem regarding a lack of standards. If you add 2 and 3, you will get 5 regardless of whether you use paper and pencil, an abacus, a pocket calculator, or an Excel spreadsheet. This constancy has not been true of simulation. "The industry is crying out for standardized representations of distributions, so that any two financial planners, working with the same client, would come to the same conclusion no matter what software they use." The problem is that even if the users of the simulations made identical assumptions, each software package has its own method for generating random numbers. The power of the DIST representation of pregenerated distribution samples is that any two simulations using the same assumptions will get exactly the same answer.

The Parisian Meter Stick

Dubis has articulated one of the main aspirations of the new field of Probability Management: to develop libraries of standardized distributions for use in various industries. Just as there was once a defining platinum meter stick in a museum in Paris, there should be publicly available online benchmarks for the distributions of returns of major asset classes. And it could come in several flavors. According to Dubis, "Many of us are anxious for the day that inputs go beyond simple lognormal distribution and include real life scenarios that 'Fat-Tails' and 'Mandelbrot distributions' would incorporate." Michael couldn't contain himself there and slipped in a few Red Words, but his point is that in fact asset prices can be modeled in several standard ways, and they could all be represented. If your portfolio looked safe under all of the standard distribution assumptions, you would feel safe indeed. If it looked safe under all but one set of assumptions, it would encourage you to learn more about that standard, maybe even discussing it around the water cooler. And getting people to discuss probability at the water cooler is perhaps the ultimate goal of Probability Management.

Smoothing Things Out

Reconsider the example of the $200,000 fund that began this chapter. If there had been no year-by-year fluctuations in return, Figure 21.1 would have been an accurate picture of the future. In fact, the smoother the ride, the lower the chance of ruin. This is

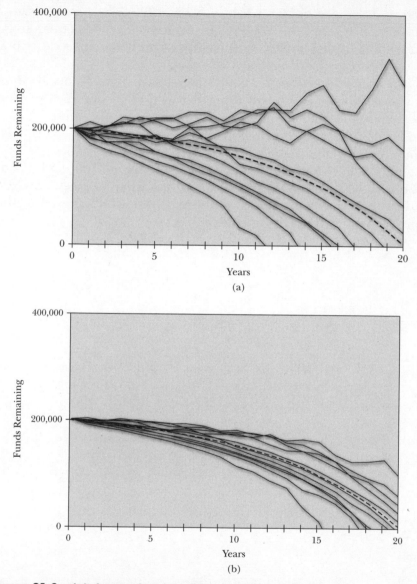

**Figure 21.3   (a) Approximately 20 percent chance of ruin;
(b) approximately 8 percent chance of ruin.**

shown in Figures 21.3a and 21.3b, which shows the results of the
same simulation with reduced level of uncertainty.

So if smoothing out the ride of retirement funds reduces the
chance of ruin, why hasn't someone done something about it? Two
people did and won Nobel Prizes for their trouble. modern portfolio

theory, developed by Harry Markowitz and Bill Sharpe, can design a portfolio that keeps the investor on the interstate, allows them to go off-roading, if they prefer, or try anything in between, as described in the next two chapters.

Of course the crash of 2008 has made people skeptical of all financial modeling. But if anything it should only reinforce the need to understand the implications of uncertainty in your portfolio. An acquaintance of mine who really understands portfolio simulation unloaded all his equities months before the crash. People who attempted to smooth out their portfolios, as in Figure 21.3, but who used only historical data, were hurt to various degrees, but were at least braced for the shock. However, those who adhered to the approach of Figure 21.1 were hammered.

The Birth of Portfolio Theory: The Age of Covariance

Recall the absurd example of hijacking an airliner, asking for $1 billion, and having one chance in a thousand of getting away with it. On average you get $1 million. However, equating this with $1 million in cash is a clear commission of the Weak Form of the Flaw of Averages. Yet technically that's what the academic literature in finance did until the mid-1950s. Let me take you back to the beginning. It's 1955. The picture is black and white. The sound track crackles.

"Harry, you've got a problem."

It is the voice of the renowned economist, Milton Friedman, and it's not what the young Harry Markowitz wanted to hear at the oral exam for his doctoral dissertation.

"This is not economics," Friedman went on. "It's not business administration. It's not mathematics."

"It's not literature," quipped Jacob Marschak, the head of the dissertation committee.

No, it was *not* economics, business administration, mathematics, or literature. But it *was* the birth of modern portfolio theory, for which Markowitz would share the Nobel Prize decades later. The committee is to be forgiven for not immediately grasping the full import of his thesis. These were men of letters and equations. Harry, on the other hand, was a student of computers, who had used this infant technology to manage investments in ways unimaginable up to that time.

Risk Is the New Dimension

A few years earlier, as Markowitz was studying the academic literature on investment theory, he discovered that it was based solely on
the average return of assets. Yes, *average*, as in the Flaw of Averages
"That can't be right," he said to himself. "If people are just trying to
maximize average return, why aren't they putting all their money
into a single high-yield stock?" The answer was clear. Having all
your eggs in one basket would keep you awake at night with worry.
Markowitz realized that there must be another dimension to investment decisions beyond average return, and that dimension was
risk. The risk of losing one's shirt was what differentiated the movie
portfolios of Rick Medress. The risk of a bullet through the head or
a life behind bars is what differentiates a hijacking from a million-
dollar bank account. Yet the concept had not been formalized in
the theory of finance before Markowitz.

A vision sprang into Harry's mind. It was a graph, with the horizontal axis representing the degree of risk and the vertical axis
representing average return. Every investment would have its own
position relative to these two coordinates, as shown in Figure 22.1.

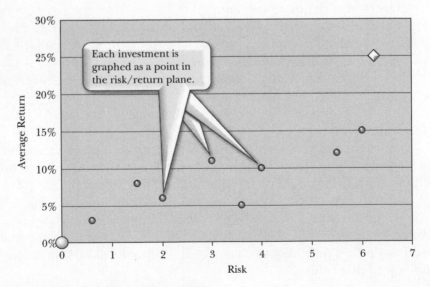

Figure 22.1 The risk/return graph.

The white dot at the origin corresponds to putting all your money under the mattress; you earn nothing, but the investment is risk free. The diamond in the upper right displays the investment with the highest average return but also high risk. In 1952, for example, this might have been Xerox, whose whacky idea for replacing carbon paper would not bear fruit for another 12 years.

Defining Risk

Markowitz defined the risk of a portfolio in terms of its **VARIANCE**, that is, the square of **SIGMA**, the Steam Era measure of uncertainty denigrated in Chapter 10 and defined at FlawOfAverages.com. Although he readily admits that **VARIANCE** in its pure form is not intuitive to most investors, it led to important models that helped explain human behavior. Furthermore, the early 1950s *was* still the Steam Era. Now that everyone and their dog has a microcomputer, Markowitz is inclined to bury the math in a simulation that shows investors how *bumpy* a ride they can expect (see Figure 21.3 and the associated web animation at FlawOfAverages.com).

Minimizing Risk

What Markowitz did next was something that generations of slick talking stockbrokers and snake oil salesmen had failed to do. He came up with a legitimate scientific method for choosing investments. The idea was to minimize the risk of a portfolio for any given average return. Recall the hypothetical investments in petroleum, airlines, and licorice introduced in Chapter 13. All three portfolios had the same average return, but the combination of petroleum and airlines had lower risk because the assets moved in opposite directions. Markowitz modeled the interrelationship between each pair of stocks with the Red concept known as **COVARIANCE**, mentioned in Chapter 13.

Markowitz was able to automate this process with a computer program, as described at FlawOfAverages.com.

The results of this program may be understood as follows. A complete butt-coverer who can't tolerate any risk would put their money in the mattress even though there is no return. The total go-for-broker, on the other hand, wants the absolute greatest average return and would put all their money in Xerox at 25 percent. For any average return between zero and 25 percent, the computer program calculates the minimum risk portfolio. This results in a trade-off curve, known as the *efficient frontier* (Figure 22.2), where each point on the line corresponds to a portfolio consisting of a different mixture of the original candidate investments.

There are no portfolios to the northwest of the frontier, or the program would have found them already. And for any portfolio to the southeast of the frontier, the average return could be increased by moving up to a point on the frontier, or the risk could be reduced by moving left to the frontier. So the only sensible portfolios lie on the frontier itself. The one that's right for you depends on your risk attitude.

This was an elegant approach in theory, but it taxed the computational power of the time. Markowitz managed to solve a problem with 10 stocks, but he tried and failed to reach 29 stocks due to computer limitations.

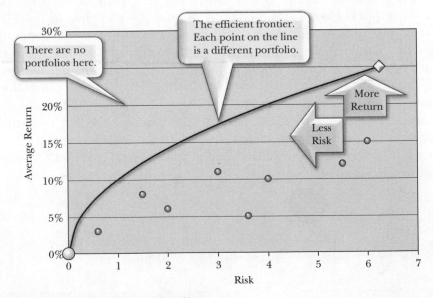

Figure 22.2   The efficient frontier.

Mutual Funds

At the end of the 1950s the most common way to invest in the stock market was through a portfolio of individual stocks. It was also possible to invest in a diversified collection of stocks chosen by someone else, that is, a mutual fund, but only a few were available. Mutual fund management was the perfect environment in which to apply Markowitz's portfolio optimization. But like so many revolutionary ideas, it was hardly noticed at the time, and, in any case, most financial organizations did not have the required computer power. Thus, in spite of having made a discovery that would eventually revolutionize investments, Markowitz devoted most of his career to technical aspects of computing, and he was best-known for codeveloping SIMSCRIPT, a language for specifying computer simulations.

Then in 1981, the economist James Tobin won the Nobel Prize. Markowitz, who was attending professional meetings when he heard the news, was stunned. Because Tobin had also done work in the area of portfolios, Markowitz assumed that this would have been his only shot at the prize himself. "I went for a long drive in the country to regain my composure," he told me, then he returned to the meeting and got on with his life.

But time was on his side. Computers were becoming faster, cheaper, and easier to use. Bill Sharpe, whom you will meet again in the next chapter, was building on Markowitz's original concepts, while enthusiastically carrying the torch of innovation to the financial community. When Markowitz got the news of his own Nobel Prize (shared with Bill Sharpe and Mert Miller) in 1990, he was stunned for the second time. Today, a search for "Markowitz" along with "portfolio" yields about 400,000 hits on Google. His name has become ubiquitous in investment management. There are now thousands of mutual funds, and the efficient frontier provides a clear framework for product differentiation by risk attitude. Furthermore, it is not just financial risk as bracketed by the butt-coverers and go-for-brokers anymore. Now there are green funds for those concerned about risk to the environment, social responsibility funds for those concerned about the risk of sweatshop labor, and feminist funds for those concerned that women aren't getting a fair shake.

The mathematics of statistical dependence was around long before Harry Markowitz and was of interest to almost no one.

But by showing how these concepts could be used to systematically reduce investment risk, he ushered in the age of **COVARIANCE**, in which the idea of statistical dependence became institutionalized in the financial community. In a November 2008 *Wall Street Journal* article on the financial crisis,[1] Markowitz reaffirms that diversification between independent investments can greatly reduce risk, but then, referring to the mortgage-backed securities that created the problem, he says "[F]inancial engineers should know that's not true of a portfolio of correlated risks."

Later I will show how the age of **COVARIANCE** has evolved into the age of the scatter plot, in which new methods of computation have the potential to illuminate such pitfalls. Today, Markowitz teaches at the University of California, San Diego, and at 81 still consults to the investment industry and engages in research driven by an energetic intellect.

When Harry Met Bill(y)

Bill Sharpe strode into class with a newspaper under his arm, sat on the edge of the table in front of the blackboard, leg dangling, and launched into an animated monologue on the day's scams, scandals, and other stories, weaving them seamlessly into the theory of finance.

It was the early 1990s and Sharpe had already shared the Nobel Prize in economics with Harry Markowitz and Merton Miller. I had recently started teaching at Stanford University's School of Engineering, and Sharpe graciously allowed me to audit his course in the Business School. I had come for the education, but I stayed for the entertainment.

A Simplified Model of the Relationships Among Securities

Sharpe met Markowitz in 1960 in Santa Monica, California, when they were both working at the RAND Corporation, the government think tank for which the term "think tank" was coined. Sharpe had a master's degree in economics from UCLA and was searching for a PhD thesis topic. His advisor suggested that he brainstorm with Markowitz.

The original formulation of Markowitz's computer model required the interrelationship between every pair of individual investments. Markowitz and Sharpe realized that most of these interrelationships were not significant but that each stock had a relationship to the stock market as a whole. So, as the Dow Jones went up or down, it dragged other securities with it to varying degrees. They felt that it would not be a bad approximation to ignore the other interrelationships and just keep this main one. This led to Sharpe's thesis topic: "Portfolio Analysis Based on a Simplified Model of the Relationships Among Securities."

Beta: Diversifiable Versus Nondiversifiable Risk

This relationship is shown in Figure 23.1 for an individual stock. Here historical changes in the stock price are plotted against historical changes in the Dow Jones. Sharpe referred to the slope of the line as *beta*, and it was calculated for each candidate stock.

Beta provides a measure of nondiversifiable risk. To understand this concept, let's start with diversifiable risk. Consider an investment in which someone flips a coin. Heads, you get $2, and tails, you get nothing, yielding an average of $1. You might think that this investment is pretty risky, but if you could diversify by investing a single penny with each of 100 people flipping coins, you could be very sure of getting almost exactly $1 of total return. This sort of risk can be diversified away.

Contrast that to spreading an investment across 100 stocks that tend to go up and down together with the market. If the Dow Jones

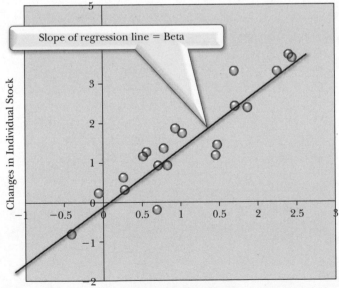

Changes in Dow Jones

Figure 23.1   Scatter plot over time of a single stock and the Dow Jones.

tanks, your whole investment is at risk. You can't diversify your way out of it with more stocks because they too will tend to move with the market. This is *nondiversifiable risk*. Each stock's beta is the measure of how it contributes to nondiversifiable risk when it is added to your portfolio.

Computational Efficiency and a New Frontier

The computations of the simplified model made it more efficient. And Sharpe, no slouch on the computer himself, was soon cooking up his own efficient frontiers, which ran faster and could handle more stocks than the original Markowitz formulation.

Then Sharpe had another idea for improvement. In Markowitz's model, butt-coverers were assumed to put their money under the mattress. But in reality they would probably put their money in Treasury bills and earn a few percent. This had a dramatic effect on the efficient frontier, as shown in Figure 23.2. With the T-bill replacing the mattress for the butt-coverers, those with slightly more pluck would split their investment between T-bills and a particular portfolio on the frontier marked **I**. Because this involved various proportions of one riskless and one risky investment (**T** and **I**), the risk/return trade-off is a straight line that is just tangent to the frontier at **I**. The points on the original frontier between **I** and

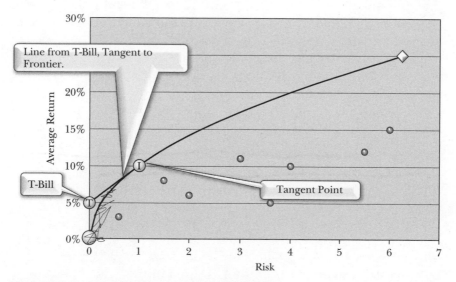

Figure 23.2   The efficient frontier with T-bill.

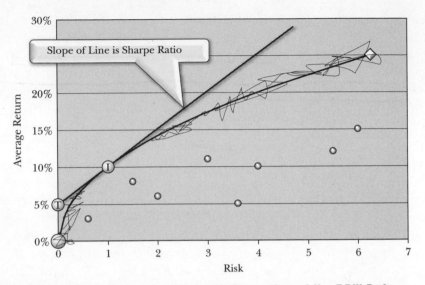

Figure 23.3   The Efficient Frontier with Borrowing at the T-Bill Rate.

the mattress can be ignored because they are now dominated by the less risky points on the straight line.

Now consider a large institutional investor who can borrow money at close to the T-bill's rate and invest it in portfolio **I**. By leveraging—that is, borrowing the amount invested—this investor could beat the original frontier at every point except for portfolio **I** itself, where they would tie it. This has the effect of extending the straight line beyond the portfolio **I**, as shown in Figure 23.3. The slope of this line is known as the Sharpe ratio. Note that if the investor paid a higher rate on the amount borrowed, the upper part of the straight line would have a lower slope.

We can now ignore the original frontier between **I** and Xerox, and the entire frontier is transformed from a curve to a straight line. The investment decision changes from which stocks to invest in to how to split money between T-bills and portfolio **I**.

CAPM and the Index Fund

But wait, there's more.

Up to this point, both Markowitz and Sharpe had modeled the optimal behavior of a single rational *investor*. Now Bill and other economists, notably Jack Treynor, John Lintner, and Jan Mossin, turned their attention to how *markets* would behave given that *investors* behaved in a Markowitzian manner.

In 1964 Sharpe published a paper that evolved into what is now known as the Capital Asset Pricing Model (CAPM).[1] This provides a simple framework for determining a fair average return of any stock based on its beta (as defined in Figure 23.1). The straight line in Figure 23.3 describes the rate at which a risk premium must be added to the return of risky stocks in order to get people to invest. The farther to the right of the T-bill you go on the graph, the greater the risk becomes, and the greater the average return must be to compensate investors for this risk.

Another important discovery was that portfolio **I** has the risk/return properties of the entire stock market. This gave impetus to the creation of index funds, whose portfolios are designed to mimic the behavior of the market as a whole.

Although Sharpe has held academic positions at the University of Washington, the University of California at Irvine, and then Stanford University, for much of his career, he has had at least one foot firmly planted in the financial industry. In the 1970s he helped major investment houses develop index funds. In 1996 he founded Financial Engines, the firm, mentioned earlier, that provides investment management and advice to investors based on simulations of their individual portfolios.

Now in his early seventies, Sharpe has just published a new book and software explaining his latest ideas on financial markets.[2] Far from an academic treatise trumpeting his Nobel Prize–winning theories, this book starts from scratch and lets readers connect the seats of their intellects to the seats of their pants with computer simulations. On page 3 of the book he describes the software, which can be downloaded from his web site.

> Instead of formulating complex algebraic models . . . one can build a computer model of a marketplace, populated by individuals, have them trade with one another until they do not wish to trade any more, then examine the characteristics of the resulting portfolios and asset prices.

All Models Are Wrong

Recall the quote that "All models are wrong, but some models are useful." Isaac Newton's models of physical motion, for example, were ultimately superseded by the relativistic models of Einstein. But Newton built the foundations from which Einstein started.

Although the models of Markowitz and Sharpe are only approximations, they were a great start and opened the floodgates of research into financial economics, leading to important new markets and a another Nobel Prize, as described later in this section.

After Markowitz and Sharpe, investors were correctly concerned not with *average* return, but with *risk/reward* ratios. The crash of 2008 was in large part caused by the fact that due to greed, negligence, or models that would not allow for negative growth in housing prices, many people got these risk/reward ratios wrong. In the 2008 *Wall Street Journal* article cited in the last chapter, Markowitz points out that "[T]he fundamental exercise of the analysis and understanding of the trade-off between risk and return has no shortcuts." He worries for this very reason that any government bailout plans that do not clearly illuminate the risks in funds of troubled assets will have the effect of keeping investors out of the market and therefore perpetuating the problem.

Yet, in spite of modern portfolio theory, naive investors still get roped in. Consider the infamous investment fund of Bernie Madoff, which had ostensibly greatly outperformed the market for years. You might have been tempted to invest, even though the prospectus no doubt carried the admonition that "past performance is not necessarily indicative of future results." Markowitz and Sharpe would disagree with this last statement, and would argue that if the investment had indeed delivered exceptional returns in the past, that it *does* indicate something about the future. That is, that this was an exceptionally *risky* investment that you should be wary of. Sadly, some of the victims of this scam flouted their theory to an even greater extent and had *all* their money with Madoff.

Mindles for the Financial Planning Client

Harry Markowitz recently told me that most investors can't relate to the STANDARD DEVIATION of a portfolio and need some more accessible explanation of risk, such as the output of a simulation. Here is how two financial advisory firms address this issue: Bessemer Trust and Financial Engines. The firms are at opposite ends of the spectrum, in that Bessemer manages money for high-net-worth individuals, whereas Bill Sharpe's Financial Engines has been designed to reach more of a mass market.

Bessemer Trust

In 1901, Henry Phipps and his childhood friend Andrew Carnegie sold their steel company to J. P. Morgan to form U.S. Steel. Phipps set aside some of the proceeds in a family fund that he called Bessemer Trust, in honor of the British inventor, Sir Henry Bessemer, who had invented the steel-making technology that had generated the wealth. By the 1970s the trust began managing the holdings of those outside the family, and today it oversees more than $50 billion. Before rushing to the phone to have them manage your money, however, you should be advised there is a $10 million minimum.

In Bessemer's wood-paneled reception area of its offices in Manhattan, oil paintings from the early 1900s celebrate the Industrial Revolution with scenes depicting steel mills and long freight trains full of coal—a reminder that this country's great wealth was not forged in a smoke-free environment.

Andy Parker is Bessemer's director of quantitative strategies. His college degree was in economics and physics, and he had taught himself how to program a computer. So when he graduated, although he initially took a dull job at a bank, he also worked evenings for a small brokerage firm writing programs on their Radio Shack TRS-80 computer. "They were really simple programs but way back when, anyone who could program a computer was a 'genius,'" recalls Andy. His programming experience led quickly to a career in the burgeoning derivatives business at several major banks and eventually to his current position.

His job is not just to get the analytics right, but to assure that it can be understood by Bessemer's clients. One approach he uses to explain the concept of risk return trade-offs is to compare the performance of a few benchmark portfolios over a specified time period. The example below was based on the period from 1946 to 2005. Although somewhat out of date, this period does include such calamities as the Korean War, the Cold War, the Cuban Missile Crisis, Viet Nam, 9/11, the collapse of Enron, the invasion of Iraq, and the advent of reality television. Each benchmark portfolio is a different mix of low-risk, low-return government bonds and a given set of high-risk, high-return equities, as shown in Table 24.1.

TABLE 24.1   Four Benchmark Portfolios

PERCENTAGE (%)	PORTFOLIO 1	PORTFOLIO 2	PORTFOLIO 3	PORTFOLIO 4
Equities	0%	50%	70%	100%
Bonds	100%	50%	30%	0%

The behavior of each portfolio is simulated over the entire period, with the average returns shown in Table 24.2 along with the ending value of $100 invested at the beginning. Clearly, the higher

TABLE 24.2   Returns over Historical Data

	PORTFOLIO 1	PORTFOLIO 2	PORTFOLIO 3	PORTFOLIO 4
Average return	5.7%	9.6%	10.9%	12.6%
Value of $100	$2,819	$24,246	$49,578	$125,302
Standard deviation	10.3%	10%	12.1%	16.5%

the percentage of equities, the greater the average return will be. It has become customary in financial planning to display the STANDARD DEVIATION as a relative measure of volatility, but Andy doesn't count on scoring lots of points with Red Words. Note that portfolio 2 with 50 percent equities is actually a little less volatile than 100 percent bonds, as it is more diversified against the effects of inflation.

Because risk is in the eye of the beholder, Andy presents this example from the perspective of various types of investors with different time horizons, as shown in Table 24.3.

- *Ten-year horizon.* Suppose you do not expect to retire for at least ten years. The first row of Table 24.3 displays the return over the worst ten-year period for each investment over the history of the data. In spite of the highest volatility, ten years is enough time to smooth out the ride with pure equities.
- *Five-year horizon.* Suppose you will need your money in five years. A portfolio of pure equities is just too risky, and 100 percent in bonds is also still unattractive. Either 50 percent or 70 percent equities seems about right.
- *Three-year horizon.* If you are retiring in three years, it looks like you had better be down to 50 percent in equities.
- *One-year horizon.* If you plan to remove all your money in one year, you don't have time to recover from the loss potential of a high equity portfolio. The pure bond portfolio looks like the best bet.

With this concept under their belt, the client is better equipped to discuss his or her own portfolio. For this analysis, Bessemer considers a much broader universe of investments. They use a mix of history *and* forward-looking estimates, recognizing that the interrelationship between assets change over time. Furthermore they may

TABLE 24.3   Worst Behavior by Time Horizon

	PORTFOLIO 1	PORTFOLIO 2	PORTFOLIO 3	PORTFOLIO 4
Worst 10 years	−0.1%	3.8%	4.2%	4.5%
Worst 5 years	−2.1%	3.6%	2.1%	−0.8%
Worst 3 years	−4.9%	−1.6%	−6.0%	−14.6%
Worst 1 year	−9.2%	−10.6%	−16.6%	−25.6%

"stress" the portfolio by simulating its performance with data from specific historical market episodes.

Interactive Simulation at Bessemer

In another effort to provide a seat of the pants understanding of risk, Andy has been a pioneer in the area of interactive simulation. He has led the development of a model in which his account managers can enter the portfolio of a client along with their cash needs. At that point a 1,000-trial simulation is run nearly instantaneously, and a graph is displayed describing the potential levels of remaining value over the time horizon of the fund.

A demo version of this model is available for download from ProbabilityManagement.org and is displayed as an animation at FlawOfAverages.com.

Figure 24.1 shows an example in which $15,000 per year is withdrawn from a $200,000 fund. The graph shows that after ten years, there is a 50 percent chance that the fund will still have about $200,000. There is only a 10 percent chance that the fund will be below

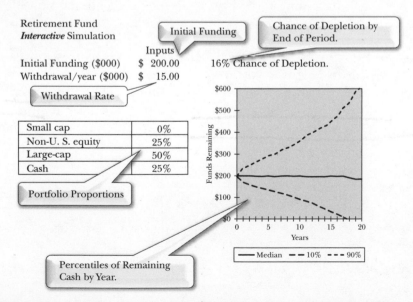

Figure 24.1   Demo version of the Bessemer Interactive Retirement Simulator.

$100,000 and only a 10 percent chance that it will be above $350,000. By 17 years, there is a 10 percent chance the fund will be exhausted.

Andy discusses the role of models below.

The Benefit of Portfolio Modeling

By Andrew Parker

Studies have shown that investors tend to buy at the top and sell at the bottom. This is something we want to help our clients avoid. Portfolio modeling is an exercise in defining uncertainty for them. Of course we are making some estimates of asset behavior which will clearly contain errors. If we could perfectly predict future asset behavior, we wouldn't need any models. But with thoughtful, conservative inputs, these models can give investors a realistic sense of risk which in turn allows them to them to create a portfolio that can "stand the test of time" The benefits are enormous, especially in the conditions we face today.

Financial Engines

Unlike Bessmer Trust, Financial Engines allows investors to run their own web-based simulations. I recently test drove their approach on a hypothetical portfolio.

The process begins by entering basic age and income information on a secure web site. It then asks when you plan to retire. I entered hypothetical data with a retirement age of 70.

The next step is to enter your retirement portfolio in as much detail as possible. I entered a portfolio that I considered typical of someone about ten years from retirement. The system then runs a simulation displaying a distribution of potential sustainable income levels at retirement, as shown in Figure 24.2. Whaddayaknow, it's a shape!

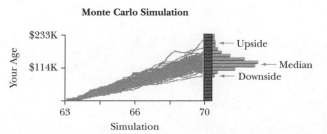

Figure 24.2 Simulation results from the Financial Engines' web site.

Source: Financial Engines

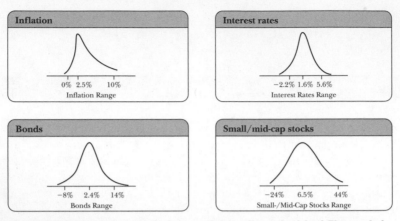

Figure 24.3   Four of the underlying distributions behind Financial Engines' simulation.

Source: Financial Engines

The program then explains how it arrived at its forecast as follows: "We don't *pick a single average number* for inflation or interest rates. Instead, we look at many different economic *scenarios*."

And it lets the user dig deeper into the various uncertainties underlying the forecast. I found this to be particularly interesting and have displayed four of them in Figure 24.3. Note that not all the uncertainties are symmetric.

You then input your target retirement income, and depending on how ambitious you are, the program returns a familiar Mindle in terms of a weather forecast. The goals I set ranged from over two-thirds to less than one-third of the working income entered at step 1. The calculated chances of meeting those goals ranged from less than 5 percent to greater than 95 percent, as shown in Figure 24.4, which looks a lot better in color on the actual web site.

Finally, the program lets you improve on your portfolio using any of the thousands of investments stored in the Financial Engines distribution database.

Figure 24.4   Financial Engines' display of the risk of not meeting retirement goals.

Source: Financial Engines

CHAPTER

Options: Profiting from Uncertainty

A security whose value is derived from the value of another security is known as a *derivative security*, and the security that it is derived from is known as the *underlying security*. Derivative securities include such contracts as *futures, forwards, options*, and *swaps*. For most derivatives, the average value is *not* what you get by plugging in the average value of the underlying. They live in the land of the Strong Form of the Flaw of Averages.

If the portfolio theory of Markowitz and Sharpe is analogous to Newton's laws of physics, simple enough to be taught in middle school, then the option theory of Fischer Black, Robert Merton, and Myron Scholes is more like the work of Einstein and is even related to it mathematically. Although almost no one knows how to derive Einstein's famous $E = MC^2$, everyone can grasp the power of the atomic bomb that it unleashed. The famous Black-Scholes equation looks like this:

$$C(S,T) = S\Phi(d_1) - Ke^{-rT\Phi(d_2)}$$

$$\text{where } d_1 = \frac{\ln(S/K) + (r + \sigma^2/2)T}{\sigma\sqrt{T}} \quad \text{and} \quad d_2 = d_1 - \sigma\sqrt{T}$$

For most of us, including me, this is about as useful as the bicycle equations. However, as interpreted by computers and programmable calculators, it launched the trillion-dollar market in derivative securities. Furthermore, it is easy to gain a seat of the pants understanding of options. This in turn can allow you to actually benefit from uncertainty, rather than fear it.

Stock Options

One of the most basic derivatives is the *stock option,* and the simplest stock options are the *call* and the *put.* For this kind of option, the underlying security is a particular stock. A *call option* gives its owner the right, but not the obligation, to *purchase* a share of the stock at a particular price (the *strike price*) on a particular date (the *maturity*). A *put option* gives its owner the right, but not the obligation, to *sell* a share of the stock at the strike price on the maturity date. These options are known as *European options.* Options that can be exercised *at any time up to* the maturity date are known as *American options.*

Suppose, for example, that I sold you a 12-week European call option with a strike price of $21 derived from a stock currently selling for $20. If the stock is above $21 at maturity (12 weeks hence), that is, *in the money,* then you will buy the stock from me at $21 and sell it on the market, pocketing the difference. Otherwise, you will do nothing and get nothing.

Figure 25.1 depicts five randomly generated trajectories that the stock price might take over the next 12 weeks (see FlawOfAverages .com for an animation of this graph). If these five paths were the only possible outcomes, then the average payoff of the option would be ($3.39 + $2.06 + $0 + $0 + $0)/5 = $1.09. Of course, in reality, an infinite number of paths might occur, which can be

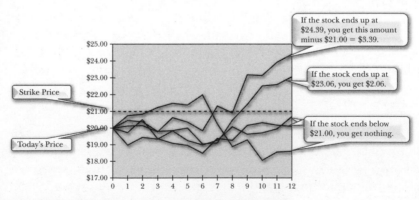

Figure 25.1   Possible outcomes of a call option.

approximated through simulation or described theoretically by the Black-Scholes equation. Note that the payoff here does not subtract off the cost of the option, which will be discussed later in the chapter.

In this example, the average, or expected, price of the stock in 12 weeks is less than $21. So the payoff of the option, based on the *average price* of the stock, is zero because at its average price you wouldn't exercise it. But since the actual payoff is either positive or zero, the *average payoff* of the option must be greater than zero.

To recap, the *average value* of the option is not the value given the *average future stock price*, so this is a classic example of the Strong Form of the Flaw of Averages. The greater the uncertainty in the price of the underlying, the greater the upside will be, but because the value is never less than zero, the downside does not increase with uncertainty. So counter to intuition, the greater the uncertainty in the price of the stock, the greater the value of the option will be.

Connection with the Value of Information

Think of buying or selling a particular stock in terms of a decision tree. You must decide what to do with the stock today, but you don't find out until later if it will go up or down. Through the use of options, you get to decide whether to buy the stock *after* you know whether it will go up or down. Thus, the prices of options are governed by the concept of the value of information, as discussed in Chapter 15.

What should the market price be of the option just described? Hint: If you had answered this question in 1973, you would have won the Nobel Prize in economics in 1997. Actually, even if you were Nobel Prize–winning material, you couldn't answer this without also knowing the volatility (degree of uncertainty) of the stock.

Option Charts

Call Option Chart   It is common to chart the payoff and profit of an option against the price of the stock at maturity. Figure 25.2 is the payoff chart for the option in our example.

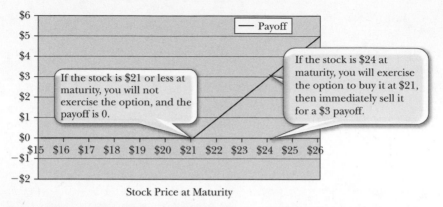

Figure 25.2   Call option payoff chart.

The profit is found by subtracting what you paid for the option from the payoff. For example, suppose the price was $1. The chart displaying both payoff and profit would look like Figure 25.3. Notice that you would exercise the option for any price greater than $21, but you don't make your dollar back until the stock reaches $22.

Put Option Chart

Now suppose that instead of a call, I had sold you a 12-week put option on the stock with a strike price of $21. According to a principle known as put-call parity the cost of the put would not be the same as the cost of the call in general. However, for the purposes of this

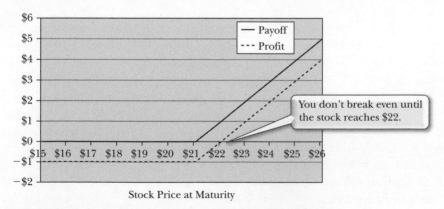

Figure 25.3   Call option chart of payoff and profit.

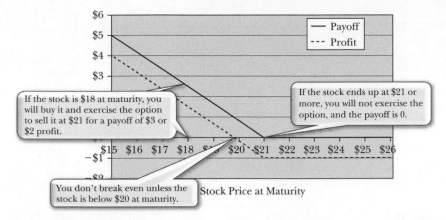

Figure 25.4   Chart of a put option with a strike of $21 and a cost of $1.

discussion, I will assume that it is again $1 (see Figure 25.4). If the stock price at maturity is greater than the strike, you will not exercise the option. But if the price is below the strike, then you will purchase it at the market price and *put* it to me (so to speak) at $21, pocketing the difference.

When you buy an option, you are *long.* When you sell an option, you are *short.* The charts for someone shorting the option are the mirror image of those who are long because the money simply goes in the opposite direction. The four types of contracts, charted in Figure 25.5, form a set of building blocks with which you can construct a wide variety of risk-mitigating contracts known as *nonexotic,* or *vanilla,* options. Notice that when you are long on the option, there is potential for great reward, but only limited loss (the price of the option itself). On the other hand, if you short an option there is only a limited reward, but the potential for loss is large, just as there is in selling insurance. Thus people who sell options typically cover their risk in various ways. For example, selling a call is *not* risky if you already own the underlying stock in case you must provide it to the option holder. This is called a covered call.

These charts form a powerful Mindle, which if fully understood, can change the way you think about and manage risk. Notice that they fall neatly into two of the categories described by Ludwig William Valdemar Jensen a century ago, as shown earlier in Figure 12.1.

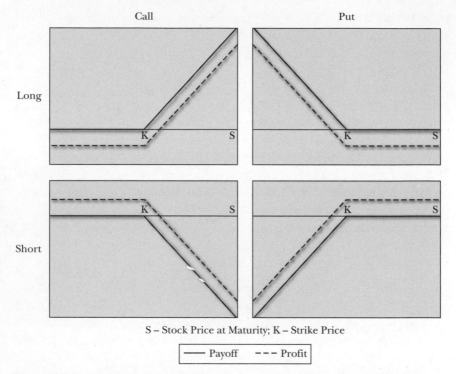

S – Stock Price at Maturity; K – Strike Price

——— Payoff   - - - Profit

Figure 25.5   The building blocks of nonexotic, or vanilla, options.

How Options Are Used

Case 1: Protecting an Undiversified Portfolio   Imagine that years ago you worked at a start-up company and purchased its stock for pennies. Recently your old firm went public. Your investment is now worth $1 million and constitutes your entire net worth. Having read up on diversification and efficient portfolios in earlier chapters, you now realize that you are ridiculously undiversified. "I know," you say to yourself, "I will sell the stock and split the cash between T-bills and an index fund, just like Bill Sharpe said I should." "Great," says the IRS, "we will snag $200,000 in capital gains taxes. That's enough to fund one full minute of war. We know you'll be proud to see your tax dollars at work on the nightly news." "Hmm," you say. "Is there another way I can protect myself against my one and only stock going south?"

What should you do to protect yourself in this situation? The answer lies in the upper right quadrant of Figure 25.5: buy puts on your stock. If you choose a put with a strike price equal to today's stock price, it will act as a nondeductible insurance policy on a share of stock. Suppose that your stock is currently selling for $100 per share and that a one-year put option with a strike price of $100 costs you $5. If the share of stock goes up to $105 over the next year, then when you subtract the cost of the option, you are back to the original $100. The more the stock goes up, the more you make, always, of course, less the $5 you paid for the option. If the stock stays the same, then you are down by $5. But that's as bad as it gets. If the stock falls to $95, the option pays you the difference of $5, which is what it cost you, so you still net out at $95. If the stock tanks to $50, the option will pay off the full $50, less the $5 you paid for it you; so you still end up at $95.

If you had bought an option with a strike price below the current price, it would have acted as a deductible insurance policy. That is, it wouldn't have paid off until you had lost the difference between the current price and strike price. Of course, the option with the higher deductible would have cost you less, just as it does with conventional insurance.

Case 2: ACME Pharmaceuticals and the Mystery Ingredient   Imagine that you live across the street from ACME Pharmaceuticals, a firm that has a blockbuster drug under development that may cure cancer. The drug has not yet been released for human testing because the FDA believes there is a 50/50 chance that it actually *causes* cancer instead of curing it. The active agent in the drug, which does either the curing or causing, is a highly guarded ACME secret, which will be divulged when the FDA publishes their final report in 30 days.

As you gaze absentmindedly at the ACME complex across the street, you catch a glimpse through a window of a PowerPoint presentation revealing that the mystery agent is licorice!

What do you do? (And fast, I might add.) What do you *know* is going to happen to the price of licorice? It will either go way up or way down from the current price. Therefore, again referring to Figure 25.5, you should buy a *call* and a *put* with strikes at the current price, and with maturities of at least one month, to give the FDA time to finish its report. This combination of options is known as a *straddle* and is charted in Figure 25.6. Let's again assume that the calls and puts cost $1 each. This time you need to buy one

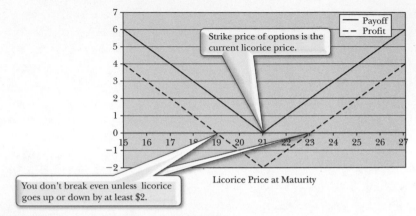

Figure 25.6   A straddle on licorice.

of each, so the straddle costs $2. Now if the price of licorice goes either up or down by at least $2 (which is likely once the FDA's report gets out), you are in the money one way or the other. You have turned the *uncertainty* in licorice prices into *profit*. How cool is that!

Case 3: ACME Pharmaceuticals and the Mystery Ingredient Version 2   This is the same as case 2, except that instead of seeing the PowerPoint presentation through your window, you see it on the CNN news channel, as transmitted by a roving satellite up-link truck that happens to be parked in front of ACME on some unrelated news story.

What do you do now? Nothing. As soon as CNN broadcasts the information that licorice is the mystery ingredient that either cures or causes cancer, everyone and their dog will start buying puts and calls on licorice. This drives the prices up, let's suppose to $3 for each option. The chart now looks like Figure 25.7, and the only way you make money is if licorice deviates at least $6 either way from today's price. The market has just erased the opportunity that existed in the previous case.

Beyond the straddle, other option combinations include the butterfly, collar, strangle, bull spread, and bear spread. If you want to learn more, the Chicago Board Options Exchange (CBOE), which launched the options industry, has a set of online tutorials on options and options trading.[1]

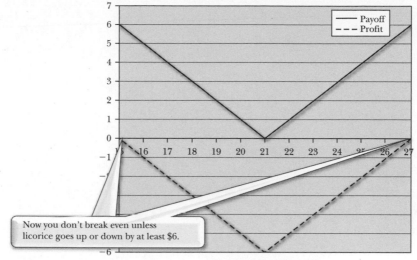

Figure 25.7 Straddle on licorice after the CNN broadcast.

Implied Volatility, the Uncertainty Gauge

For millennia, people could determine the real-time price of commodities, such as gold or ostrich feathers, by going down to the market and buying a piece of gold or an ostrich feather. And for millennia, people knew that future prices were uncertain. Historically, people could see that the price of gold was more stable than the price of ostrich feathers. However, there was no real-time measure of market *uncertainty* until options.

Let's return to the case of ACME Pharmaceuticals and the CNN satellite truck. A trader in Singapore, on the opposite side of the world, is monitoring the prices of options on petroleum, airlines, and licorice on his computer screen (Figure 25.8). At 8:45 p.m. he says to himself, "Yikes, I wonder what put the jitters in the licorice market?"

The jump in uncertainty in future licorice prices is revealed nearly instantaneously on the other side of the world through its option price. This is known as *implied volatility*. A profound result of option theory is that you can read the current price uncertainty of an asset straight off the price of its options. The trader mulls over the past week's new stories and shouts "Eureka! The mystery ingredient in ACME's new drug must be licorice."

Real Time Options Tracker

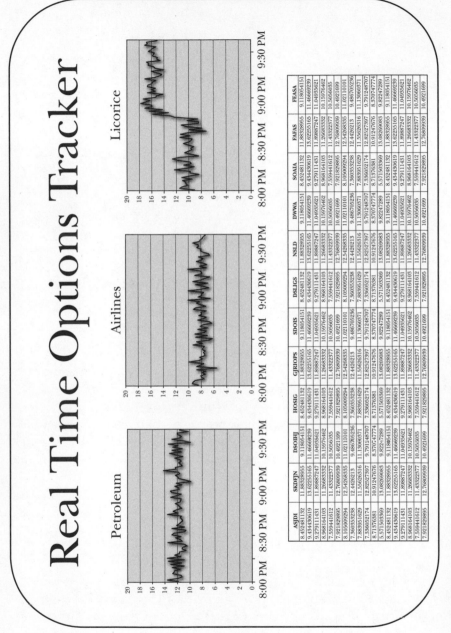

	ASJDI	SKDFIN	DSOHJ	HOSIG	GJKOPS	SDOIS	DSLICS	NSLD	DWWA	SOAIA	FAFAS	FEASA
	8.452481132	11.88328955	9.118054151	8.452481132	11.88328955	9.118054151	8.452481132	11.88328955	9.118054151	8.452481132	11.88328955	9.118054151
	9.434430619	13.62255165	11.46669239	9.434430619	13.62255165	11.46669239	9.434430619	13.62255165	11.46669239	9.434430619	13.62255165	11.46669239
	9.279111431	11.89887247	11.04935621	9.279111431	11.89887247	11.04935621	9.279111431	11.89887247	11.04935621	9.279111431	11.89887247	11.04935621
	8.968164103	11.26683332	10.15976462	8.968164103	11.26683332	10.15976462	8.968164103	11.26683332	10.15976462	8.968164103	11.26683332	10.15976462
	7.559441612	11.43322377	10.5056035	7.559441612	11.43322377	10.5056035	7.559441612	11.43322377	10.5056035	7.921829805	11.43322377	10.5056035
	7.921829895	12.76809939	10.4921699	7.921829895	12.76809939	10.4921699	7.921829895	12.76809939	10.4921699	7.921829805	12.76809939	10.4921699
	8.105009294	12.54268335	11.02110101	8.105009294	12.54268335	11.02110101	8.105009294	12.54268335	11.02110101	8.105009294	12.54268335	11.02110101
	7.360353238	12.4426213	9.486705296	7.360353238	12.4426213	9.486705296	7.360353238	12.4426213	9.486705296	7.360353238	12.4426213	9.486705296
	7.889951629	11.56626316	11.13060371	7.889951629	11.56626316	11.13060371	7.889951629	11.56626316	11.13060371	7.889951629	11.56626316	11.13060371
	7.336052174	12.82527397	9.791248707	7.336052174	12.82527397	9.791248707	7.336052174	12.82527397	9.791248707	7.336052174	12.82527397	9.791248707
	8.71376381	10.91247676	8.370747774	8.71376381	10.91247676	8.370747774	8.71376381	10.91247676	8.370747774	8.71376381	10.91247676	8.370747774
	5.571503369	13.08269083	9.82247289	5.571503369	13.08269083	9.82247289	5.571503369	13.08269083	9.82247289	5.571503369	13.08269083	9.82247289
	8.452481132	11.88328955	9.118054151	8.452481132	11.88328955	9.118054151	8.452481132	11.88328955	9.118054151	8.452481132	11.88328955	9.118054151
	9.434430619	13.62255165	11.46669239	9.434430619	13.62255165	11.46669239	9.434430619	13.62255165	11.46669239	9.434430619	13.62255165	11.46669239
	9.279111431	11.89887247	11.04935621	9.279111431	11.89887247	11.04935621	9.279111431	11.89887247	11.04935621	9.279111431	11.89887247	11.04935621
	8.968164103	11.26683332	10.15976462	8.968164103	11.26683332	10.15976462	8.968164103	11.26683332	10.15976462	8.968164103	11.26683332	10.15976462
	7.559441612	11.43322377	10.5056035	7.559441612	11.43322377	10.5056035	7.559441612	11.43322377	10.5056035	7.559441612	11.43322377	10.5056035
	7.921829895	12.76809939	10.4921699	7.921829895	12.76809939	10.4921699	7.921829895	12.76809939	10.4921699	7.921829895	12.76809939	10.4921699

Figure 25.8   Option trading screen in Singapore.

190

Things to remember:

- The charts (see Figure 25.5) for calls and puts and the things you can build with them.
- The average value of an option is not the value of the option given the average future price of the stock (Strong Form of the Flaw of Averages).
- Buying a call or put has a potentially large upside and limited downside.
- Selling a call or put has a limited upside and potentially large downside.
- The greater the current stock price, the greater the value of calls and the less the value of puts.
- The greater the strike price, the less the value of calls and the greater the value of puts.
- The greater the time to maturity, the greater the value of both calls and puts.
- The greater the discount rate, the lower the value of both calls and puts
- The greater the volatility (i.e., the uncertainty in the price of the stock), the greater the value of both calls and puts.
- One can actually read the volatility of the stock from the option price. This is known as the implied volatility.

Things to forget:

- The Black-Scholes equation (unless you are an options trader and have it programmed on your computer or calculator).

When Fischer and Myron Met Bob: Option Theory

It is 1969. Myron Scholes, with a freshly minted PhD in finance from the University of Chicago, joins MIT's Sloan School as an assistant professor. He meets Fischer Black, a consultant at Arthur D. Little with a Harvard PhD in applied mathematics. They are both up to speed on the Capital Asset Pricing Model of Bill Sharpe and are trying to apply it to options instead of to stocks. Fischer and Myron meet Bob Merton when he arrives at Sloan for a job interview as an assistant professor of finance. Bob lands the job, and it emerges that he too is investigating option valuation. I encourage you to read Peter Bernstein's *Capital Ideas* and the Nobel Prize acceptance lectures of Scholes and Merton to see whether you can untangle the intellectual paternity issues involved.[1,2] But clearly all three of these pioneers share credit for deriving the theoretical value of options, and Fischer Black would certainly have shared the Nobel Prize with the other two in 1997 had he not sadly passed away in 1995.

Risk-Neutral Pricing

Here is the basic argument by which the team arrived at a theoretical price for options:

1. Recall from the last chapter that options can behave like fire insurance policies on stocks. Therefore it is possible to bundle a combination of stocks and options into a portfolio, which, like a house and its insurance policy, is essentially risk free.

2. According to CAPM, such a bundle would be priced by the market to be the same as a T-bill. If it weren't, you could become fabulously wealthy by buying whichever one was cheaper and (since they are mathematically equivalent) selling it at the price of the more expensive one.
3. Step 2 gives you the price of the bundle, but now all you need to do is subtract the price of the stock and you're left with the price of the option.

Because their pricing argument was based on the theoretically risk-free bundle, it is known as *risk-neutral* pricing. A more detailed description follows.

The Risk-Free Portfolio

Here is how to create such a risk-free portfolio for the 12-week call option of Chapter 25. Consider an idealized world in which there are only two time periods: today and 12 weeks from now. There are also only two possible scenarios in 12 weeks for the underlying stock. It will either move up from $20 to $24 or drop from $20 to $18. Now consider a portfolio created by buying 5 shares of the stock and selling 10 call option contracts (Figure 26.1).

Let's analyze this portfolio under each of the two future scenarios.

- If the stock goes up to $24, then your 5 shares of stock are worth $120. Unfortunately, the option holder gets to buy 10 shares of stock from you at $21 even though it is now worth $24. So you take a $3 haircut on each, for a loss of $30. At the end of the day you are left with $90 ($120 − $30).

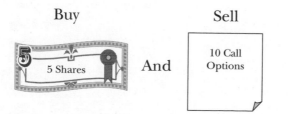

Buy   Sell

5 Shares   And   10 Call Options

Figure 26.1 The risk-free portfolio.

TABLE 26.1   Payoffs of the Risk-Free Portfolio

	States of the World	
	$24	**$18**
Stock price in 12 weeks		
Value of 5 shares of stock	$120	$90
Payout on 10 options	−$30	$0
Total	$90	$90

- If, on the other hand, the stock drops to $18, then your 5 shares are worth only $90. However, because the stock is selling for less than the strike price of $21, the option holder is *not* going to buy shares from you, and there is no cost associated with the options. Again you end up with $90. This is summarized in Table 26.1.

In this idealization, the portfolio has exactly the same value under both states of the world. It is therefore risk free, behaving like $90 stored under your mattress for 12 weeks (Figure 26.2).

Consider the value of each element of this formula. The stock in the portfolio is 5 shares times the $20 price, or $100. Since you have sold the 10 options, their value must be subtracted. We represent the as yet unknown price of the option as P. And, of course, there is the $90 lying under the mattress without the benefit of interest income for 12 weeks.

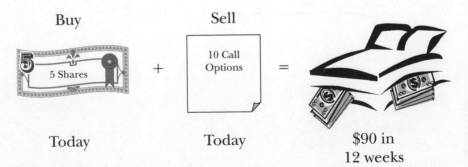

Buy		Sell		
5 Shares	+	10 Call Options	=	
Today		Today		$90 in 12 weeks

Figure 26.2   Risk-free portfolio equation.

This may be rewritten as

$$\$100 \quad - \quad 10 \times \$P \quad = \quad \$90 \text{ in 12 Weeks}$$

Or dividing both sides by 10 *& reavringing*

$$10 \times \$P \quad = \quad \$100 \quad - \quad \$90 \text{ in 12 Weeks}$$

To solve for P, we need the value of $9 in 12 weeks.

$$\$P \quad = \quad \$10 \quad - \quad \$9 \text{ in 12 Weeks}$$

The Time Value of Money

Have you heard the one about the million-dollar lottery in which the winner gets a dollar a year for a million years? This old joke highlights the time value of money. That is, a dollar in a million years is obviously not worth as much as a dollar today. So what is $9 in 12 weeks worth in today's dollars? If you had $9 today, you could invest it in T-bills (which let's suppose are earning 4 percent per year). Then in 12 weeks (roughly a quarter of a year), your money would grow 1 percent and be worth $9 × 1.01, or $9.09. Conversely, how much would you need today to be worth exactly $9 in 12 weeks? The answer is $9 ÷ 1.01, or $8.91. Therefore the price of the option is:

$$\$P \quad = \quad \$10 \quad - \quad \$8.91 \quad = \quad \$1.09$$

This is fairly easy to understand, but it applies only to an idealized world with two time periods and two outcomes. The real world has continuous time and continuous possibilities for price outcomes.

Dynamic Hedging

All it took to make this example applicable in the real world was pages of hideously complex calculations using an obscure branch of mathematics called Ito calculus, related to Einstein's 1905 work on the diffusion of gas molecules. The resulting Black-Scholes equation showed how to continually update the portfolio in the example, to keep it essentially risk free as market conditions changed. As an analogy, think of investing as sailing a small boat under changing wind conditions. To extract energy from the wind, you must continually move around the boat to balance the force on the sail, trying to tip the boat over, with the force of gravity, pulling it back down. The Black-Scholes equation showed how to automatically stabilize the boat under certain conditions.

Publication

Fischer Black and Myron Scholes wrote their famous paper on option pricing and submitted it to the *Journal of Political Economy* (*JPE*) in 1970. It was rejected without even being reviewed! Mert Miller, Scholes's thesis advisor at the University of Chicago who would share the Nobel Prize with Markowitz and Sharpe 20 years later, came to their rescue. He insisted that the journal accept their paper, which after some revisions, it did.

In 1973 the Black-Scholes paper appeared in the *JPE*,[3] and a seminal paper by Bob Merton was published in the *Bell Journal of Economics and Management Science.*[4]

The Black-Scholes equation cured a special but important case of the Strong Form of the Flaw of Averages. With a standardized approach to valuing options, the Chicago Board Options Exchange (CBOE) was formed for trading calls and puts. Today, the CBOE has an annual volume of a couple of hundred billion dollars, which is itself a drop in the bucket of the total derivatives industry.[5]

Buttoned Up

In his Nobel Prize lecture, Scholes relates this amusing story about sharing a spot on a calculator button:

> Texas Instruments marketed a hand-held calculator in 1977 that gave the Black-Scholes model values and hedge ratios. When I asked them for royalties, they replied that our work was in the public domain. When I asked, at least, for a calculator, they suggested that I buy one. I never did.

Long-Term Capital Management: The Perfect Storm

In 1994, long after their revolutionary theories had permeated the world of finance, Merton and Scholes helped found a hedge fund called Long-Term Capital Management (LTCM). For the first few years the returns were astonishing. Then, in August of 1998, less than a year after they received the Nobel Prize for option theory,

LTCM ran into trouble. On September 2, LTCM sent a confidential letter to their investors warning of trouble ahead. This was promptly leaked to the press, nearly triggering a worldwide financial crisis. The story has been chronicled by Roger Lowenstein, in his book, *When Genius Failed: The Rise and Fall of Long-Term Capital Management*, which provides a detailed blow-by-blow account.[6] Although technically their investment strategy was not dynamic hedging, I will present the story as a docudrama in terms of our sailing analogy.

LTCM avoided bets that markets would go up or down, but instead made lots of diversified investments in spreads, or the differences between markets. In particular, they bet heavily that, as markets became ever more efficient, the difference in risk premiums between various classes of debt would continue to narrow. This was like sailing in small waves with steady winds. With their sophisticated trading schemes, they were easily able to keep the boat balanced, making modest but dependable profits on most trades. They could not increase the profit per trade, but they could do *more* of them if they had *more* money. And the sailing was so smooth and the profits so dependable that LTCM decided to borrow the money, thus leveraging their investment. In effect, they had now put up a huge sail and were hiked way over the edge of the boat, streaking along at an incredible 40 percent profit per year.

But as their market position increased and others got into the game, LTCM quickly evolved into an 800-pound gorilla, now jammed onto a 20-foot yacht with a bunch of other sailors—major investment banks around the world, who were making similar investments. Then in 1998 a Black Swan paddled across their bow: A nuclear power, Russia, defaulted on its national debt. The differences between various classes of debt were suddenly magnified, and the spreads on the prices between them, which were supposed to keep coming down, skyrocketed instead. Where there had once been small waves, a perfect storm now kicked up a financial tidal wave that swept toward the yacht. To escape the onslaught, all the other sailors suddenly rushed to the gorilla's side of the stricken craft. The yacht swamped, and the gorilla was knocked overboard, getting tangled in the anchor chain.

At this point, the Federal Reserve Bank sailed up in a Coast Guard cutter and pointed out to the investment banks that they were all in the same boat, which was about to be dragged to the bottom by the gorilla if they did not attempt a rescue. Everyone involved got soaked except the Fed, which never actually bailed

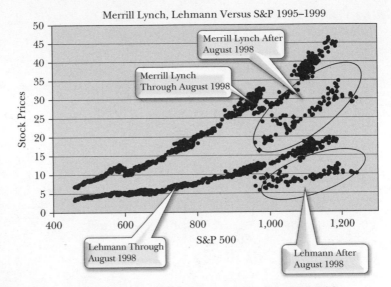

Figure 26.3   Scatter plot of JP Morgan versus the S&P 500.

anyone out, but merely sang sea shanties while the other bankers hauled in the half-drowned gorilla.

In the final analysis the aspect of the Flaw of Averages that tripped everyone up was that strong unanticipated interrelationships suddenly developed in prices of debt instruments, worldwide. In retrospect, the Black Swan that did them in should not have been that difficult to imagine before the entire banking community had sailed out over their heads.

The Russian financial crisis left a wake that is still visible today in the historical prices of investment bank stock. Figure 26.3 displays a scatter plot that I created from data available at Yahoo Finance. It shows the level of the S&P 500 on the *x* axis and the stock prices of Merrill Lynch and Lehmann Brothers (two of the banks that were impacted) on the *y* axis. The data for each bank falls into two neat clusters: one before the crisis and one after. Between these periods each stock lost roughly one-third of its value relative to the S&P 500.

 Similar patterns appear in the scatter plots of other investment banks of the time. An animation and spreadsheet at FlawOfAverages.com allow you to explore this in more detail.

Skin in the Game

Financial upheavals conjure up images of insiders unloading their stock on unsuspecting investors at the first sign of trouble. Just the opposite occurred with LTCM. In fact, shortly before the excrement engaged the ventilating device, the partners actually bought out many of their investors. Like the Wright Brothers, who did their own flying (one of whom was badly injured in a crash), Merton and Scholes had plenty of skin in the game. Orville Wright's crash, which killed an Army officer riding as a passenger, did not invalidate the laws of aerodynamics that they had struggled so hard to develop. Similarly, and contrary to some interpretations, LTCM's crash, and indeed, the current fiasco, do not invalidate the accomplishments of Black, Scholes, and Merton. All three crashes will fade into history. Manned flight and financial modeling will endure.

CHAPTER

Prices, Probabilities, and Predictions

The second half of the twentieth century was devoted to debating the relative merits of planned economies versus free markets. In case you missed it, the winner was announced with the collapse of the former Soviet Union and the rise of China. As Adam Smith pointed out in his 1776 *Wealth of Nations*, the best way to generate wealth is through free markets, in which prices guide the allocation of goods and services.[1]

A recent endorsement of this principle came from a surprising source: Russian Prime Minister Vladimir Putin in his January 28, 2009 address to the World Economic Forum in Davos Switzerland.[2] He warned that in a financial crisis: "Instead of streamlining market mechanisms, some are tempted to expand state economic intervention to the greatest possible extent." But, he continues, "In the 20th century, the Soviet Union made the state's role absolute. In the long run, this made the Soviet economy totally uncompetitive. This lesson cost us dearly. I am sure nobody wants to see it repeated."

Prices are, in effect, the neurotransmitters of society, reflecting wants, needs, fears, estimates of future supply, outcomes of horse races, and so on. Prices are also intertwined with the concept of probabilities, which in turn drive predictions. My father was an early advocate of subjective probability. He encouraged me from a young age to think of the probability of an event as the amount of money I would gamble to win a dollar if the event occurred.

Portions of this chapter appeared in Sam L. Savage, "Predictions and Probabilities," *ORMS Today*, Vol. 31, No. 3 (June 2004).

In the Information Age, the relationship between prices and probabilities is even more intimate. An elegant essay, "Nuclear Financial Economics" by Bill Sharpe, clearly shows the connection.[3] It's on the web; don't miss it. Two types of financial transactions are particularly tied to probabilities and predictions—futures and options—which are derived from underlying uncertainties.

Futures and Probabilities

Imagine the dismay of a farmer who has slaved away in his cornfield for months only to find that when the September harvest arrives, a glut in the market has driven prices to a new low. Suppose he could find someone willing to buy 100 bushels of corn in June, for delivery in September, at a discounted but prespecified price. Then the farmer would be protected from corn price risk. But who would buy such a contract? Due to the discount, this September corn future is a good deal when averaged over the long run, and if one diversifies by also buying pork belly, soybean, and petroleum futures, then an unexpected glut in any one of these markets would not be enough to wipe you out. If a large number of buyers and sellers are in such a market, then the prices of the futures carry a lot of information.

For example, a classic 1984 paper by UCLA finance professor Richard Roll shows that the futures market in frozen concentrated orange juice is a better predictor of Florida weather than the National Weather Service.[4] This is a beautiful example of what James Surowiecki calls the Wisdom of Crowds;[5] that is, a crowd of futures traders are collectively wiser than the weather experts.

To see how this might work, consider an idealized world in which there are two time periods: now and six months in the future. There are also two possible states of the world: warm or freezing weather. If it's warm, a quart of juice in six months will be selling for exactly what it does today. If it freezes, supply will be reduced, and the price will be $1 higher. Now consider the six-month juice future, that is, the price today of a quart of juice to be delivered in six months. If the price of the future equals today's price, it indicates that the market estimates no chance of a freeze. If the price of the future is $1 higher, it indicates a certain freeze. If the future price is $0.50 higher, it indicates a 50 percent chance of freeze, and so on. In this somewhat contrived example, the future price is just the perceived probability of freeze, but in the general case the price will be proportional to the probability.

Given how terrible individuals are at estimating probabilities, it is a profound result that marketplaces usually get them right. And getting good estimates of probabilities is a big step toward curing the Flaw of Averages.

Options and Uncertainty

Although the futures markets predict the average future values of assets, as we have seen, option prices indicate the degree of uncertainty. Between options and futures, it's a little like having the average and the volatility. But it doesn't stop there. Many other types of derivatives exist, including some that indicate the interrelationship between various uncertain assets.

Prediction Markets

Corn and Colin Powell Futures

In 1995, while idly searching the web for stories on Colin Powell, who was considering a U.S. presidential run, I stumbled onto a link identified as the Colin Powell Nomination Market. Intrigued, I followed it to an electronic futures market run by the University of Iowa.[6] They grow a lot of corn and hogs in Iowa, so I wasn't surprised to find a futures market there. But Colin Powell? It turned out this was a market where you could trade Powell Yes futures, which would pay $1 if Powell accepted the Republican nomination (and zero otherwise), and No futures, which would pay $1 if Powell did not accept the nomination (and zero otherwise).

How would you start such a market? The ingenious Iowa exchange sold these futures in bundles of one Yes and one No. Each bundle was worth exactly $1 because exactly one of these two bets would pay off. But once people owned the futures, they were free to trade them at any price they pleased, and the prices were recorded daily, as shown in Figure 27.1. Those who correctly predicted the final outcome made money, whereas those who didn't lost money. But everyone else benefited by being able to watch the prices on a daily basis.

Market reaction to such events as the beginning of Powell's book tour and the O.J. Simpson verdict are clearly visible. Also notice that

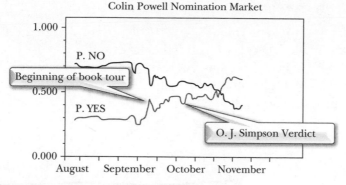

Figure 27.1   The Colin Powell nomination future.

the sum of the two prices remains very close to $1. If the sum was less than $1, then you were guaranteed to make money by buying both. This would drive up demand for both, and prices would rise. If the sum of the prices was greater than $1, you were guaranteed to make money by selling both. This would drive down demand for both, and prices would fall. This also demonstrates that the sum of the probabilities of mutually exclusive events must equal to 1. The fact that the graph is not completely symmetric indicates that the market is not perfectly efficient, but it seems pretty close. The Iowa Electronic Market, which is underwritten by the University of Iowa, is still going strong today, along with a growing number of others.

Predicting Terror Attacks

As discussed previously, a put option is a gamble that a stock price is going to fall. In February of 2000, a denial of service attack on the online trading firm E-TRADE caused its stock price to plummet. This is an attack in which hackers arrange for thousands of hits to flood a computer server, rendering it unavailable to the intended visitors. I wrote to a colleague:

> Has it occurred to you that if the hackers had bought put options the day before that they are now millionaires?

I went on to conjecture that

> You might discover a twitch in the options market that would actually tip you off to an impending attack.

Put Options on 9/11?

Fast forward to September 11, 2001. Unusually high numbers of put options were taken out on American and United Airlines just before the attack. This was reported by Dave Carpenter of the Associated Press and others.[7] To check out Carpenter's story, I created a graph (shown in Figure 27.2) from data available at the Options Clearing Corporation.[8] It displays the ratio of put and call trading volumes just before 9/11 for the following stocks: United Airlines), Southwest Airlines, Delta Airlines, American Airlines, and General Motors. Typically the volume of call contracts is twice that of puts. So one would expect the ratio to be about one-half. Thus the value for United Airlines on Thursday September 6, 2001, is 50 times above normal. Notice that there is no trading on weekends, so the spike in AMR puts occurs on the Monday before the Tuesday attack. Furthermore, there was no such spike in either Southwest Airlines or General Motors.

Could proper interpretation of this data have provided advance warning of the attack?

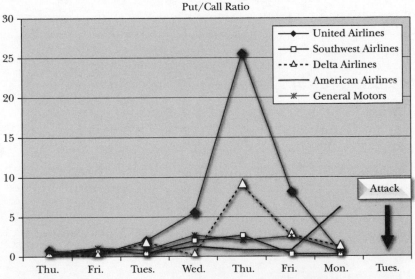

Figure 27.2   Put option volume on airlines and General Motors stock before the 9/11 attack.

According to an article by Allen M. Poteshman in the University of Chicago's *Journal of Business*, which investigated these trades,[9] the

> finding is consistent with informed investors having traded options in advance of the attacks.

And if you Google 9/11 put options, you will find all sorts of conspiracy theories. For example, 911Research.com displays the graph in Figure 27.2,[10] apparently taken from the online version of my 2004 article in *ORMS Today*. The same site also contains a host of other financial anomalies surrounding the 9/11 attack. But don't jump to conclusions. According to page 499, paragraph 130 of the 9/11 Commission Report:[11]

> A single U.S.-based institutional investor with no conceivable ties to al Qaeda purchased 95 percent of the UAL puts on September 6 as part of a trading strategy that also included buying 115,000 shares of American on September 10.

Did the 9/11 terrorists actually take advantage of the opportunity? It's hard to imagine suicidal maniacs, intent on killing thousands of innocent people, who would nonetheless draw the line at a little market manipulation to benefit of their heirs.

DARPA Gets into and out of the Picture

The idea of using prices to estimate probabilities is not just the domain of a few academicians and traders. In July of 2003 the Defense Advanced Research Projects Agency (DARPA) announced its Policy Analysis Market (PAM) to exploit the power of free markets to "focus on the economic, civil, and military futures of Egypt, Jordan, Iran, Iraq, Israel, Saudi Arabia, Syria, and Turkey and the impact of U.S. involvement with each." PAM was just preparing to issue prediction instruments whose prices would hopefully shed light on these important foreign policy issues when the entire program was summarily scrapped due to public outrage, forcing the resignation of DARPA head, John Poindexter.[12] See the graphic from the now defunct Policy Analysis Market (PAM) web site.[13]

A Market in the Future of the Middle East

Predictomania

I thought PAM was a creative idea. My main objection was that an exchange run by the U.S. Department of Defense could hardly be considered unbiased. Also, why waste taxpayer's money on something that already existed?[14] At the time, there were already several prediction markets up and running on the web, with people putting money where their mouths were on issues as wide-ranging as the outcome of the Kobe Bryant trial to the capture of Osama bin Laden.[15] Some of these exchanges are offshore to skirt gaming laws, and they use real money. Others offer the chance to win prizes. Google "prediction markets" to learn more.

Irony of Ironies

Within days of the public announcement of PAM in July 2003, in what CNN Money calls an "irony of ironies," TradeSports.com (now called Intrade.com), a Dublin-based exchange using real money, had a wager that Poindexter would lose his job by September.[16] He did.

WMD Futures

Another of my favorites on TradeSports were contracts that paid off if weapons of mass destruction were found in Iraq by various dates in 2003 (Figure 27.3).

While the U.S. administration said, "We'll find them, we'll find them, we'll find them," the markets were saying, "Yes, you will . . . no you won't . . . no you didn't," and all trading was subsequently halted. Comparing what I heard on the evening news to what I saw on my laptop computer, I felt strangely liberated from the traditional news media.

Insider Trading in an Insider Trading Scandal?

I was checking the markets every evening during the run-up to the 2004 election, and on July 15, 2004, something caught my eye. One of the most actively traded contracts on TradeSports.com was

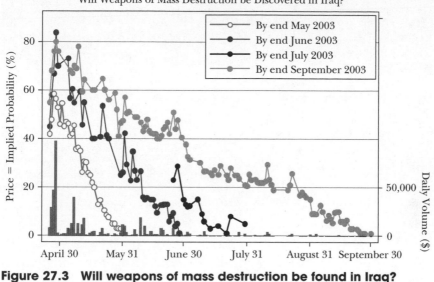

Figure 27.3   Will weapons of mass destruction be found in Iraq?

Source: Justin Wolfers and Eric Zitzewitz, "Prediction Markets," *Journal of Economic Perspectives,* Vol. 18, No. 2 (Spring 2004).

the MARTHA.TIME.+14Mths, which had just lost more than 50 percent of its value, as displayed in Table 27.1. Martha Stewart, the well-known TV and magazine personality, had been convicted of lying in an insider trading investigation, and there was great speculation about the severity of her upcoming sentence. The contract in question paid off if she received a sentence of greater than 14 months. Note that the last price (Last) was 20, and it had just dropped by 25 (Chge). The following day she was sentenced to five months, the minimum allowable under federal guidelines.

How had TradeSports predicted a light sentence the night before? I then wondered how the stock of her company, Martha Stewart Living Omnimedia, had reacted. It had opened only slightly higher the morning of July 16, but then shot up when the judge

TABLE 27.1   TradeSports Contract on Martha Stewart the Night Before Her Sentencing

TradeSports Contract	Bid	Ask	Qty	Last	Vol	Chge	Thursday
MARTHA.TIME.+14Mths	33 5.0	35	100	20	1643	−25	7/15/2004 9:48PM

announced his sentence (see Figure 27.4). I am surprised that more people didn't buy MSO early on the 16th based on the signal from TradeSports. If they had, they would have made a bundle.

The 2008 Election

Figure 27.5 shows Barack Obama's and John McCain's prices for the two years preceding the election. In early May 2008, Obama won the North Carolina primary in a landslide. Thereafter, the market assumed that Obama would be the ultimate Democratic nominee, and it became essentially a zero sum game with McCain. Thus if McCain went up, Obama would by necessity go down, and vice versa, resulting in a very symmetric graph from then on.

Real-Time Predicting

It is also possible to watch the predictions change in almost real time, as events unfold. I once brought my laptop to a San Francisco Giants baseball game at AT&T Park, which has wireless Internet. One could see the prices of the various wagers on the game change within a few seconds of events on the field.

As another example, Figure 27.6 shows Obama's price during his final debate with John McCain. Throughout the campaign,

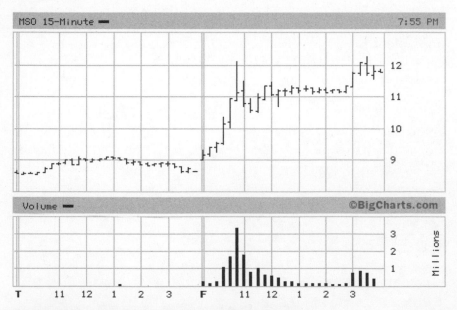

Figure 27.4   MSO Stock the Day of the Sentence.

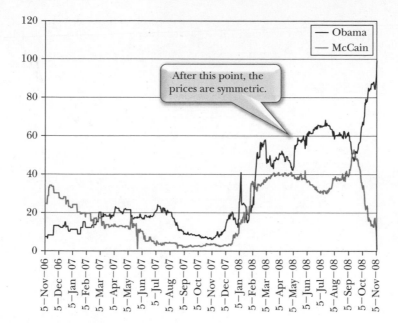

Figure 27.5 Obama's and McCain's prices.

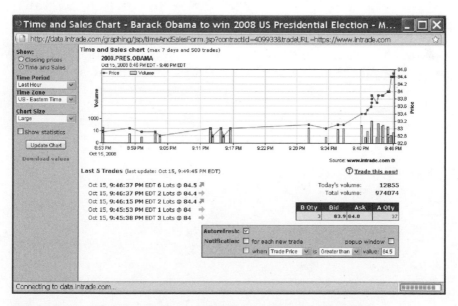

Figure 27.6 Obama-McCain debate on October 15, 2008.

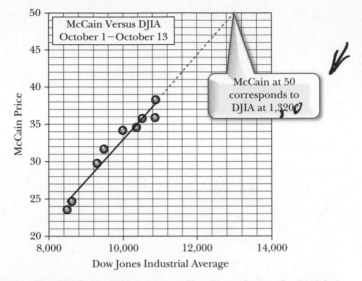

Figure 27.7   The McCain Price versus the Dow Jones Industrial Average, October 1–October 13.

newscasters kept saying we would need to wait until the next poll to see the results of some campaign-related event, but those events were probably already reflected in the prediction markets.

To what extent did the economy influence the election? It is well-known that a sour economy is bad for the incumbent party in general. But how clear was the picture with John McCain and the 2008 meltdown? The prediction markets tell a lot. Figure 27.7 is a scatter plot of McCain's price on Intrade versus the Dow Jones Industrial Average from October 1 through October 13, 2008. It displays a strong relationship that could not have happened by chance. For what it's worth, I couldn't resist calculating the value of the Dow that would have brought McCain up to a 50/50 chance during this period if this had been the only variable and there had truly been a linear relationship (both big IFs).

Of course, the true picture is more complicated but contains plenty of interesting patterns. Figure 27.8 displays the time period from January 2 through the election. I have made this data available at FlawOfAverages.com if you wish to explore it further on your own.

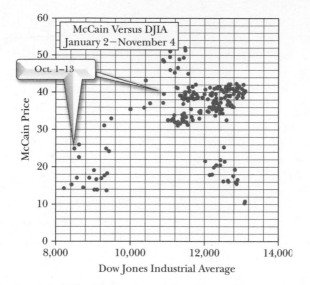

Figure 27.8   The McCain Price versus the Dow Jones Industrial Average, January 2–November 4.

When Does This Stuff Work?

A key component of Probability Management involves estimating probabilities. The prediction markets may prove to be an important resource in this regard.

Several authors have explored prediction markets.[17] They indicate some criteria for successful wagers.

1. The terms of the wager must be stated with great specificity so that there will be no ambiguity.
2. The participants must have some knowledge of the field. For example, Joe Grundfest of the Stanford Law School has pointed out the futility of a market to predict the veracity of String Theory.[18]
3. The bet must pay off well enough to make it worth investing one's time and revealing one's true opinion. This presumes that the main players in the market are more motivated by money than, for example, by martyrdom. As a counterexample, Grundfest describes how such markets might be manipulated. "Suppose you were a terrorist. If you wanted

to blow up a bridge, you would try to get everybody to look everyplace else by buying the futures that would say, 'No, what we're going to do is blow up a power plant.'"

If my father were still alive, he would be fascinated and no doubt gratified by the attempt to harness subjective probability as an economic force. But will prediction markets work in the long run? To answer this question, he would have no doubt suggested that we float a wager on the prediction markets that will pay $100 if the volume of prediction market trading has doubled in five years and that will pay zero otherwise.

PART

6

REAL FINANCE

In the late 1970s people began to investigate portfolios of industrial projects from the perspective of modern portfolio theory, and the term "real option" was coined for things like the gas property in which having the option not to pump was worth $500,000 on average.

This part will discuss the application of the Nobel Prize–winning principles of Part 5 to real assets, an area in which Probability Management has the potential to play a central role.

CHAPTER

28

Holistic Versus Hole-istic

I
t was the late 1980s in Chicago when I was still involved in the development and marketing of What's*Best!*, the **LINEAR PROGRAMMING** software package discussed in Chapter 2. I was spending many Saturdays and evenings alone at the office trying to make up for lost time. On such occasions the rare phone call was usually a wrong number, but that afternoon a Texas drawl thick enough to spread with a knife said, "Hi, this is Ben Ball." He got right to the point. "When people invest in portfolios of oil exploration sites, they rank the places to drill hole by hole, then start at the top and go down until they have exhausted their budget. Why don't they do Markowitz style portfolio optimization instead? Can you help me do this with **LINEAR PROGRAMMING**?"

Although I had never spoken to Ben before, I knew the name, because he had been quoted in *The Wall Street Journal* as a user of our software. I remember being struck by three things that afternoon. First, it was a good question. Second, the tone in Ben's voice indicated commitment. Third, the way he pronounced "oil" rhymed with his last name.

At the time, the top ten things I did *not* know about Ben were:

10. He started doing **LINEAR PROGRAMMING** at oil refineries in the early 1950s.
9. He had a bachelor's degree in chemical engineering from MIT.
8. He had also a master's in chemical engineering from MIT.
7. He had been vice president of strategy for Gulf Oil.
6. He had learned about portfolio optimization at the Harvard Business School.

5. He was now an adjunct professor at MIT.

4. He had been thinking about this problem since the early 1970s while still at Gulf.

3. He had published a preliminary paper on the subject in 1983.[1]

2. He had been an expert witness in numerous legal cases.

1. He was not the kind of guy to give up on something just because he hadn't had a breakthrough in 15 years.

Without realizing that this call would lead to a turning point in my own career, I simply told Ben that it was a sensible idea but that Markowitz optimization required NONLINEAR PROGRAMMING, in which I had little expertise and which What's*Best!* did not do at the time. And even if it did, Markowitz had had to calculate a COVARIANCE to model the interrelationship between every pair of stocks, and how the heck would you do that for oil wells?

In 1990 I moved to Stanford and forgot the whole incident.

But Ben was persistent. He tracked me down and arranged to meet me in person at a seminar I was giving in the Midwest. We talked more about the problem, but I still didn't have any ideas.

Then, over a two-week period in October 1992, everything changed.

A Serendipitous Sequence of Events

I was on one of those crazy spreadsheet seminar tours for the University of Chicago where I would start with a full-day course in New York, then fly to Chicago for a second day, and then on to Los Angeles for a third, picking up extra hours to unwind with each time zone.

The Methodology

I got to New York a day early and visited Mark Broadie, a finance professor at Columbia University, who had claimed in a phone conversation to have a way to do Markowitz portfolio optimization with LINEAR PROGRAMMING, as opposed to the standard NONLINEAR approach. I was skeptical when Mark described this over the phone, and it was before I had email, so he couldn't send me his computer file at the speed of light as we can today. When I arrived at Columbia and saw his spreadsheet, I immediately grasped the Mindle.

Mark's methodology *did* use **LINEAR PROGRAMMING** instead of **NONLINEAR PROGRAMMING!**

It did *not* use the Steam Era **COVARIANCE** approach, but instead relied on a more general way to model interrelationships, flexible enough to model the uncertain outputs of *petroleum prospects.*

The Model

Before reaching Los Angeles, I had spent several hours shackled to a chair in a confined area (courtesy of United Airlines). This solitude provided the opportunity to develop a prototype model of a portfolio of oil wells based on Mark's approach. I used Lotus 1-2-3, What's*Best!,* and my first Thinkpad laptop computer. I'll never forget excitedly calling Ben from my hotel room that night with the news that we now had a path forward. It was several days before I could FedEx him a computer disk. How times have changed.

The Motivation

The following Monday I returned to my office at Stanford and found a package on my desk. A note from someone named Peter Bernstein said that he had enjoyed my seminar in New York and hoped *I* would enjoy *his book.* It was *Capital Ideas: The Improbable Origins of Modern Wall Street.*[2]

A few pages into the first chapter, I read that the current explanation of stock price movement dates back to a 1900 dissertation by an obscure French mathematician named Bachelier and that his "thesis was lost until it was rediscovered quite by accident in the 1950s by Jimmie Savage, a mathematical statistician at Chicago." *It was?*

Learning something new and important about my late father caught my attention, and I decided to keep reading. Actually, I had trouble putting the book down. Although I had taught management science at the University of Chicago and had met several of the protagonists in the book, I knew little about finance. Here was the big picture of a big subject exposed clearly in a small book. More than that, *Capital Ideas* made me appreciate that Ben Ball in his own way was trying to follow in the footsteps of Harry Markowitz, but in the parallel universe of petroleum exploration investments.

The book whetted my appetite and motivated me for the challenges that I knew lay ahead.

Then coincidentally, later that week, our departmental colloquium was delivered by Hiroshi Konno, a Japanese management scientist, who had coauthored an important paper on the portfolio modeling approach that Mark had shown me the week before in New York.[3] Two weeks earlier, I had never heard of SCENARIO OPTIMIZATION, as it is called, and I had now received a double dose. Furthermore, at the same colloquium I met Bill Sharpe (of CAPM fame) for the first time, who has served as another important source of inspiration over the years.

Thus over a two-week period, through no particular brilliance on my part, I had stumbled onto the methodology, the model, and the motivation to help Ben put his ideas into practice. I had taken a fork in the road that would ultimately lead to Probability Management.

We Win Some and Lose Some

Ben and I teamed up on numerous occasions to spread the word of project portfolio optimization within the petroleum industry. We were often, but not always, well received.

In 1993, for example, we were invited to consult with a large oil firm (that no longer exists). They had written thousands of lines of FORTRAN programming code to simulate the potential economic output of a large set of petroleum projects. Ben and I were excited as they described their model. Choosing which of these projects to invest in was exactly what our approach was designed to do.

The prices of oil and natural gas generally do *not* rise and fall in lockstep. Thus there is an opportunity to diversify over these two commodities. I asked whether they modeled the prices of oil and gas separately. They said they only modeled oil price. For valuing gas, they used a formula that translated a volume of gas into its energy equivalent of oil, and then used world oil price. I kicked Ben's leg under the table. If nothing else, I knew we could improve their model by using two interrelated price distributions instead of a single one. Then Ben asked what distribution they used for the price of oil, and we were flabbergasted to hear that they used a single *average* price per barrel. They had written thousands of lines of computer code to model the portfolio of hundreds of uncertain projects, each containing price-sensitive embedded options, and they were guilty of *both* forms of the Flaw of Averages. This time I just about broke Ben's knee cap.

We were buoyant at dinner that night, scarcely believing our luck at finding a firm that could benefit so directly from our methodology.

We never heard from them again.

Our Ideas See the Light of Day

Someone who *was* receptive to our approach was John Howell, a former employee of a major oil company who had started a small consulting firm. John realized, however, that individual oil companies might be reluctant to take the lead on this new management approach, so in 1997 he organized a consortium of major and independent oil and gas companies under the sponsorship of Columbia University. Ben and I gave the kickoff workshop in Houston for this program, which was well received. Howell worked tirelessly on this project, further evolving the models and developing approaches to effective implementation. In 1998 he started Portfolio Decisions, Inc. (PDI) to meet the increasing demand for assistance with portfolio management issues. Happily, PDI is still going strong a decade later.[4]

Ben and I published our methodology in the *Journal of Petroleum Technology* in 1999 in a paper that compared the modern approach of modeling portfolio effects with the old method of ranking the prospects hole by hole. Ben came up with the title: "Holistic vs. Hole-istic Exploration and Production Strategies."[5]

 Further explanation of this approach, along with an Excel model for generating optimal portfolios, is available at FlawOfAverages.com.

In 2004 I attended a conference in Houston on Portfolio Optimization in Oil & Gas and was heartened to discover that our paper had become widely known within this group. Most people would have given up after a couple of decades, but Ben Ball had persevered to become the Harry Markowitz of the Oil Patch.

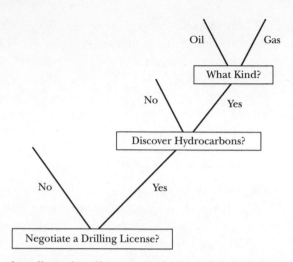

Figure 28.1   An oil exploration project viewed as a tree.

The Decision Forest

Conceptually the approach that Ben and I developed can be applied to portfolios of projects of any sort. For example, a firm introducing a new product lineup should use a portfolio approach to avoid risks due to both cannibalization and potential competitive products. A portfolio of pharmaceutical R&D projects would be designed with both competitive drugs and potential governmental regulation changes in mind. Most people working on such problems, however, continue to simply rank their projects instead of taking true portfolio effects into account. For such folks, I offer the following Mindle to help you better grasp the situation. Think of each project as a decision tree reflecting uncertainties that pertain only to that project. An oil exploration project is displayed in Figure 28.1. This results in a bunch of decision trees or a *decision forest*.

But modeling all of the individual projects as decision trees is not enough, because, as discussed earlier, portfolio decisions must reflect the interrelationships between the constituent parts. For this, I model global uncertainties such as the price of oil or political upheaval as the winds of fortune, which blow through the entire forest, influencing all the trees at once, as shown in Figure 28.2.

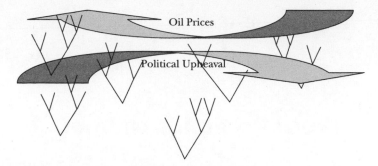

Figure 28.2   The winds of fortune.

Once the entire decision forest is modeled, it remains to choose a good portfolio. If, for example, there were 100 possible projects, there would be more distinct portfolios than stars in the universe. But once the problem is properly formulated, readily available optimization software can guide you to an optimal choice, as discussed at FlawOfAverages.com.

CHAPTER

Real Portfolios at Shell

In a leather jacket and jeans, riding his Harley Davidson up St. Charles Avenue after work, he blends seamlessly with the New Orleans scene of the mid-1990s. But looks can be deceiving. In his previous five years, he has worked in the Netherlands, Brunei, Sarawak, Thailand, Vietnam, China, Oman, Nigeria, and Canada. Daniel Zweidler is a geologist working for Shell, and he is Swiss.

The Planets Were Aligned

I met Daniel in the fall of 2004, when Stefan Scholtes and I were assisting with a course for Shell executives at the Judge Business School at Cambridge University. We were planning to present portfolio management in the course and had sought Daniel's input. But Daniel was also working on Shell's real-life exploration portfolio as well, and invited me to help.

By then several firms had developed software focused on this area (some based on the methods published by Ben Ball and me). But, as discussed earlier, enterprisewide risk models could not easily be built up out of subcomponents. Daniel had experience with some of these complex systems, which, although technically sound, had not gained traction within the decentralized decision-making structure of the firm. This time the planets were aligned.

First, Shell had recently drawn its exploration investment decisions back into their headquarters at The Hague. Matthias Bichsel, then the executive vice president of Shell International Exploration and Production, describes the problem: "I had the challenge of moving our dispersed and disparate exploration efforts (and exploration barons) under one common roof and with one common agenda: maximizing our returns from the Global portfolio."

Second, Bichsel supported a holistic approach to this problem because the company's managers had all suffered through a painful capital allocation process based on ranking the year before. "Building an exploration portfolio is like building a house out of bricks," says Bichsel, "but our bricks were all different shapes, different colors, different sizes, including bricks whose core was rotten or that were chipped."

Third, unlike earlier systems, Daniel and I based our data structures on a scenario library (also known as a stochastic library), as discussed in Chapter 3. As a reminder, this is a database containing Monte Carlo trials of uncertainties concerning the various projects under consideration. This allowed the model to be assembled from the separate bricks described by Bichsel. Furthermore, the use of interactive simulation provided a seat of the pants understanding for management. Bichsel describes how this aided the transition to portfolio thinking. "This mind shift was helped by actually seeing the outcome when we put the various bricks together. We could also see how the house would look under different scenarios, technologies, costs, fiscal regimes, etc." And he describes the ultimate goal: "To see how we could build a large solid house for the least amount of money."

Instrument Panel of the Enterprise

After modeling the exploration projects and the winds of fortune (oil price, world scenarios, and other factors), we were at the point described in the last chapter of having an astronomical number of potential portfolios, which we called the Universe. To winnow this down, we then performed a mathematical optimization to leave us with a few hundred portfolios of interest, which we called the Galaxy.

Like pilots who become fixated on their instruments, managers can easily be mesmerized by the output of complex management science models, so Daniel and I designed an instrument panel that provided intuition at a quick glance without drawing executive attention away from the windshield of day-to-day business. A simplified version is shown in Figure 29.1.

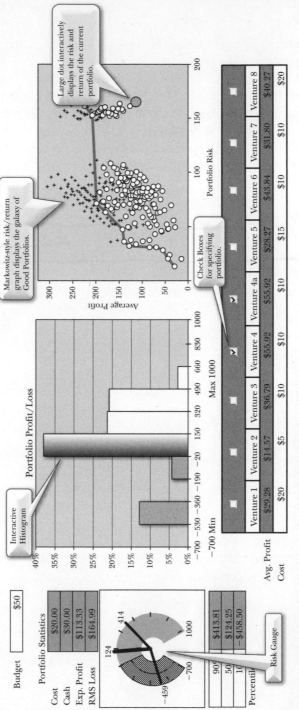

Figure 29.1 The user interface of the Shell demo model.

The user can click a checkbox to select or deselect a project in or out of the portfolio. With each click of a checkbox, a 1,000-trial simulation is run instantaneously, whereupon the histogram updates, and the portfolio position is displayed in the risk/return graph. Alternatively, the user can click on a Galaxy point in the risk/return graph, and the associated portfolio is indicated by the check-boxes. I call this interface the Markowitzatron, in honor of Harry Markowitz and the Orgasmatron from Woody Allen's 1973 movie, *Sleeper.*

A demo version of the model in Excel is available for download at ProbabilityManagement.org. Here I have merely provided a feel for the model's interactivity.

Consider, for example, a project that hedges the risk of the cur-rent portfolio. Figure 29.2 displays the effect in the risk/return graph when the hedge is clicked in or out of the portfolio. If you do not want to download the Excel demo model, you may visit FlawOfAverages.com to see an animation.

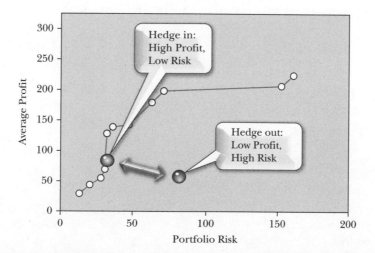

Figure 29.2   The interactive response of the system when a hedge is added or removed.

Level of Detail

Perhaps the most critical decision in any modeling effort is the intended level of detail. Too much detail, and you will never complete the model or get your hands on the data to drive it. Too little detail, and the model doesn't tell you anything that you didn't tell it to tell you, as Jerry Brashear would say. Daniel describes the approach finally arrived at:[1]

> At Shell, the stochastic library had to be assembled from vast amounts of data gathered world-wide. The first decision was the level of granularity at which to model projects. The level chosen was the "exploration venture," which included a number of projects within a single geographical region.

The next problem is that, just as Eskimos have no word for snow but rather many words to describe various forms of frozen water, oil companies have no word for oil. The model needed to reflect numerous metrics for oil in various states of discovery, such as the oil in Region 6 that you haven't discovered yet, the oil you have discovered but haven't figured out how to extract, and so on. Furthermore, multiple time periods needed to be modeled. As a result, there was no simple two-dimensional efficient frontier, as shown in Figure 29.2. Instead, in choosing the portfolio, management needed to visualize a large number of trade-offs that evolved through time.

Managerial Response

The model was introduced in two sets of workshops in the spring of 2005, the first with the regional planning managers only, and the second with the senior exploration executives. Daniel describes the results:[2]

> It became apparent at the first meeting that the planners were surprised that the points on the graph represented portfolios, rather than individual projects. They quickly grasped this concept. . . . For the first time the question shifted from "how does my venture rank?" to "how does my venture contribute to the portfolio?" Managers who were accustomed to silo thinking were confronted with Big Picture issues on the spot.

Then came the second meeting.

> The acid test was certainly the next workshop with senior executives who were also not accustomed to looking at portfolios of ventures, albeit they had some prior exposure to the methodology. The same phenomenon was observed, as they were not presented with a direct ranking of exploration projects, they had to shift to a more global perspective. Members of the group now had a source of motivation to operate as a cohesive team in optimizing the overall portfolio. Although there were still obvious temptations for a member to promote their own ventures, thereby increasing their own budgets, the adverse consequences, if any, were now immediately apparent to the entire group.

The Model Survives a Hurricane and Management Changes

After the introduction of the model in the spring of 2005, the good news was that Daniel became the head of Exploration Planning and Portfolio for Shell. The bad news was that after ten years he had to leave his beloved New Orleans for Shell Headquarters in The Hague.

Just as the Zweidlers were preparing their belongings for shipment to the Netherlands, Hurricane Katrina hit, and they lost most of their furniture along with the treasured Harley. "It sure has made packing up easier," Daniel told me when I called just after the storm to find out how they were doing.

At the beginning of 2006, a change in top exploration management proved the model's ability to engage senior executives. It survived the transition. Then in 2008, Daniel Zweidler, the most experienced "pilot" of the exploration cockpit, took a position with Merck & Co.. The tool was retained and again successfully used during Shell's 2008 strategy update. Improvements in the underlying technology, as discussed in future chapters, have significantly enhanced the performance and capabilities of the system while simplifying the basic architecture. As of this writing, the current Shell pilots on this mission are Bryan Baker and Jan van de Sande, who are investigating additional enhancement, which will enable the system to be flown further into exploration space.

Real Options

Recall the example of the gas well, presented in Chapter 11, that was worth $500,000 given the *average* price of gas but was worth $1 million on *average*. The increased value was due to the option not to pump in the event that the gas price was below the production cost. An opportunity such as this is known as a *real option*, and it is analogous to a call option on the gas, with a strike price equal to the pumping cost.

Life is full of such options, and they all exploit uncertainty.

- Should I save money by making my plane reservations early or pay more for the option of flexible travel dates?
- Should I hire full-time employees, who cost less per hour, or have the option to easily reduce my workforce by using more costly temporary labor?
- Should I commit to my production quantities today to get the lowest per-unit cost, or should I maintain the option to produce what I really need after I have a better estimate of market demand?

Keeping Sailplanes Aloft

Before learning to fly sailplanes, I would watch them from the ground, circling so slowly in the sky, with no idea what kept them up.

The answer is real options. Here the uncertainty is what the air you are flying through will do. Still air represents complete certainty. On a still day, after you are pulled aloft by the tow plane, the best a pilot can do is descend at around 100 feet per minute, making for a short, boring flight.

In uncertain conditions, that is, turbulent air, the sailplane will again descend at 100 feet per minute on *average* if it simply holds a straight course. However, if the pilot exercises the option to circle when in an updraft, and the option to fly somewhere else when in a downdraft, the sailplane can climb for thousands of feet and stay up for hours. This is truly buying low and selling high. Sailplane pilots don't even waste time going out to the airfield if there is no meteorological uncertainty.

Cambridge's Stefan Scholtes believes that superior managers should crave uncertainty in the same way that sailplane pilots crave unstable air. It affords them a challenging environment in which to beat the averages.

Case Study: Restoring a '64 Porsche

In 1999, I decided to restore a 1964 Porsche. Although shiny when I bought it in 1976, it had taken on the color of yellow chalk, and my kids were embarrassed to be seen in it.

Step 1 in restoring an old Porsche is to buy another car to drive during the many months the project will take. This second car must be inexpensive, due to the high cost of steps 2, 3, 4, and the others in the restoration. A friend recommended a visit to Lazlo, a mechanic and curator of aged Mercedes, for this purpose.

After studying the condition of my Porsche, Lazlo confirmed that my backup car would indeed need to be *really* cheap. "How about $900?" he asked, and beckoned me to a 1976 Mercedes diesel. The interior was trashed, and the color was no longer identifiable. But Lazlo had rebuilt the engine and transmission a couple of years earlier, and it ran like a top. I had always wanted a diesel, and suggested that an additional $3,000 in paint and interior would make this one presentable. "You're nuts," said Lazlo, "if you want a better car, buy a better car."

So I surfed the web and, sure enough, found the same model and year, with a claimed 98,000 miles (still youthful for a Mercedes diesel). The seller brought it to my house, it looked great, I drove it around the block, offered $3,000, and it was accepted.

That's the preface to the story.

The story itself is about risk mitigation, and took place over the next 30 seconds.

I now had to walk back in my house, a trip of 20 feet, and explain to my wife, that "Well, you know I'm restoring my thirty-six-year-old Porsche, so as a first step I . . . er, um . . . just spent three thousand on a twenty-four-year-old Mercedes." I am now down to 15 feet and wondering what might go wrong with a 24-year-old car in the first few months? Anything, I decide. Ten feet and closing and beginning to sweat. Then I have a good idea. Why not buy Lazlo's $900 car for parts, hedging the risk of major mechanical calamity? Five feet. Had I done that, I would no doubt have a junk Mercedes sitting in my front yard to this day. Then I have a sophisticated idea. I know just how to mitigate the risk. I enter the house with supreme confidence. "Sweetheart," I say, "I just picked up a great car for three thousand dollars."

What was my risk mitigation strategy? I bought a call option on Lazlo's Mercedes.

And how would you negotiate the price of such an option?

"Lazlo, I'll give you fifty bucks to hold on to that piece of junk for six months during which time you agree to sell it to me for $900 if I need it." (I figured there was no law against writing an American option on a European car.)

But Lazlo knew his option theory. "Too long," he said, "three months for $100." And *I* knew my Mercedes Theory: If there were no loud, clanking noises in the first three months, I was probably home free. The market cleared at $100, as shown in the illustration.

The Mercedes and Porsche, after restoration, are shown in the photograph.

Bottom line: My Mercedes was great, and the option expired worthless at the end of three months. Well, actually, not completely worthless. The stress that it relieved probably increased my life expectancy by a couple of months, and it also serves as an exhibit in this book.

Supplying Thrust in Podunk

Now imagine that, instead of keeping an old Mercedes running, I had to do the same with a fleet of passenger jets. One of my biggest worries is that an engine breaks down on a plane that has made a stop in Podunk. I now have 110 irate passengers who want to get from Podunk to Toledo, and 130 more in Toledo who were scheduled to take the same plane on to Memphis. Since Podunk is

No. 2442   WRITTEN BY   Date   19

Name

Address   _From_

Sam Savage   Model

Phone   _10/7/99_

Date Wanted

INSTRUCTIONS	AMOUNT
Attached is a check for $100.00 to secure the option to purchase 1976 MB 300D * sunroof for an additional $900.00 on or before Jan 7th 2000. * VIN 115.114.12 050154 Agreed	
	Tax
	Total

I hereby authorize the repair work to be done along with the necessary materials. You and your employees may operate vehicle for purposes of testing, inspection or delivery at my risk. An express mechanic's lien is acknowledged on vehicle to secure the amount of repairs thereto. You will not be held responsible for loss or damage to vehicle or articles left in vehicle in case of fire, theft, accident or any other cause beyond your control.

SIGNED X _____   Date _10/7/99_
TERMS CASH UNLESS ARRANGEMENTS MADE PRIOR TO AUTHORIZATION

REPAIR ORDER

not long on maintenance facilities, I will need to fly a mechanic in from Detroit and the parts in from Chicago. Besides the expense of repairing the engine, it will take at least $100,000 to sort out the mess of having the plane out of service for 24 hours. Why can't someone just sell me engines that are guaranteed to work?

According to Jim Scanlan, an engineering professor at the University of Southampton in England, business is moving in precisely this direction. "In many sectors including transportation, civil engineering and even healthcare, customers are increasingly demanding long term performance and cost guarantees," says Scanlan. In other words, instead of selling jet engines, firms are selling the thrust that they produce. This is in effect a derivative contract for which the underlying asset is the engine itself.

"Currently," according to Scanlan, "most civil and military purchasers of gas turbines insist on a contract that guarantees a long term performance against a fixed rate of expenditure, called 'power by the hour.' "

In this new environment, the engine malfunction in Podunk becomes the manufacturer's problem. "This increases the business risk for gas turbine suppliers enormously," continues Scanlan, "because these guarantees are often entered into early in the design process when full knowledge of the sensitivities and product performance is not available."

And to make matters more complicated, he goes on, "Recent changes to certification now allow the use of third-party spare parts in aircraft." So not only do the manufacturers not get as much revenue from selling spares, which used to be their bread and butter, but they must now guarantee the performance of their engines while running with competitors' parts! Recall from Chapter 25 that, if you buy an option, there is potentially a huge upside and a limited downside, whereas if you sell an option, the upside and downside potentials are reversed. The manufacturer is, in effect, selling a call option on engine thrust. And if the value of thrust in Podunk suddenly goes through the roof, they could get hammered.

Scanlan describes how this has impacted the design of engines themselves. "As a result of this change in business paradigm companies such as Rolls-Royce have to radically change the design process to address this increase in risk. In particular the mechanical design considerations must be intimately integrated with business process modeling and business risk analysis."

Scanlan is developing a computerized design system called DATUM to allow collaboration between multidisciplinary teams with expertise in supply chain, logistics, operations, law, marketing, as well as traditional mechanical design, materials, and manufacturing.[1] There is no way such a system could be completely developed in spreadsheets, and Scanlan has been making use of the Vanguard system, one of several alternatives to the spreadsheet described later in this book.[2]

As a former hang glider pilot (the type of gliding where you strap a kite to your back and jump off a cliff) and aerospace engineer, Scanlan has a full-spectrum understanding of both risk and airplanes. Recently he was in the United States to present his research at a conference in Reno. We agreed to meet at the San Francisco airport where he was arriving from the United Kingdom before renting a car to make what is normally a four-hour drive across the Sierra Mountains to Nevada.

He arrived hours before the fiercest storm to hit the Bay Area in years, with torrential rains and gale force winds. The mountain roads had already been closed due to snow, and the National Weather Service had issued a stern warning. "Do not attempt to travel across the Sierra passes," the Weather Service said on its web site. "Attempting to travel in the Sierra will put your life at risk!"[3] I tried unsuccessfully to dissuade Scanlan from making the trip in his rental car, but clearly the weather only heightened his sense of adventure. He had developed a risk-based plan and was eager to try it out. "We'll try to get as far as Sacramento," he said, "If the roads don't open tomorrow, we'll have the *option* to take the train from there to Reno."

Meanwhile Back at Wells Fargo

Matthew Raphaelson of Wells Fargo, mentioned earlier, is definitely not a quant. His limited interest in mathematics was, in his own words, "driven by a desire to calculate the latest baseball statistics." Nonetheless, since the mid-1990s he has played a central role in the effort initiated by Terri Dial to improve analytical modeling at the bank. Now an executive vice president, he has achieved a seat of the pants understanding of the Flaw of Averages and has a keen grasp of options, wherever they appear.

A certificate of deposit (CD) is a type of savings account that pays a higher interest in return for leaving your money in the bank for a set period, typically at least six months. Raphaelson describes the bank's analysis of a new offering in this area. "The product development team was pitching the idea of an 'upgradeable CD'— if market interest rates moved up during the period, the customer would also get a higher rate." Obviously such a product could be sold for more than a normal CD because the rate could only go up. The product team had proposed a price premium of 0.10 percent, but Raphaelson wasn't sure that was enough.

"The business case appeared to have used just a single number to represent interest rates in an otherwise complex and elegant Excel model. The justification was that rates hadn't changed much in the past few years," he recalls. "This was a classic options problem. With an 'upgradeable CD,' the customer had a right, but not obligation, to upgrade the CD when interest rates changed. Using a single number for interest rate in this situation immediately raised red flags."

Sure enough, when Raphaelson ran a simulation using historical interest rates instead of the current rate, he discovered that the price would need to be roughly five times higher to make it attractive for the bank to sell. It is all too easy to create large, beautifully formatted Excel models that are built on the quicksands of the Flaw of Averages. According to Raphaelson, "Just because a model looks great in Excel doesn't mean it couldn't lose us real money."

My Intuitive Approach to Options

By Matthew Raphaelson

My general philosophy is to be a holder of as many options as possible, especially since many times you will be granted them for free. My wife and I always ask for the option to check out late at a hotel, for example. Or in a business deal, we try to get a "right of first refusal" to lease the property next door for future expansion.

However, be extremely cautious about granting options to others, or holding short positions. Many of these have a small risk of unlimited loss. Banks can diversify this risk; but it is much harder for an individual to do so. If you do grant an option, protect yourself.

When Lazlo sold me the Mercedes call option, he was protected in two ways. First he shortened the period from six to three months. Second, the car in question was sitting on his lot. He would not need to go find a running 1976 300D in the market if I exercised the option.

Things to remember:

- Real options are everywhere.

Things to forget:

- The Black-Scholes equation, in case you didn't forget it the first time I asked you to because you are an options trader. When it comes to most real options, it is about as useful as the differential equations of motion are to riding a bicycle.

CHAPTER

Some Gratuitous Inflammatory Remarks on the Accounting Industry

The Enron debacle reminded me of an old joke. Three accountants interview for a job. When asked to evaluate 2 plus 2, the first responds, "Four." The second, thinking it's a trick question, says, "Five." But the third, whom they hire on the spot, says, "What do you want it to be?"

I wasn't laughing, however, when Marc Van Allen, a partner at the Chicago law firm of Jenner & Block, informed me in 2001 that generally accepted accounting principles (GAAP) might be guilty of the Flaw of Averages. Marc and I had worked together on a case the year before, and with degrees in both economics and law, he had a good understanding of probability and statistics. Marc explained that a statement on accounting for contingencies by the Financial Accounting Standards Board (FASB) might give a green light to the behavior of job applicant number three.

"I can't believe that," I told him. "I'm calling Roman Weil." Roman, a prominent professor of accounting at the University of Chicago and former colleague, as well as an expert witness in accounting cases, confirmed Marc's suspicion. Furthermore, he had coauthored an article on rules for recording uncertain numbers in financial statements in 1993 in the journal *Accounting Horizons*.[1] The piece exposes a smoking arsenal of FASB-sanctioned accounting

---

Portions of this chapter appeared in the *Journal of Forensic Accounting*, 1524-5586/Vol. IV (2003), pp. 351–354.

ambiguities and inconsistencies, raising important questions about how accounting deals with uncertainty. I want to make clear that the authors of this article, which included an FASB board member, were not oblivious to the problems discussed in this chapter but were, in effect, whistle blowers who continue to be ahead of their time.

FASB and the Weak Form of the Flaw of Averages

I found the following example from the *Accounting Horizons* article particularly striking. It involves the manner of assessing the value of accounts receivable, and I have slightly changed the numbers from the original to make the arithmetic easier without materially changing the results.

> *Case 1:* A firm has $400,000 in receivables with a single customer who has a 90 percent chance of paying in full and a 10 percent chance of defaulting.
>
> *Case 2:* A firm has $100 in receivables with each of 4,000 customers, all of whom have an *independent* 90 percent chance of paying in full and a 10 percent chance of defaulting.

How should we compare these two situations? The answer is through their shapes, of course, as depicted in Figure 31.1. In case 1, the firm gets either the full $400,000 or nothing. The average value of $360,000 appears at the black dot. In case 2, there could be

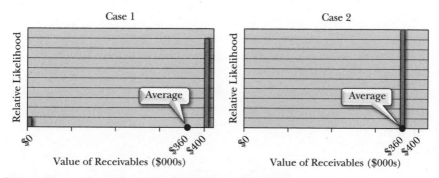

Figure 31.1   The value of accounts receivable.

numerous outcomes depending on exactly how many of the 4,000 customers defaulted. However, the width of the bars in the graphs is $10,000, and, thanks to the diversification across customers, virtually all possible outcomes would lie within the bar centered at $360,000.

What are the market values of these two receivables? The Nobel Prize–winning theory of Markowitz and Sharpe states that, when two assets have the same average value, the market will place greater value on the one with smaller risk. Thus the diversified receivables in case 2 would, if anything, have higher market value than the single large receivable in case 1.

But back to the accountants. According to the article, FASB would value the 4,000 diversified assets of case 2 at $360,000. So far, so good. Given that the asset of case 1 has *greater* risk, it should have a *lower* value. However, the FASB rule for case 1 is that, with only a 10 percent chance of default, "it is not probable that an asset has been impaired." Therefore they would apply the full value of $400,000 to the *less* valuable asset. If FASB had valued both cases at $360,000, it would have presented a classic case of the Weak Form of the Flaw of Averages, that is, that average value alone does not fully specify the value of an asset. But to place a higher value on the *riskier* of two assets with the same average is utterly at odds with modern finance. This is worse than the Flaw of Averages because, instead of even attempting an average value of the receivables, FASB allows the maximum value of the receivables if impairment is not probable and zero if it is. It's too bad that "probable" isn't well defined.

If 2 = 1, I'm the Pope

So what's all the fuss over a little inconsistency in our accounting standards? Bertrand Russell pointed out that if you accept any particular falsehood, you can prove any other falsehood. "What?" he was reportedly asked. "Do you mean that if we assume that two equals one, you could prove that you were the pope?" "Of course," replied Russell. "The pope and I are clearly two, but if two equals one, then the pope and I are one. Hence I am the pope." How might this play out in business if we accept that asset 1 has a paper value of $400,000 and asset 2 has a paper value of $360,000?

Consider a firm whose only asset is the receivables of type 2 with a paper value of $360,000. Now assume an unscrupulous party wishes to increase the firm's paper value even if it reduces its real value.

The firm swaps their type 2 asset for someone else's type 1 asset (there will be a lot of takers because it is worth more on the market). The firm's paper value has increased while its real value has decreased. This makes it easier for them to raise more money to pursue more such bad deals that drive their paper value even higher and their real value even lower, without the blink of a warning light on the FASB's instrument panel. When Enron's Skilling said that he had relied on his accountants, it explains a lot.

FASB and the Strong Form of the Flaw of Averages

You may recall that the 1973 Black-Scholes option formula cures the Flaw of Averages for stock options. As a reminder, consider the European call option, discussed in Chapter 25, involving a stock that is currently selling for $20. The option provides the right to purchase the stock for $21 in 12 weeks. If in 12 weeks the stock takes on its average value (which is less than $21), then you would not exercise the option, and it would expire worthless. Therefore the value of the option based on the *average* stock price is zero, but given that there is some chance it will exceed $21, the *average* value of the option is clearly *greater* than zero. In fact, the greater the uncertainty of the stock price, as measured by its volatility, the greater the average value of the option.

In 1995, over two decades after the Black-Scholes publication, the FASB finally issued a statement that acknowledged the basic principles of option theory.[2] The statement says that the fair value of an option "is determined using an option-pricing model that takes into account the stock price at the grant date, the exercise price, the expected life of the option, the volatility (degree of uncertainty) of the underlying stock and the expected dividends on it, and the risk-free interest rate over the expected life of the option."

So compared to the inertia of our accounting standards, an aircraft carrier bobs around like a rubber duck, but better late than never, I say. However, in 1995 the game was still in early innings, and there was a lot riding on placing a zero value on out-of-the-money call options. This way a firm could give them away to its employees as an incentive to increase its stock price, and if they weren't "worth" anything, the firm would not need to write off any expense. Thus in 2003, the *Harvard Business Review* published an article entitled "For the Last Time: Stock Options Are an Expense."[3] Its authors included none other than Robert Merton (Nobel Laureate in options theory). Finally in December of 2004, FASB issued Statement 123R, in which it acknowledged that all forms of stock compensation, including options, must be treated as an expense.[4]

Decades after the Black-Scholes equation, accounting standards are slowly adjusting to it. But how about other analogous forms of the Flaw of Averages? Recall the natural gas property that included the option not to pump if the price was below the cost of production. Similar options also exist for most petroleum properties and indeed for many other natural resources as well. The values are due in large part to the price volatility of oil, gas, and minerals, and they cannot be estimated on current price alone. Thus I was surprised by a 2005 *Wall Street Journal* article on the valuation of petroleum reserves stating that "[t]he SEC stipulates that their evaluations of petroleum properties must be based on a snapshot of oil prices at the companies' year end, usually Dec. 31."[5] My (unanswered) letter to the *Journal* follows:

> I enjoyed your article on the evaluation of oil reserves in the *Wall St. Journal* on 2/14/05. I find it astonishing that the SEC still values petroleum reserves based on *average* oil price. In fact an oil property is a type of Call Option on oil, in which the Strike price is the marginal cost of production. Thanks to Black and Scholes, it is well understood that the value of a Call Option on a Stock depends not only on the **average** price of the stock, but also to a great degree on both the *volatility* of the stock and the *duration* of the option, that is the length of time one has to exercise it. Evaluating stock options based on *average* stock price is now acknowledged to be a fallacy as fundamental as the belief that the earth is flat, yet the same principles apply to oil reserves. Given the high *volatility* of oil price, and the long *duration* of the life of an oil property (for ever) I believe that the SEC's approach may grossly undervalue such properties.

There are material consequences of this false perspective. For example, Jeff Strnad, a professor at the Stanford University Law School (no, that is not a typo, Jeff's Czechoslovakian heritage has left him with a congenital vowel deficiency), has shown that by ignoring the real options underlying petroleum exploration, our tax code may actually have an adverse effect on the country's energy development.[6]

I have heard that Saddam Hussein would speculate on future oil prices, whereupon he would threaten war by rattling his saber and then cash in. Whether this story is true or not, countries or politicians with energy interests may stand to profit not just from higher oil prices, but simply from more volatile prices.

Inspired by the *Accounting Horizons* article, Marc Van Allen and I further investigated the manner in which GAAP deals with uncertainty in financial statements, publishing our own observations in an article entitled "Accounting for Uncertainty" in the *Journal of Portfolio Management.*[7]

Some Constructive Criticism for the Accounting Industry

Nothing changes in commerce unless there's something in it for someone. In this case, there would seem to be quite a lot in it for quite a few. In 2002, in the aftermath of scandals at Enron, WorldCom, Tyco, and other firms, Congress passed the Sarbanes-Oxley Act. This legislation requires CEOs of publicly traded companies to certify their financial statements. Hmm. . . . Our financial codes contain mathematical falsehoods, and CEOs are required by law to certify those falsehoods. There must be an entrepreneurial opportunity in there somewhere.

Rules Versus Principles

Current U.S. accounting standards are *rules based,* that is, instead of being derived from broad underlying principles, a *new* rule is added each time something falls between the cracks of the *current* rules. This reminds me of the second century Ptolemaic model of the solar system. It starts out well enough with the sun and moon revolving smoothly around the earth, each on its own transparent sphere. But when you start to add the other heavenly bodies, all hell breaks lose. Each planet requires spheres rotating on the surfaces of other spheres, with their moons rotating on additional spheres, ad nauseam.

In the mid-1500s, Copernicus posed an alternate model that had the sun at the center. In the early 1600s Galileo used a primitive telescope to verify this perspective and was rewarded for his efforts with imprisonment by the Vatican. Later that century, the Copernican model inspired Kepler and Newton to derive a few simple principles of gravitation, from which all planetary motion could be worked out. This led to a *principles-based* model of the solar system that was easily generalized to predict the motion of human-made satellites centuries after it was proposed. As a happy footnote to this story, the Vatican pardoned Galileo in 1992.

Sarbanes-Oxley urges a *principles-based* form of accounting. Given that there are well developed principles for dealing with uncertainty, why can't they be applied here? The International Accounting Standards Board (IASB), for example, is also principles based and at least recognizes that they must deal with probability somehow.

FASB has already suggested several choices for calculating the value of options: the original Black-Scholes formula, a model called the binomial lattice, or Monte Carlo simulation.[8]

A big problem remains, however, which raises its ugly head every few years: the *concentration* of risk. It happened with Long-Term Capital Management, and it happened again with subprime mortgages. Recall the analogy between an investment strategy and balancing on the deck of a sailboat. A simulation model could indicate your chances of falling down or going overboard. Now imagine that everyone on the boat runs his or her own model, where the wind and waves represent interest rates, GDP, housing prices, and other conditions. What is typically missing today is a way to tie those models together to warn regulators when everyone is *concentrated* on the same side. For example, when my model has the boat rocking right, your model might have it rocking left. Add up enough models, and it looks like the boat is perfectly level. But if regulators could provide us with a single common model of wind and waves, then our individual models would be coherent, and they could be added up to show the true likelihood of capsizing. This would be similar to the modular approach in which Shell manages the concentration of risk in its portfolio of exploration projects.

In June 2008, FASB issued the draft of an amendment on accounting for contingencies such as potential losses from lawsuits, the area that Jenner & Block's Marc Van Allen first brought to my attention in 2001.[9] "Unfortunately," according to Van Allen, "the draft does not tackle the 'elephant in the room' regarding the use of a single (wrong) number to measure contingent liabilities." Instead he says that "[t]his ad hoc patch-work solution is equivalent to adding additional epicycles to the broken Ptolemaic model. What is needed is something akin to the Copernican revolution in which FASB recognizes (once and for all) that (1) the values of a firm's assets and liabilities are uncertain and (2) the best way to account for uncertainty is with distributions, not single numbers."

Roman Weil recently commented on the June amendment in a letter to FASB and argues for the IASB approach that at least recognizes the principles of probability theory. Weil argues:

"Economic scholars teach us that in setting policy we shouldn't let the best be the enemy of the good so that we should adopt less-than-ideal solutions if we can't get the best one. Here, I advocate that the best (IASB approach) should be the enemy of the good that might come from increased disclosures under current FAS 5 rules. That is, the cost of acting now will make more difficult doing the right thing later."

7

THE FLAW OF AVERAGES
IN SUPPLY CHAINS

The Flaw of Averages is central in managing supply chains. Chapter 32 describes a the basic Mindle of the problem. Chapters 33 and 34 contain examples from the pharmaceutical and chemical industries.

CHAPTER

32

The DNA of Supply Chains

Recall the perishable antibiotic inventory example at the beginning of the book. This is, in effect, the DNA of all inventory problems. Think of it as a single link in the supply chain. Management scientists call it the Newsboy Problem, because it is analogous to the dilemma faced by someone purchasing newspapers for a particular day's uncertain demand. If demand is less than the number of papers purchased, the excess will be wasted, whereas demand greater than the number on hand results in lost sales. In the case of the pharmaceutical firm, too much inventory resulted in a $50-per-unit spoilage cost, and too little inventory required paying air freight charges of $150 for each unit that they were short.

Suppose the average demand was five. If the firm kept five units in stock and if the demand actually *was* five, the cost would be zero because there is no penalty. When I falsely claim in class that zero is therefore the *average* cost, nearly all of my university and executive education students dutifully nod their heads in agreement.

But the graph of operating cost versus demand (Figure 32.1) makes it clear that a deviation of demand either way from the average of five results in a penalty, so average cost must be greater than zero. But how much greater?

We need the distribution of antibiotic demand to find out. Suppose that demand fluctuates from month to month with no systematic seasonality. Then Figure 32.2, the histogram of 36 months of historical demand, gives us a good idea of the distribution of next month's demand.

A simple approach to this problem is to use the computational technique of resampling that Rick Medress and I used on

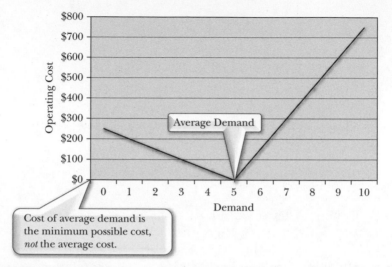

Figure 32.1   Operating cost versus actual demand with inventory of five units.

his historical movie revenues. Conceptually it would work like this: Starting with 36 ping-pong balls, paint the number 1 on one of them, the number 2 on two of them, the number 3 on seven of them, the number 4 on five of them, and so on, until you have accounted for the entire histogram. Then throw all the balls into a lottery basket.

Now repeatedly draw balls from the basket, run them through the cost formula depicted in Figure 32.1, and toss them back in the basket. Because the number of ping-pong balls associated with each

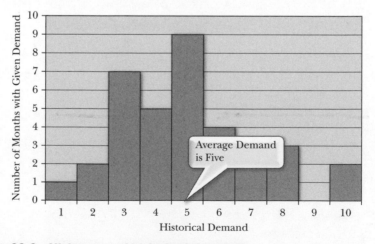

Figure 32.2   Histogram of historical demand.

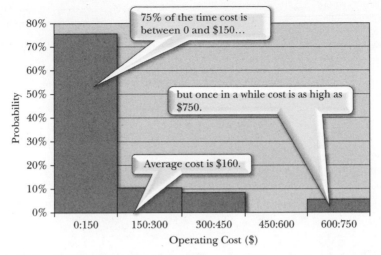

Figure 32.3   Distribution of operating costs with uncertain demand of Figure 32.2.

demand level is proportional to the likelihood of that demand level, the demand distribution has been faithfully reproduced. The resulting histogram of costs will look like Figure 32.3. This process is essentially instantaneous with interactive simulation. A working spreadsheet version of this model is contained in my textbook,[1] and at FlawOfAverages.com.

Besides the histogram, the simulation also indicates that the average cost is $160, not zero, if we stock five units, but who said five was the right number to stock in the first place?

Just Plain Nuts

By repeatedly simulating this situation with different quantities stocked, you can come up with an optimal inventory policy. Figure 32.4, shows the simulation results for stocking levels between 1 and 9.

The bottom line shows that the average cost is slightly lower if we stock six, rather than five. This is not surprising, given that the air freight costs exceed the expiration cost. But the upper line, the 95th percentile, tells a story of risk. There is only one chance in 20 (5 percent) that cost will be as high as the upper line, so you can think of this as a worst-case scenario.

This graph reminds me of the "Far Side" cartoon in which a psychiatrist is taking notes about his patient, lying on a couch. His diagnosis is "Just Plain Nuts." The graph in Figure 32.4 doesn't tell

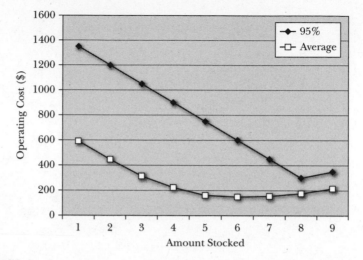

Figure 32.4   Average cost and risk associated with various stocking levels.

us exactly what level of inventory to stock, but it tells us that most of the levels are just plain nuts. Any level below six has both a higher average cost and higher risk of a very high cost, than stocking six, so levels one through five are nuts. And nine has both higher average cost and higher risk than eight, so nine is nuts. Levels six, seven, and eight are not nuts, and the one you choose will depend on your willingness to trade off the risk of high cost against average lower cost.

When Less Is More

Sometimes a very simple model is all you need to have an impact. Martin Farncombe is a British consultant who, after a career with several large accounting firms, now has a private practice in the area of procurement. Using the basic Newsboy Problem model, he was able to quickly help a large European IT company improve its costs. The firm had been ordering a certain piece of communications gear on a monthly basis, with demand fluctuating between 2,500 and 5,000 units. The supplier was offering a 10 percent discount if they ordered in batches of 10,000.

"The obvious thing was to order 10,000 units quarterly instead of smaller monthly amounts," recalls Farncombe. "But the company was worried that if they ran short it would delay their customers' delivery." That was the shortfall penalty, analogous to the airfreight in the antibiotic example that began this chapter. "However," he continues, "they were even more worried that if they over-ordered they would have to pay finance charges for the unsold stock." And that's the overstock penalty, the other half of the double whammy that characterizes the Newsboy Problem.

Once he had the historical demand data, it took Farncombe about 60 seconds to construct a spreadsheet model with three cells, each of which randomly resampled one of the previous demand levels. The sum of the three monthly cells simulated quarterly demand. "I was able to demonstrate to the client that ordering 10,000 units each quarter would adequately supply their customers, and leave them with excess stocks only about once every four years. And this was accomplished within two minutes of being given the problem," says Farncombe. The client was reassured, and agreed to the larger quantities. "The IT company saved money, the supplier was happy, and I was happy. If only every day was that good!" he concludes. Unfortunately every day isn't that good. More complex supply chains become much harder to optimize.

The Bullwhip Effect

The Newsboy Problem is a supply chain consisting of a single link. But most supply chains contain numerous such links, one each for the retailer, wholesaler, distributor, producer, and so on. Each of these links holds a certain amount of inventory, and, when they are chained together, something horrific can occur.

Due to lags in the system, the inventory levels can begin to fluctuate wildly and get out of control, much as your airspeed probably did if you tried the flight simulator at FlawOfAverages.com described in Chapter 5. Instead of pilot-induced oscillation, in this context, the loss of control is called the *Bullwhip Effect*, as displayed in Figure 32.5. It is one of the reasons that supply chain management can make or break an organization. These problems cannot be solved in two minutes on a spreadsheet, and a whole industry of supply chain consulting and software tools has arisen in this area.

The Beer Game

Jay Forrester was born in 1918 on a Nebraska cattle ranch that did not even have electricity until he built a wind-powered generator from junk car parts in high school.[2] By 1944, as an electrical engineer

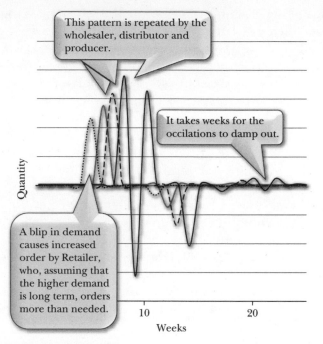

Figure 32.5   The Bullwhip Effect.

at MIT, he was working on an early computerized flight simulator for the military. Forrester realized that similar dynamics applied to many complex systems including businesses, and he founded the field of systems dynamics around these ideas in the late 1950s.[3]

Many executives have been exposed to this work through a classic management simulation called the *Beer Game*, which models a supply chain from brewery to retailer. Professor John Sterman, the Forrester Professor of Management at MIT's Sloan School, has done research on management behavior using the Beer Game as his laboratory.[4] Reflecting its heritage, Sterman calls the Beer Game a Flight Simulator for Management Education.[5] When managers are initially exposed to this game, many of them crash and burn due to the bullwhip effect.

It starts when they stock out due to what may have been a temporary increase in demand. Now in a panic, they put in a big order for more beer, forgetting the two weeks' worth in the pipeline. Just when things seem to have settled down again, the large panic-induced order arrives, and the whole place is awash in beer. "Smooth flying arises only if people take into account the inventory on hand, and the time delays in the supply chain," says Sterman.

Visit FlawOfAverages.com for an interactive simulation of the newsboy problem and links to the Beer Game. Also explore a spreadsheet model of the bullwhip effect created by Cambridge's Stefan Scholtes, which was used to generate Figure 32.5.

CHAPTER

A Supply Chain of DNA

Anyone managing an inventory must attempt to forecast future demand, and there are numerous software systems available to assist in this task. Typically, these programs provide an estimate of *average* demand, a single number, and also an indication of the distribution of uncertainty in demand. For the example in the last chapter, the average demand was five, and the distribution was described by the shape in Figure 32.2. Unfortunately, most organizations don't know how to deal with distributions. They generally ignore *that* part of the forecast, relying instead on the single number, and, presto, they're back to square one with the Flaw of Averages. People use the centerline of the highway as the drunk's average position and think he will survive. But he's dead, so the next thing you know, people are marching up and down chanting, "We need better forecasts. We need better forecasts. We need. . . ."

You have no doubt observed this activity within your own organization. The problem was not the forecast at all, but rather the fact that ignoring the distribution and keeping the average was like throwing out the baby and keeping the bathwater. Some firms, however, are taking steps to keep the distribution of demand alive.

A Supply Chain at Genentech

Just to visit the place quickens one's pulse. Spectacularly located on a promontory jutting into the bay north of San Francisco's airport is the sprawling campus of Genentech, the firm that practically founded the field of biotech. I couldn't help thinking about the people who would not have pulses at all if it weren't for the exotic pharmaceuticals cooked up here. Getting their drugs manufactured and out to the patients who need them constitutes a truly vital network of Newsboy Problems.

In fact, this may be why Darren Johnson got his job there. With an MBA from Carnegie Mellon University, concentrating in supply chain management, Johnson was well versed in the subject. During his interview he was questioned about a case on capacity planning and said, "This is similar to the Newsboy Problem." He credits this simple statement with landing him the job, though the interviewers claim he did have a few other strengths.

Johnson understood that optimal inventory strategy must balance the risks of overstocking with the risks of running short of supply. Typically, this is measured as the percentage of demand that you are actually able to fill on average, and, being new to the job, he innocently asked what this was. The response was that "No patient goes without," which is part of the mission statement at Genentech. Now anyone trained in probability knows that nothing can happen with 100 percent certainty, so Johnson innocently said, "OK, so we're talking ninety-nine percent?" They again replied, "No patient goes without." "Ninety-nine point nine percent?" Johnson asked. "What part of 'no patient goes without' don't you understand?" was the response.

With this sort of commitment to maintaining supply, Genentech must not only consider the uncertainty in future demand for their drugs, but also possible disruptions of their manufacturing process due to various Black Swans, including natural disasters.

Forecasting Done Right

Johnson made a presentation at a technical meeting in Vancouver that I attended in 2007, at which he described certain aspects of this problem. When he had arrived a year earlier, parts of the firm were already adhering to the most basic principle of Probability Management. When the marketing department provided forecasts of demand to production planning, they did *not* use single average numbers, but instead *were* using distributions.

Unfortunately, as delivered to the production people, the distributions of demand did not preserve the interrelationships between the products. However, because these forecast distributions were known to be the result of a simulation, the production team requested that marketing output the actual Monte Carlo trials to a file, which would preserve the interrelationships. Marketing kindly complied, and now production could receive a scenario library from the marketing group.

An Interactive Dashboard

Johnson recognized an opportunity to leverage the distribution of demand to help ensure that "no patient would go without." In Vancouver, he presented a prototype application using falsified data, which would potentially allow management to visualize the distribution of demand supplied by the marketing group.

Figure 33.1 shows one of the screens of Johnson's prototype, which allows planners to interactively switch strategic options in or out. For example, they could model the risk implications of obtaining FDA approval to produce product B at plant 2 or outsourcing some manufacturing to a third party, and instantly see the probability of meeting demand in year five. Although at an early stage, it proves the concept that a scenario library, independently created on one simulation system in one department, can be used in a different system in a different department.

Johnson's interactive dashboard, which he built himself using low-cost, readily available desktop software, would have been as impossible a couple of decades ago as would the pharmaceuticals that it was designed to track.

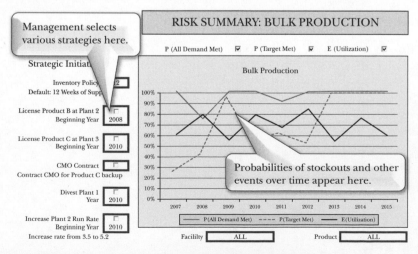

Figure 33.1   Darren Johnson's strategic dashboard.

Cawlfield's Principle

Anyone who has seriously mastered Microsoft Excel will understand why I refer to this skill as a folk art, passed down in the oral tradition. I joke in my classes about learning Excel secrets from a master craftsman in the hills of Tennessee. When I met David Cawlfield in 2006, it was soon clear that he was in fact such a master. David is principal engineer at Olin Chemical's Chlor-Alkali Division and works at their plant in Charleston, Tennessee. They produce inorganic chemicals such as chlorine, caustic soda, bleach, and other things that you don't want to touch but that we can't live without.

From Remedial Math to Chemical Engineer

When David was in fifth grade, he found multiplication tables particularly boring. Thus his teachers determined he was bad at math and should be put into a remedial program. Luckily his father, a math editor for a major publisher, knew a thing or two about math education himself. David's parents quickly taught him multiplication using flash cards and then convinced his teachers to put him into the advanced math program instead of the remedial one. No longer bored, David flourished. He went on to become a chemical engineer, but his activities at Olin have taken him as far afield as mathematical optimization, computer control systems, and, of course, Microsoft Excel.

A Problem at Olin

Recently David grappled with an ongoing problem at a chemical production facility. The plant had enough capacity to fill 110 percent of average customer demand, and it was served by a fleet of company-owned freight cars that could handle 105 percent of average customer demand. Yet these two divisions of Olin, working together, were meeting only 80 percent of demand on average. The manufacturing flow is outlined in Figure 34.1. According to David, "When I heard about the Flaw of Averages, I realized that this was a textbook case."

There were three fundamental uncertainties driving the problem: customer demand, production rate, and the availability of freight cars. Some days there were few back orders left to fill, and the plant was cranking out plenty of material, but there were not enough freight cars to deliver the stuff. The plant manager would scream over the phone at the head of Olin's railcar logistics division to get more cars there in a hurry. Other days, there would be a production glitch or such high demand that manufacturing couldn't keep up, and empty freight cars were lying idle at the plant. The head of the logistics division would scream over the phone at the plant manager for not running the plant properly and for not shipping the same number of cars each day. This situation resulted in constant tension between these two groups that should have been working as a team.

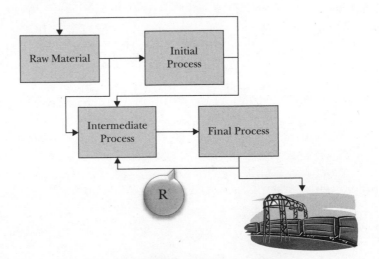

Figure 34.1   Chemical manufacturing flow at Olin.

Source: Courtesy of Olin Corporation

A Real Option

More flexibility was needed to get the system to run smoothly, but you can't just turn a plant like this on and off like a kitchen faucet. "What made the situation worse," says David, "was that when the plant had a good day, and there was more product made than could be loaded into rail cars, there was nowhere to store the excess, so potential production was lost." Then he made a discovery. The intermediate processing module had storage tanks with significant capacity. Its level was set so as to avoid the possibility of overflow during the inevitable ebb and flow of production. David reasoned that if they could increase the allowable level of this tank, it would present them with the following real option:

- In the event that no freight cars were available, they could flow material back to the intermediate process through line R in Figure 34.1.
- If empty freight cars were available, having the added material in the intermediate tank would increase the chance that they could fill them all.

David built an interactive simulation of 1,000 trials of 60 days of operation. This was based on a scenario library of uncertain customer demand, uncertain production level, and uncertain freight car availability. Figure 34.2 shows the results of increasing the tank

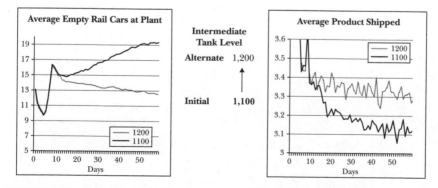

Figure 34.2   The effects of increasing intermediate tank level.

level from its initial value of 1,100 gallons to 1,200 gallons. Note: These results are based on using David's model with hypothetical data so that it could be released for publication.

The left-hand graph shows the number of empty freight cars waiting at the plant by day, averaged over 1,000 simulated 60-day periods. The black line represents the status quo with a tank level of 1,100 gallons, and the gray line shows the result of increasing the tank level to 1,200 gallons. Note that at day 0, the plant and freight cars were started up in an arbitrary state, so it takes a couple of weeks for transient effects to die out. But then the higher tank level results in a significant reduction in average number empty cars at the plant. By 60 days out, this average is still declining, but if a longer simulation had been run, it would have eventually leveled out.

The right-hand graph shows the average product shipped per day, which is also improved through increased tank level. Similar transients appear here as well, along with a similar long-term improvement in operation. "The simulation showed us that the only way to make progress was to increase the number of rail cars in service to the plant and at the same time change the plant operating policies as well," David recalls.

David now had the daunting task of convincing two distinct management teams to both try something new simultaneously. So he shuttled between both divisions with his model, encouraging each of them to improve on his initial design. Because the model is interactive, as the tank level is changed, the graphs change immediately (this requires 60 times 1,000 trials, or 60,000 simulated days). See FlawOfAverages.com for an animation depicting these graphs during interactive simulation.

The logistics manger loved the left graph because it meant fewer idle freight cars. The production manager loved the right graph because it meant greater shipments. It was a classic win/win. But there was still the worry of tank overflow. Once David had the model, it was easy to simulate both the probability of overflow as well as average delivery shortfall. When these probabilities were plotted on the same graph, a tank level of 1,200 was clearly the sweet spot, as shown in Figure 34.3.

This interactive model served as a communications channel that in David's words "healed the organization." Because it takes several

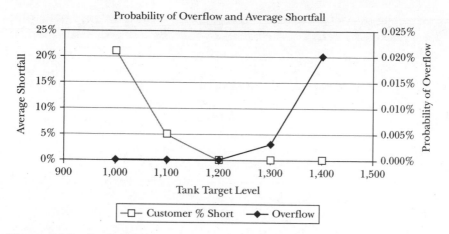

Figure 34.3   Probability of overflow and average shortfall, by tank level.

real weeks for initial conditions to be overcome, and then several months to observe the average beneficial effects, "there is no way that this could have been arrived at by trial and error," he goes on.

The General Principle

While developing this model, David had a simple insight: The Flaw of Averages creates trouble at organizational boundaries.

"Of course, how obvious," I thought when I heard this, followed by "why didn't I think of it myself?"

- At Olin, the boundary was between manufacturing and logistics.
- At Shell, the boundary was between the reservoir engineers in the field and the portfolio managers in The Hague.
- At Genentech, the boundary was between the marketing group and their supply chain managers.

I call this elegant idea Cawlfield's Principle, and David explains it better than anyone else in his own words. He confirms what I have long believed: that managers at many levels are just bursting with probabilistic knowledge, which if properly channeled can be put to good use.

The Flaw of Averages at Organizational Boundaries

BY DAVID CAWLFIELD

Of course, the Flaw of Averages occurs everywhere, but often the flaws are small and go unnoticed, or the consequences are insignificant. At organizational boundaries the Flaw can cause real damage. This is where most of the cross-communication occurs between upper level managers, and involves decisions with large consequences. Lower in the organization, experts with the most knowledge about variability leave out the gory details about day-to-day ups and downs by communicating only the "big picture" to the boss.

In my experience with modeling the chemical plant, I found that expert engineers and supervisors were pleased to provide details about variability that had previously been ignored. Not only did they know how often different parts of the process broke down; they even shared details about the likelihood that a particular part of the plant would need maintenance again shortly after it broke down once. On the transportation side of the problem, the railroad experts shared their observation that cars "bunched up" during shipment, resulting in a very non-uniform distribution of cars available for loading at the plant. Management had ignored these details in the past, and the engineers were gratified that our model reflected their hard-won experience.

The resulting credibility of the model gave local decision makers the confidence to experiment with new strategies. I used this inside track into both organizations at once to get them working together, but without exposing the guts of the issue at too high a level.

A corollary is that an understanding of variability constitutes a large portion of the value of long work experience. The secret of successful Probability Management is learning to capture this understanding in a stochastic library.

8

THE FLAW OF AVERAGES AND SOME HOT BUTTON ISSUES

There is nothing like life-and-death issues to get people thinking irrationally and making bad decisions. The Flaw of Averages only makes this tendency worse.

This part begins with the hotbed of World War II statistical research in which my father's career was forged. Next I discuss the War on Terror, which is poorly understood from a statistical perspective. Climate change and health care provide many additional opportunities for misunderstanding. Part 8 concludes with some observations on the differences in the genetic portfolios of men and women.

CHAPTER

The Statistical Research Group of World War II

In the spring of 1942, a young economist and statistician teaching at Stanford University received a telegram requesting his assistance in the war effort. He had been asked to come to New York to help run a statistical research group at Columbia University devoted to military problems. He accepted. Allen Wallis had a bachelor's degree in psychology from the University of Minnesota and had done graduate work in economics at the University of Chicago, where he developed lifelong relationships with Milton Friedman and George Stigler, both future Nobel Laureates in economics. Wallis himself, perhaps due to the arrival of the telegram that fateful day, never finished his own PhD. He did, however, go on to become dean of the University of Chicago Graduate School of Business, greatly elevating its stature, then chancellor of the University of Rochester, and finally undersecretary of state for economic affairs under President Ronald Reagan.

In a 1980 article in the *Journal of the American Statistical Association*, Wallis reminisced about his wartime experiences at the Statistical Research Group, or SRG, as it was known.[1]

"Exploring the history of one's professional field is often a mark of maturity. Reminiscing about it is usually a mark of senility," Wallis wrote. However, he was still far from senile when I last met him in 1998, a few months before his death.

There were a total of 18 researchers in the group, comprised of future Nobel Laureates Friedman and Stigler, as well as many others who would go on to prominent careers in statistics. My father was lucky to be among them. In fact, according to Wallis, "The effect of SRG on the subsequent careers of its members was probably greatest on Jimmie Savage, who came to SRG as an applied mathematician, innocent of Statistics." Their offices were in an apartment on 118th Street, a block from Columbia. The problems they worked on were fascinating and urgent. Again quoting from Wallis's article, "The first project assignment of the SRG was to evaluate the comparative effectiveness of four 20 millimeter guns on the one hand and eight 50 caliber guns on the other as the armament of a fighter aircraft."

He then goes on to list a few other odd jobs they got around to: ". . . geometry and tactics of aerial combat . . . probability of hitting . . . vulnerability of aircraft . . . pursuit curves . . . automatic dive-bomb sight(s) . . . homing torpedoes . . . guided missiles . . . submarine searches . . . use of shrapnel against directly approaching planes . . . rockets in air-to-air combat . . . acceptance testing of bomb sights."

The SRG made a major contribution to the field of statistics itself, in the development of what is known as **SEQUENTIAL ANALYSIS**. This provides rules for halting tests once the value of the additional information you will gain falls below the cost of subsequent experiments. Wallis relates the events leading up to this result.

The SRG had been asked to evaluate a calculation derived by a Captain Schuyler of the Navy on the probability that a dive bomber would be brought down by antiaircraft fire. The analysts found the calculation to be worthless. Wallis, who had been warned that Schuyler was one of the "orneriest" characters in the military, was the designated messenger to bring him the bad news.

According to Wallis, he told Schuylar that "we were now in a position to tell him how good his formula was. He barked, 'How good is it?' and I replied 'Not good at all.' He snapped, 'What's wrong with it?' This had been anticipated and my reply planned: 'What's right with it? We were unable to see any sense in it at all.' From then on, he and I were good friends." It was, in fact, Captain Schuyler's subsequent discussions of the sequential test firing of rounds of experimental ordinance that planted the seeds of **SEQUENTIAL ANALYSIS** within the SRG.

At one point, my father wrote a paper with Fred Mosteller, another member of the group. Wallis gave their work to Milton Friedman, five years their senior, who was executive director of the project. "We were . . . rather pleased with ourselves for the way we had written it," recalls Mosteller.[2] But when they got the paper back from Friedman, he goes on, "We could scarcely believe what he had done to the manuscript . . . the pages were black with corrections, and the backs full of extended notes and rewriting."

"Jimmie and I held an indignant meeting of the 'He can't do that to us' variety, and we studied the literally hundreds of suggestions that had been made. The more we worked, the more we found that Friedman was occasionally; well, often; let's face it; usually right. We finally made a list of 100 or so objections to Milton's changes and went up seven flights to do battle with him. Milton was just delighted to see us. In no time he showed us that he was right in about 85 percent of the objections. He gave us credit for one or two complaints, admitted that one or two items were matters of taste, and the rest we agreed to disagree about. Milton kindly explained to us that we knew little about writing, that there were books from which we could and should learn, and he recommended several to us." Mosteller went on to a long and illustrious career in statistics at Harvard, while my father developed a close professional relationship with Friedman.

This was the environment into which I was born down the street at the Columbia University Saint Luke's Hospital in late 1944.

After the war, Wallis and Friedman went to the University of Chicago, and my father followed in 1947. Images of Friedman—short, feisty, and supremely confident—and Wallis—tall, slow-talking, and supremely confident—fill my earliest memories. My father wrote two important papers with Friedman, and he and Wallis founded the department of statistics at the University of Chicago.[3] At a young age, I could sense the respect and friendship that had grown up among these three great intellectual colleagues. To this day, they remain a daunting triumvirate role model for me.

German Tanks

In the mid-1990s, I was giving regular seminars around the country on management science in spreadsheets for the University of Chicago. One day I received a note from Wallis, inviting me to visit him in Washington, D.C., on my next visit. I was thrilled. When we met for dinner, I was full of questions about the war years.

The first thing I asked involved estimating the number of German tanks during World War II. Without guaranteeing the authenticity of this story, I had been teaching it to my students as a powerful example of statistical thinking. The allies had captured a certain number of German tanks complete with serial numbers, as the story goes, and, of course, they knew how the orderly Nazis would number their tanks: ein, zwei, drei. . . . Thus the serial numbers of captured tanks would appear as numbers generated from a spinner that went from 1 to N, where N was the total number of tanks. Recalling that the spinner running between 0 and 1 had an average of $1/2$, then this spinner would have an average of $1/2$ times N. This led to an incredibly simple but accurate estimate for the total number of tanks produced. Just take the average of all captured tank serial numbers and multiply by 2, as displayed in Figure 35.1.

When I asked Wallis if this story was true, I got more than I had bargained for. "Not only is it true," he said, "but in 1948 while I was consulting on statistical quality control at a plant that manufactured atomic bombs, I kept note of the serial numbers on the bomb casings." He described how at that time, the number of atomic bombs in the U.S. arsenal was the most highly guarded secret in the free world. "At the end of the day," he went on, "I told the Air Force colonel running the place what I thought that number was and how

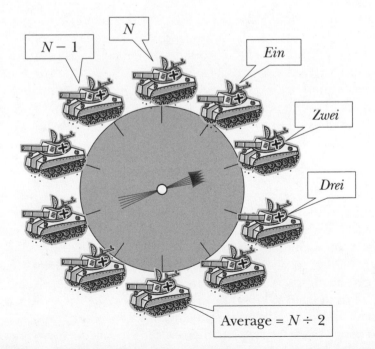

Figure 35.1   Captured tank serial numbers are like numbers from a spinner.

I had arrived at it. The officer didn't bat an eyelash at the time, but three decades later I ran into him at a cocktail party in DC, and he told me I had been dead on."

Protective Armor on Bombers

How do you know where to put protective armor on a fighter or bomber? According to Wallis, "The military was inclined to provide protection for those parts that on returning aircraft showed the most hits."[4] This seems pretty obvious. I mean if your roof leaks, you patch the place with the hole. But Abraham Wald of the SRG pointed out the statistical sample used for these decisions consisted only of the planes that had returned. In other words, the only bullet holes you would see are those that don't matter. So where should you really put protective armor? Anywhere you never see a bullet hole. The original analysis was off by a minus sign!

Wallis tells a funny story about Wald, who, being an émigré from Nazi-controlled Europe, was technically an enemy alien and could not receive a security clearance. However, he was one of the key architects behind SEQUENTIAL ANALYSIS, which was highly classified. One day in frustration, Wallis exclaimed, "What do they expect us to do, snatch the pages away as each one is written and keep it secret from him?"

Half a Battleship

Columbia, of course, was not the only place where mathematics was turning the tide of the war. Perhaps the most famous of all was Bletchley Park in England, where Alan Turing, one of the fathers of computer science, cracked the Germans' military code. And 60 miles southwest of Columbia, at Princeton University, another group of U.S. scientists were also doing their part for the war effort. Ted Anderson, currently an emeritus professor of statistics and economics at Stanford University, was a research associate there. One of their projects involved the evaluation of long-range weather forecasts. "We found that there was very little accuracy beyond two days," Ted recalls. (Things haven't changed much.) Another study involved the statistical testing of explosives. They needed to be sensitive enough to be detonated by a trigger, but not so finicky that they would blow up in the ammo truck.

When I ran into Ted recently at the Stanford faculty club and described what I was working on, he recalled a classic example of the Flaw of Averages (see "The Flaw of Averages in Naval War Games").

The Flaw of Averages in Naval War Games

BY TED ANDERSON

During World War II at the Naval War College "games" were played on a huge board (as large as a football field) simulating a naval battle involving two fleets of battleships, cruisers, etc. To evaluate the effect of a shot of one gun on a battleship of the opposing fleet, use was made of a table of the probabilities of a gun hitting a target ship at a given range.

Play consisted of the moves of one fleet alternating with moves of the other fleet. If Battleship A was firing at Battleship B at 5 miles, say, and the probability of a hit was 1/2, then instead of either hitting or missing with equal probability, play would continue with half of Battleship B.

Later in the war IBM provided the Naval War College with computers which would furnish outcomes using the actual probabilities; that is, with probability 1/2 Battleship B would be removed from the board.

Statistics played a tremendous role in the war. And when the SRG and related groups dispersed, they spread peaceful applications of statistics across academia and industry. When Wallis asked former members of the group to send him letters of reminiscences to help him with his 1980 article, there was a universal recognition that they had been involved in "one of the great creative periods in statistical science." But one letter added a sentiment that Wallis says was felt by all: "Ghastly that such progress should have involved, even depended on, the deaths of millions of people thousands of miles away."

I visited Wallis several more times, and, although frail near the end, he was the same old Allen I had remembered as a child. A hint of a smile would often play across his lips as it always had, because so many of the serious things he had to say were said with humor. On my last visit, we sat in his apartment under a photograph taken with Margaret Thatcher. He told me of sitting in his office as undersecretary of state one day, when he heard his old friend and colleague, George Stigler, enter the outer office. "My receptionist called through the door: 'Mr. Stigler to see Dr. Wallis.'" There was that flickering trace of a smile. "And George corrected her: 'No, that's *Dr.* Stigler to see *Mr.* Wallis.'"

We are now in a very different war. But like World War II, the War on Terror must be understood with statistics. Robert Shearer is a lieutenant colonel in the Army who used Monte Carlo simulation while in Baghdad to estimate the size of the Sunni insurgency and the number of foreign fighters entering the country. If he had given me the details and I had shared them with you, he would have had to kill all of us.

He could, however, share this: "The intelligence community had a general idea how to make the estimates," Shearer emailed me from Iraq, "but had no idea how to capture their uncertainty." The challenge, he discovered, was to explain what happens when you add or multiply distributions. So he brought a pair of dice into the briefings to test people's intuition. "I was surprised to find that a majority of those I briefed knew the general shape for the sum of two dice," Shearer says. "But," he continues, "no one guessed the shape for the product of two dice, and that's when I won them over." Shearer's unclassified slide of the histogram of the product of two dice appears in Figure 35.2. In the next chapter I will explore some things that can be deduced about the War on Terror from the basic laws of probability.

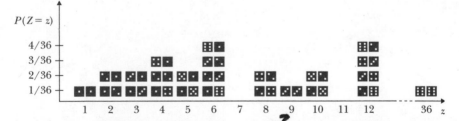

Figure 35.2   Lieutenant Colonel Robert Shearer's histogram of the product of two dice.

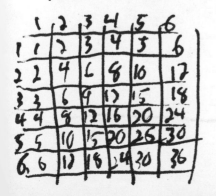

CHAPTER

Probability and the
War on Terror

A story in *USA Today* describes how Christine Anderson first learned that her son was a suspected terrorist.[1] It was at the Minneapolis-St. Paul International Airport in 2004. "We checked in at the ticket counter, and the woman said in a stern voice, 'Who is John Anderson?'" Christine pointed to her baby carriage.

To this day, young Mr. Anderson, along with 15,000 other U.S. travelers, have been unable to clear their names. John's family cannot print out his boarding passes over the Internet but must show up in person at the ticket counter to prove that he is a child. This trademark issue in the War on Terror is known as the problem of false positives, and, as we will see, it often defies intuition.

Portions of this chapter appeared in Sam Savage and Howard Wainer, "Until Proved Guilty: False Positives and the War on Terror," *Chance Magazine*, Vol. 21, No. 1 (2008).

The Magic Bullet

So how many true terrorists do you think are currently in the United States? I'm not talking about common thugs, cutthroats, or murderers, but hard-core professionals intent on mass murder. I have no idea myself, but for the sake of argument, suppose there are 3,000. That is, in the total U.S. population of 300 million, one person in 100,000 is the real deal.

Now consider a magic bullet for this threat: unlimited wiretapping tied to advanced voice analysis software on everyone's phone line. The software can detect would-be terrorists within the utterance of three words, whereupon it automatically calls the FBI, as required. Assume that the system is 99 percent accurate; that is, if a true terrorist is on the line, it will notify the FBI 99 percent of the time, whereas for nonterrorists, it will call the FBI (in error) only 1 percent of the time. Although such detection software probably could never be this accurate, it is instructive to think through the effectiveness of such a system, if it existed.

When the FBI gets a report from the system, what is the chance it will have a true terrorist?

- a. 99%
- b. 98%
- c. 66%
- d. 33%
- e. 1%
- f. One chance in 1,000

Think of it this way. When the FBI gets a warning, it either has the correct report of a true terrorist or the false report of a nonterrorist. Of the 3,000 true terrorists, 99 percent or 2,970 would actually be reported. Of the 299,997,000 nonterrorists (300 million minus the 3,000 terrorists), only 1 percent, or 2,999,970 would be falsely reported.

Figure 36.1 provides a graphic display of the target population that would trigger a report. Assuming that any given report is drawn at random from this population, you can think of the outcome as the result of throwing a dart at the target.

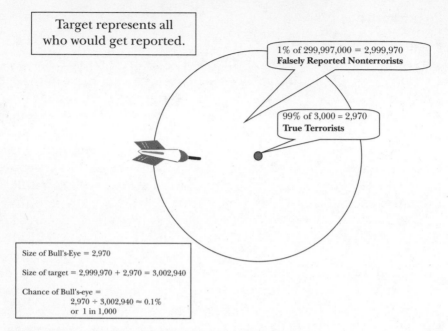

Target represents all who would get reported.

1% of 299,997,000 = 2,999,970
Falsely Reported Nonterrorists

99% of 3,000 = 2,970
True Terrorists

Size of Bull's-Eye = 2,970

Size of target = 2,999,970 + 2,970 = 3,002,940

Chance of Bull's-eye =
    2,970 ÷ 3,002,940 ≈ 0.1%
    or 1 in 1,000

Figure 36.1   The reported population as a target.

The False Positive Problem

The chance is only one in 1,000 that a report will result in the FBI's nabbing a true terrorist, even with a 99 percent accurate detector. If the number of true terrorists was smaller than 3,000, the chance of a correct warning would be even less. If the number of terrorists was greater, the chances would be greater. But even if there were 30,000 terrorists in the country, the chance of a correct warning would only be 1 in 100. What looked like a magic bullet doesn't look so attractive when you consider the number of innocent people who would be thrown under suspicion.

This is known as the problem of *false positives*, and it may be the single biggest issue in the War on Terror. When armies clash, detecting the enemy is easy for both sides. In the War on Terror, it is highly improbable that we will detect the terrorists, and it is trivial for them to detect us. No wonder this has been called asymmetric warfare.

Major Paul Kucik, an assistant professor in the department of systems engineering at the United States Military Academy at West

Point, relates an example of just how nonintuitive the false positives problem can be. A group of military analysts had been working on a statistical method to detect car bombs in Iraq. A team of Kucik's student cadets was assigned to analyze the proposed statistical test as a final class project. Just as with the hypothetical terrorist detector, the test was believed to accurately predict explosives when they were actually present.

"When the students met with the analysts who had developed the methodology, they made a case for using multiple sources of intelligence, instead of just the single test," says Kucik. "They explained to the client that even with a very accurate detector, the base rate of vehicles carrying explosives is so low that when a soldier receives a positive signal, there is only a tiny chance that the vehicle is actually dangerous," Kucik continues. "What seemed so powerful is that a group of undergrad students was able to share a very important (and surprising) insight with a group of PhDs and professional engineers who had spent over three years working on this problem."

Greg Parnell, a full professor at West Point, with decades of experience in decision analysis, confirms that even very competent senior leaders grossly underestimate the chance of false positives. "I once presented a hypothetical example to a group of high level government officials and industry leaders in Washington," says Parnell, "and they were extremely surprised when they discovered how far off their intuitive estimates were."

The Second Worst Terrorist Attack on the United States

There are other ways in which this type of probabilistic thinking applies to the War on Terror. For example, when the news first broke on April 19, 1995 that the Federal Building in Oklahoma City had been bombed, I immediately thought of Islamic fundamentalists, although I wondered what they would be doing in Oklahoma City. As it turned out, the principal instigator, Timothy McVeigh, was a decorated veteran of the first Gulf War and was involved in a white supremacist organization. Come to think of it, there may be a lot more war veterans associated with criminal gangs in the United States than there are Islamic fundamentalists, and some have had excellent training in blowing things up. Again, our intuition can be improved upon by thinking of the relative sizes of the various target populations.

The Army is aware of extremism in its ranks and takes the problem seriously. For example, the *Commander's Handbook—Gangs & Extremist Groups—Dealing with Hate*, published by the XVIII Airborne Corps and Fort Bragg Provost Marshall Office, is a 96-page manual compiled with the aid of various civilian and military law enforcement agencies.[2] It is designed to raise awareness of the problem among military officers. It contains a fascinating history and taxonomy of gangs and extremist groups, as well as methods for dealing with them.

Speaking of problems that arise from within, the terrifying anthrax attacks just after 9/11 had the galvanizing effect of confirming that "they" were really out to get us. It certainly scared the daylights out of me, and no doubt this made it easier to get support for the War in Iraq. In 2008, with the suicide of a government biodefense anthrax scientist, we learned that "they" was probably "us." Conspiracy theorists, start your engines.[3]

Your Worst Enemy

So you're having nightmares about dying at the hands of Islamic fundamentalists, rogue veterans of Middle Eastern wars, or mad government scientists? You ain't seen nothin' yet. If you have the guts to handle it and want to catch a glimpse of your worst enemy, then look in the mirror. One person in 10,000 commits suicide every year in the United States, according to StateMaster.com, a fascinating source of wide-ranging statistics.[4] That's an annual total of 30,000, more than twice the number of people murdered per year. This reveals a hidden danger of the War on Terror. Suppose either politicians trying to scare us about terrorists or thousands of false accusations of terrorism increased our rate of depression by 10 percent. The associated growth in suicides might take as many lives annually as the 9/11 attack. Furthermore, a recent study by CBS News has revealed that the suicide rate may be considerably higher among young U.S. military veterans of the wars in Iraq and Afghanistan.[5] One can conclude that an effective way to avoid violent death is to heed the advice of Bobby McFerrin: "Don't worry, be happy."

No More Excuses

The examples so far can all be characterized by the target analogy. The method for solving them is known as **BAYESIAN ANALYSIS**, and, as demonstrated, it can be counterintuitive. Thus, decision makers in business, government, and the military have had an excuse for making terrible decisions concerning rare events.

But no more.

> *In a recent article in Chance Magazine entitled "Until Proven Guilty: False Positives and the War on Terror," Howard Wainer and I introduced a freely available False Positives Calculator in Microsoft Excel.[6] You may experiment with this at FlawOfAverages.com.*

I suggest that the next time you learn of a politician or bureaucrat about to make a decision that may bring more harm through false positives than benefit though true ones, you send them the link to the above file.

There Is Nothing to Cheer but Fear Itself

It is tempting for some politicians to manipulate public opinion by raising the specter of horrific but extremely unlikely events, and it is easy to fall for their faulty logic. A few years ago, for example, a legislator, who supported an antimissile system for protecting us from rogue states such as North Korea, argued emotionally that the specter of a nuclear weapon destroying New York was so horrible that we should stop at nothing to deter it. Oddly, he didn't mention that it is more likely that such a weapon would be delivered to New York by ship and that a missile attack, aside from being far more expensive and difficult, is the only delivery method providing a definitive return address for a devastating U.S. counterstrike.

Someone who has thought long and hard about missile defense is William J. Perry, former U.S. secretary of defense. Perry has a BS, MS, and PhD, all in mathematics, but has nonetheless had a remarkably practical and productive career as an entrepreneur, academician, and public servant. He is a stellar exemplar of the benefits of connecting the seat of the intellect to the seat of the pants.

The Mother of All False Positive Problems

As undersecretary of defense for research and engineering under President Jimmy Carter, Perry received some firsthand experience in missile defense one morning at 3 a.m. The watch officer at the North American Aerospace Defense Command (NORAD) was on the phone.

"The officer said his computers were indicating an attack underway from the Soviet Union, involving a large number of missiles," recalls Perry. "He believed it must be a false alarm because of the lack of other indicators, and wanted me to help him figure out what had gone wrong," Perry continues. "Eventually we determined that a training tape had mistakenly been put in the computer that had simulated the attack on the radar screens."

National Missile Defense

One of Perry's tasks during this period was to evaluate a national missile defense system (NMD). "All the analyses were based on air defense against bombers during WWII," Perry recalls. "A typical kill rate was 5 percent, but that was enough because a bombing campaign required many missions. From the pilot's perspective, there would be a 95 percent chance of surviving the first mission, but only a 36 percent chance of surviving 20 missions. In a war of attrition, that constituted an effective defense." Perry contrasts this against the threat of a nuclear missile attack. "This would not be a war of attrition. Instead of a 5 percent kill rate, you would need nearly 100 percent. If a single warhead gets to its target, you have failed."

It's All in the Numbers

A 99 percent effective system is completely unrealistic, but suppose you could actually get from 5 percent to even 75 percent effectiveness? You would have a 75 percent survival rate against a single warhead, but what about multiple warheads? The chart in Figure 36.2 tells the story.

The intuitive explanation is that stopping warheads is a little like flipping heads on a coin. Nobody flips 15 heads in a row. Thus, as the number of warheads goes up, there is no practical means of defense, so you should put your money elsewhere. That is why Perry did not pursue an NMD in the late 1970s. Instead, he championed the development of the stealth aircraft technology that proved so decisive two decades later.

Perry confirmed that missile defense doesn't make much sense even against rogue states with only a few warheads. When I recently asked Perry about North Korea's missile capability, he replied, "I don't give a damn about their ICBMs. I worry that they sell a bomb to terrorists who try to deliver it on a freighter or drive it across the border in a truck."

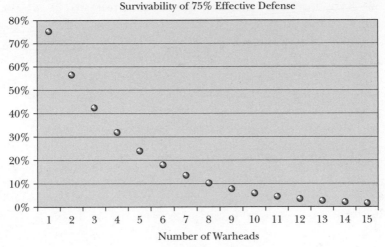

Figure 36.2   Reduction in survival probability as the number of warheads increases.

But come to think of it, there is one instance in which a rogue state might use a missile against the United States. Suppose two of our rogue enemies were also enemies of each other. Then each one would have an incentive to sneak its own ICBM into the other country and fire it at us from there, thereby killing two birds with one stone. If this is the scenario keeping you awake at night, then missile defense is for you. Otherwise, you should consider the equally daunting challenge of securing U.S.-bound shipping containers and our land borders. It would cost about the same.[7]

Loose Nukes

When the former Soviet Union unraveled, people did their best to keep track of all the nuclear warheads. The Nunn-Lugar Cooperative Threat Reduction Program went a long way toward tidying up, but no one is sure that all the weapons are accounted for.[8] The only terrorist threat that could harm us on the scale of our own suicide rate or worse would come from one of these (or some biological agent) delivered by terrorists.

How can we estimate the probability that such a weapon could be successfully smuggled into the United States? A rough approximation can be arrived at by comparing the War on Terror to the War on Drugs. A 2006 Department of Justice (DOJ) report estimates that in 2004, between 325 and 675 metric tons of cocaine were shipped to the United States, of which 196 metric tons were seized.[9] Thus by DOJ's own accounting, the <u>percentage of cocaine making it through is between 40 and 70 percent</u>. Stanford University decision analyst Ron Howard has joked that would-be WMD terrorists might well consider smuggling their weapons inside cocaine shipments.

As with the missile defense system, thwarting terrorist-borne WMDs is all in the numbers. Suppose there was a 90 percent chance of interdicting such weapons. By the time you reach 40 independent attacks, the chance of thwarting them all is less than 1 in 100, as shown in Figure 36.3. This is why a primary goal in the War on Terror, in addition to preventing such attacks, should be to reduce the number of people who want to carry them out in the first place.

Star Wars

As an historical footnote, Ronald Reagan introduced his own antimissile Strategic Defense Initiative (SDI) in 1983, which soon became known as Star Wars. It received some of the credit for ending the Cold War, even though it faced the same mathematical impossibilities as just described. Physicist Michael May, former

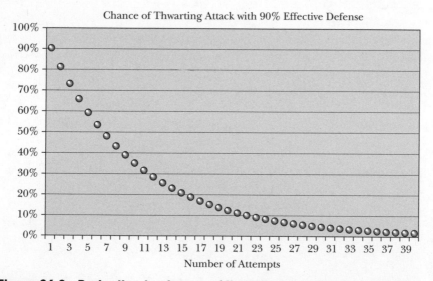

Figure 36.3   Reduction in chance of thwarting an attack as number of attempts increases.

director of the Lawrence Livermore atomic weapons lab, once asked a high-ranking Soviet physicist, "Are you guys really scared by the SDI?" According to May, "The fellow responded that 'none of our scientists consider it a threat but all of our politicians do.'"[10] May continues, "That may characterize, to a lesser extent, what went on in Washington as well. The scientists knew it wasn't even close, but politicians and I must say most media made much of it."

Rumsfeld Asks the Right Question

In a 2003 leaked memo, then U.S. Defense Secretary Donald Rumsfeld said:[11]

> Today, we lack metrics to know if we are winning or losing the global war on terror. Are we capturing, killing or deterring and dissuading more terrorists every day than the madrassas and the radical clerics are recruiting, training and deploying against us?

That was the right question to ask. By 2006, the National Intelligence Estimate had begun to develop answers. There is evidence that, at least in some areas, U.S. actions have been counterproductive. According to those who have seen the classified report, it "[c]ites the Iraq war as a reason for the diffusion of jihad ideology."[12]

People have compared fighting terrorism to fighting a disease for which surgery can sometimes be a cure and other times spread it throughout the body. In seeking answers to Rumsfeld's question, perhaps we should be taking an epidemiological perspective. In any event, too bad he didn't ask it openly because it was and still is an important issue for public debate.

An Epidemiological Approach to the War on Terror

Paul Stares and Mona Yacoubian of the U.S. Institute of Peace introduced this perspective in a 2005 article in the *Washington Post* entitled "Terrorism as Virus."[13]

According to Stares and Yacoubian, "One promising new approach builds on the parallels often drawn between terrorism and a mutating virus or metastasizing cancer." They list three benefits of this perspective.

First, it would focus attention on the nature of the threat and its spread. "Which transmission vectors—for example, mosques, madrassas, prisons, the Internet, satellite TV—spread the ideology most effectively?"

Second, it would lead to a better understanding of the dynamics of the terrorist movement as a whole. "Just as diseases do not emerge in a vacuum but evolve as a result of complex interactions between pathogens, people and their environment, so it is with Islamist militancy."

Third, it would lay the framework for a global strategy for reducing the threat. "Public health officials long ago recognized that epidemics can be rolled back only with a systematically planned, multi-pronged international effort."

A great Mindle for grasping epidemiological issues is a mathematical model known as a MARKOV CHAIN (I apologize in advance that this is a Red Word for which I know of no Green equivalent).[14] These and related models have been used with considerable success to determine the optimal management of various diseases. The idea is to predict how a population will evolve over time.

To see how this approach could be applied to the War on Terror, consider a hypothetical violent region of the world in which people fall into one of four states: peaceful, militant, terrorist, or killed. The initial distribution is shown in Figure 36.4. In each three-month period, a certain percentage of the population will transition from state to state, as described in Table 36.1.

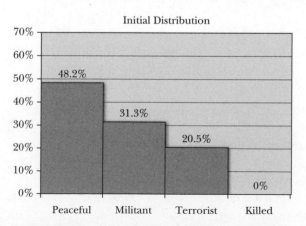

Figure 36.4   Initial distribution of terror-related attributes.

TABLE 36.1   Hypothetical States of Militancy

	Description
Peaceful	These people are the largest segment of the population, but in every three-month period, 12% will become militant, and 1% will become terrorists.
Militant	These attend rallies and proselytize but do not engage in terrorist acts. In every three-month period, 20% will lose interest and revert to a peaceful state, and 5% will become active terrorists.
Terrorist	These are hardened killers, none of whom revert to a peaceful state. However, 10% lose their nerve and return to being merely militant by the next time period.
Killed	At this point none of the population is being killed. The natural birth and death rate keep the population constant. .

Imagine that the transition rate from state to state in Table 36.1 remains constant for the next ten years. What would the final distribution of attributes be?

> *Hint. This is impossible to answer without a* MARKOV CHAIN *model. So I have provided an Excel version at FlawOfAverages.com.*

It turns out that the distribution in ten years will be *identical* to the initial distribution shown in Figure 36.4. Actually, I picked the initial distribution so that this *would* be the case. That is, I started off the population in equilibrium. The distribution over time, as displayed by the model, appears in Figure 36.5.

Hearts and Minds   Now consider what would happen if, through some act of diplomacy, the rate of transition between states could be changed to encourage less militant behavior. Suppose a strategy, which I will call Hearts and Minds, created the changes shown in

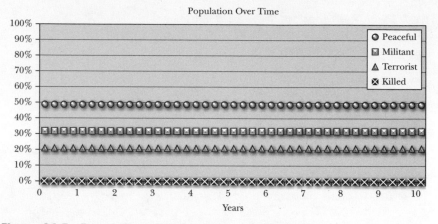

Figure 36.5 Population distribution in equilibrium.

Table 36.2; that is, the percentage transitioning from peaceful to militant is reduced from 12 percent to 10 percent, whereas the transition rate from militant to peaceful is increased from 20 percent to 23 percent, and so on.

What is the distribution of attributes in ten years? Hint: This is also impossible without a MARKOV CHAIN model, which indicates a very different distribution in ten years, as shown in Figure 36.6. Notice that what looked like fairly small changes in the transition rates reduced the percentage of terrorists from 20 percent to 4 percent, which in the numbers game of thwarting attacks could have an even bigger effect on assuring our own security, as shown in Figure 36.3. The evolution of the population is shown in Figure 36.7.

TABLE 36.2 Hypothetical Changes in Transition Behavior Induced by Hearts and Minds Strategy

To \ From	Peaceful	Militant	Terrorist
Peaceful		20% → 23%	
Militant	12% → 10%		10% → 15%
Terrorist	1% → 0%	5% → 2%	

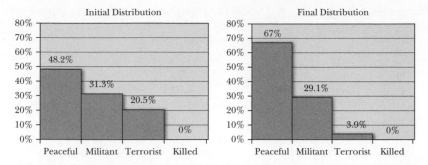

Figure 36.6   Initial and final distributions under the Hearts and Minds strategy.

A Military Strategy   Next consider a hypothetical Military strategy, with the goal of killing terrorists. But don't forget the false positives problem from the beginning of this chapter. We must assume that we will also kill some nonterrorists, whose surviving relatives will undoubtedly become more militant as a result. This is exacerbated by the fact that the terrorists exploit this by intentionally mingling with the nonterrorist population. Suppose the results of the Military strategy changed the transitions as shown in Table 36.3.

The initial and final distributions are shown in Figure 36.8. For this set of hypothetical transition characteristics, the percentage of

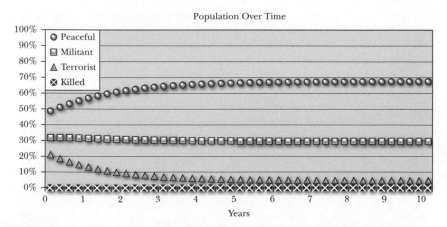

Figure 36.7   Evolution of the population under the Hearts and Minds strategy.

TABLE 36.3   Hypothetical Changes in Transition Behavior induced by the Military Strategy

From To	Peaceful	Militant	Terrorist
Peaceful		20% → 10%	
Militant	12% → 15%		10% → 5%
Terrorist	1% → 2%	5% → 24%	
Killed	0% → 1%	0% → 1%	0% → 1%

terrorists more than doubles. Furthermore, a third of the population has been killed.

For these hypothetical transition numbers, the military solution is like throwing rocks at a hornet's nest. The number of hornets killed by such an attack doesn't make up for the number that you make angry.

The MARKOV CHAIN models in these examples are purely hypothetical and, without estimates of true transition rates, do not bolster the case for either the Hearts and Minds or Military approach. But the models *do* bolster the case that transition rates between states of militancy can have a huge effect. Perhaps *these* are the metrics sought by Rumsfeld that will ultimately determine whether we are winning or losing the War on Terror.

As this book was in page proofs I came across Fareed Zakaria's March 2009 *Newsweek* article on "Learning to Live With Radical

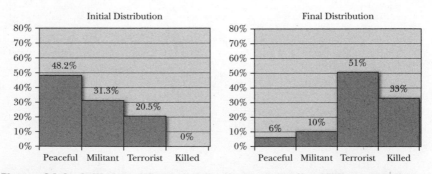

Figure 36.8   Initial and final distributions under the Military solution.

Population Over Time

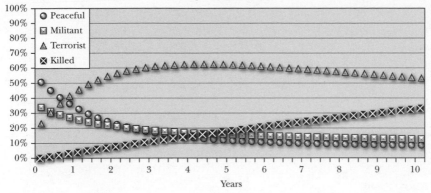

Figure 36.9   Evolution of the population under the Military solution.

Islam"[15], in which it appears that some in the defense community are now taking a view commensurate with this approach. Of course they have many more than three categories of militancy, but they are clearly talking of transitioning people between them. For example, Zakaria quotes a former CIA analyst Reuel Marc Gerecht as saying: "What you have to realize is that the objective is to defeat bin Ladenism, and you have to start the evolution. Moderate Muslims are not the answer. Shiite clerics and Sunni fundamentalists are our salvation from future 9/11s." One of General Petraeus' advisors believes that less than 10 percent of "the people we call the Taliban" are aligned with Mullah Omar or Al Qaeda. He believes that the remaining 90 percent are "almost certainly reconcilable under some circumstances." With this in mind I hope those interested in this issue will access the model at FlawOfAverages.com and try their own transition rates.

In summary, there are two big problems in the War on Terror. The first, as we saw, is the difficulty in identifying the enemy. When we read headlines proclaiming: "50 suspected terrorists killed," we should remember that most "suspected terrorists" are probably innocent civilians. General David Petraeus acknowledges this in a discussion of the use of air power in counterinsurgency in his 2006 *Army Field Manual*.[16] "Bombing, even with the most precise weapons, can cause unintended civilian casualties. . . . An air strike can cause collateral damage that turns people against the host-nation government and provides insurgents with a major propaganda victory." But Petraeus did not include numerical examples to display the magnitude of the false positive problem, and without doing the numbers it is invariably underestimated. In the next edition of the *Field Manual*, I suggest they include a False Positives Calculator like the one offered at FlawOfAverages.com.

The second problem is that the chance of preventing a terrorist attack drops dramatically as the number of people attempting the attacks goes up. Therefore, we must be mindful of the paradox that in killing suspected terrorists, we will inevitably harm innocent civilians among them, thereby motivating more people to become terrorists in the first place.

I suggest that instead of thinking just of good guys and bad guys, we look at the *distribution* of states of militancy across a population and how the distribution evolves over time. I have proposed some simple mathematical models to help us grasp these issues. But for the proper use of models, I return to the mathematician and Secretary of Defense William J. Perry. He was once asked if, during his tenure at the Pentagon, he had ever personally built a mathematical model to answer some pressing question. Although a great deal of sophisticated modeling is done in the military *for* the Secretary of Defense, when it came to his *own* decision making, he replied, "No, there was never enough time or data for me to build an actual model on the spot. But because of my training I think about problems differently."

The best models are those you no longer need because they have changed the way you think.

The Flaw of Averages
and Climate Change

Everyone is talking about it, everyone is uncertain about it, and everyone is asking questions: How much hotter will it get? How high will the oceans rise? What should we do about it? Give us the numbers.

Why the Earth's Average Temperature Is Falling

As I began my own investigation of climate change, I realized that current researchers had ignored some important aspects of the problem, which, if taken into account, indicate that average temperature is likely to *decrease* not increase.

Given the growing number of upstart nuclear-armed states, the chance of thermonuclear war is on the rise. And according to experts, the dust kicked up by a robust exchange of such weapons would significantly block the planet's solar heating, "causing surface temperatures to drop drastically."[1] Major asteroid strikes and catastrophic volcanic events would have similar effects. Taking these disasters into account drags the average temperature way down. Of course, like people with their heads in the oven and their feet in the freezer, humanity may not be comfortable in any event.

But seriously, folks, the Flaw of Averages permeates our discussion of climate change in other ways as well. Before addressing this issue I will attempt to frame the problem.

1. The earth's temperature has varied over time. Figure 37.1 shows the relative temperature over the past 420,000 years, as determined from an ice sample taken at the South Pole.

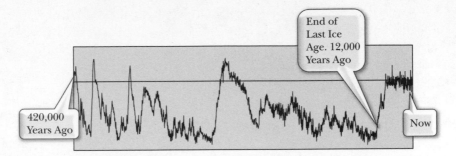

Figure 37.1   Relative earth temperature over 420,000 years.

The Vostok Ice Core data, as it is known, is widely available at web sites such as the National Oceanic and Atmospheric Administration.[2] As you can see from the graph, there would be plenty of uncertainty about future temperatures even if humans had never set foot on the planet. Although at present we are not at record high temperatures, there is more to the story.

2. There is evidence that the earth's temperature is positively interrelated with the amount of carbon dioxide (CO_2) and other greenhouse gases in the atmosphere. This is because they let sunlight in but, like the glass windows of a greenhouse, trap in heat. The CO_2 in the atmosphere has increased at an unprecedented rate in the past 50 years, and, if you are stuck in miles of traffic breathing the exhaust of the car in front of you, it is easy to imagine that humans are solely responsible for this. In fact, there is still great uncertainty surrounding the fraction of total CO_2 generated by humans, but the consensus is that it is big enough to have an effect.

3. If the earth does warm up, sea levels may rise and cause flooding, but again there is uncertainty as to how much.

Viewing these issues in terms of distributions instead of averages reveals both bad news and good news, as I will illustrate with a few examples.

The Bad News

Recall from Chapter 1 that Grand Forks would have been a lot grander if the Red River had merely reached its *average* predicted height. The damage from an average flood was negligible, whereas the damage averaged over all possible levels of the Red River was considerable. This is a classic case of the Strong Form of the Flaw of Averages (described in Chapter 12) and applies just as readily to future world sea levels.

The Uncertainty

Although most scientists believe that the earth is in a warming trend, assume for argument's sake that the expected, or average, future temperature of the earth will *not* rise, but is nonetheless quite uncertain. This leads to uncertainty about the future sea level, represented by the distribution shown in Figure 37.2. The horizontal axis represents possible future levels, with the average assumed to be where it is today. The vertical axis represents the likelihood that a given level occurs.

The Risk

Recalling that risk is in the eye of the beholder, we will take the perspective of those living in a coastal region. For them, the risk is flood damage caused by increased sea level. But don't forget

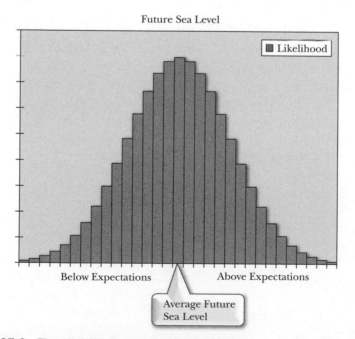

Figure 37.2 The distribution of future sea level.

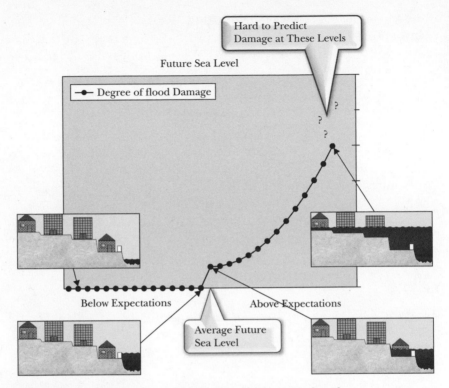

Figure 37.3   Nonlinear implications of rising sea level.

that people who have speculated in future beachfront property in Nevada are subject to the risk of losing their investments if sea level does *not* rise. Figure 37.3 depicts the nonlinear increase in flood damage with increasing sea level. The horizontal axis is the same as in Figure 37.2, but now the vertical axis is the degree of flood damage for the corresponding sea level.

Because the vertical axis represents the degree of something bad, this curve is a case of the devil's smile. (If the last sentence didn't mean anything to you, it might be a good time to revisit Chapter 12 to look at the graphs and brush up on smiles and frowns.)

Figures 37.2 and 37.3 are combined in Figure 37.4 to show a probabilistic picture of the damage. This superimposes the likelihood of future possible sea levels (the histogram) with the degree of flood damage associated with those levels (the line graph). If the sea level ends up below expectations, then damage will be a bit

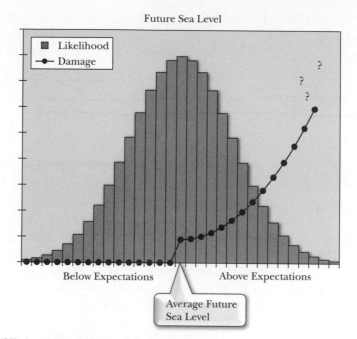

Figure 37.4 Probabilistic risk assessment.

lower than expected, but if sea level is above expectations, damage will be much worse than expected. Hence, the damage associated with the average or expected sea level may be tolerable, but averaged over all the things a scorned and furious Mother Nature might do to us, the damage could be disastrous.

The average, or expected, damage is greater than the damage of the average, or expected, sea level. This time the drunk is not on the center line of the highway, but wandering around on the edge. His chances of survival go from nil to 50/50, so on average he is half dead.

But wait, it gets worse. In addition to the uncertainty of future temperature, we are also unsure of the consequences of higher temperatures. Here's one that looks likely. In a compounding of the Flaw of Averages, guess what else global warming causes? More global warming! For example, as the polar ice cap melts, it reflects less solar energy, which further increases the temperature and makes it melt even faster.

And this was a discussion just of warming. It is also likely that storm severity will increase due to projected changes in the atmosphere. It would be erroneous to simply think of this as a separate problem. Here we have a classic case of interrelated uncertainties that make each other worse. A monster storm surge on top of coastal flooding already exacerbated by higher sea levels could make Hurricane Katrina look like an ocean breeze.

Now remember, for this analysis I assumed that the expected temperature would stay the same. Yet the uncertainty *alone* created great risk.

The Good News

The good news is that even if the climate is changing at an unprecedented rate, it is still slow by human standards. This gives us time to learn and adapt, providing us with options along the way, and options make the Flaw of Averages cut in our favor.

For example, if we continue developing sources of renewable energy at our current *average* pace, we may indeed be doomed. But we *won't* continue at this pace because there will be a *distribution of success rates*, with some technologies evolving faster than others. The technologies that *do* evolve faster will get more funding than the others, further accelerating the advances, while the below-average technologies will be abandoned. Therefore, the expected pace of progress today underestimates the true pace of progress in the future.

Furthermore, at least locally, some parts of the world will improve from the human perspective. A 2005 *New York Times* article describes something like a gold rush attitude of many countries to take advantage of the warming conditions around the North Pole.[3] Vigorous international negotiations around formerly worthless real estate are now being driven by the promise of new fishing grounds, petroleum deposits (to keep the warming trend going), and shorter shipping routes as the ice cap recedes. The article quotes Canada's minister of national defense: "[A]t the rate of present global warming, we know that it [a Northwest Passage] will be within 20 years and we have to get ahead now." If you really want to know the future temperature of the earth, I suggest that you monitor comparative real estate prices between those areas currently prone to flooding and those currently covered with ice.

There is more good news on the global warming front at the gas pump. Steep price rises not only reduce consumption but increase the motivation to invest in renewable alternatives and to reduce our dependency on foreign oil. This has happened far faster than many were predicting a couple of years ago. Paradoxically, some who have been most vociferous about global warming have also called on the government to artificially hold down gasoline prices, thereby increasing its use.

Free Markets and the Tragedy of the Commons

Adam Smith, the eighteenth-century economist, used the metaphor of an invisible hand to describe how free markets can guide individuals motivated by personal greed into benefiting society as a whole through increased commerce. By and large this works great, and we all benefit from it. However as recent economic events have demonstrated, the invisible hand occasionally drops the ball. A classic example of the failure of completely free markets is known by economists as the Tragedy of the Commons.[4] It involves an English village in which individually owned sheep graze on the commons, grassy fields belonging jointly to all inhabitants. If the commons is overgrazed, then total productivity falls with each additional sheep. But under these conditions no invisible hand leads people to remove one of their own sheep because they would penalize themselves in the process. Thus in a perfectly greedy world, more and more sheep would be added until they all die of starvation.

Before discussing the obvious parallels between too much grazing on the commons and too much carbon dioxide in the atmosphere, let's figure out what to do with the sheep. Suppose that you are mayor of a village for which the optimal herd size is 100 sheep. Unfortunately, there are currently 200. You figure that this is easy to solve, and issue 100 grazing licenses. Any sheep caught on the commons without a license will be towed away and converted to lamb chops for your personal banquets (in any system, the politicians will get their pound of flesh). But how will you dole out the licenses? Whose 100 sheep get to stay and whose have to leave? That's easy too. The traditional approach in these situations is to give the licenses to your relatives and campaign contributors. But suppose you don't have the gall for that. Then you could hold a lottery for

the 100 licenses. That sounds fair. Fair maybe, but it does not bring the maximum economic benefit into the village.

The Flaw of Averages in this setting is that when you think about sheep, you are implicitly imagining *average* sheep. In reality, however, the sheep would display a wide distribution of attributes. Suppose, for example, they fell into two categories, with their economic contribution (based on a total flock of 100 sheep on the common), as displayed below.

- *Scrawny.* These sheep are not well cared for and will produce little mutton. They will bring £100 of value per sheep into the village per year.
- *Robust.* These are well cared for animals and top mutton producers. They will bring £300 of value per sheep into the village per year.

The average economic value of a sheep is £200 and by picking the 100 sheep at random, that is what you would get. That is, there would be roughly 50 of each category with a corresponding economic contribution of £100 times 50 plus £300 times 50, or £20,000.

Cap and Trade: Harnessing Free Markets

There is a potential as before free market solution that provides the best of both worlds. The grazing licenses would be capped at 100 but this time they would be auctioned off each year to the highest bidders. Clearly the winners in this auction would be the owners of the robust sheep because the licenses are worth more to them. The total economic output would jump 50 percent to £30,000 (£300 times 100).

The owners of the scrawny sheep would lose their jobs, but the government's new source of revenue (sheep licenses auction fees) has the potential to tide them over and provide training for new jobs.

Of course, in reality there would be more than two categories of sheep. There would be many, including new ones that no one in the government had dreamt of. For example:

- Breeding stock that bring in £500 per year.
- Insulin-producing sheep that save the lives of several diabetics bringing in £1,000 per year.
- Unusually flatulent sheep that produce £5,000 worth of clean-burning methane fuel per year.

Over time, the greedy invisible hand of Adam Smith would cause this system to evolve to bring ever greater value to society from the 100 allowable sheep and ever greater license fees to the government.

The Value of Information

An argument raised for doing nothing about climate change is that we aren't even certain that there's a problem. But the Flaw of Averages tells us that it is precisely this uncertainty that we need to insure against even if the average temperature is not increasing. I believe the biggest bang for the buck in dealing with the risk of global warming is continued research, that is, in purchasing information that will reduce the level of uncertainty.

Not My Department

Another argument has been made that we should do nothing because humans may not be responsible for the problem in the first place. I understand this point of view. For example, it is known that sooner or later a major asteroid is likely to impact the earth, annihilating life as we know it. And I am personally incensed that at this very moment NASA is wasting millions of taxpayer dollars trying to develop schemes to divert these hunks of rock when clearly they are not our fault!

Learning the Controls

We have been riding this planet as passengers for a while now, and it's about time we learned to fly the thing. But if you have tried the flight simulator of Chapter 5, you will have gained a feeling for how difficult this may be due to the lags in the system. John Sterman of MIT has created a web site where you can take the controls of a simulated earth and try to keep it on an even carbon footing.[5]

Keeping excess pollutants out of our atmosphere is similar to keeping excess sheep off the common. However, at this point, we are still unclear what the long-term problems or solutions will be. Locking ourselves into a rigid regulation system with limited information is a bit like the lottery for the sheep. Instead, to ensure a solution that evolves with the problem, we need to harness the invisible hand of Adam Smith. The cap-and-trade approach, widely proposed to limit carbon emissions, is analogous to the grazing licenses that can be traded as technologies and economies evolve.

Even that bastion of free enterprise, *Economist Magazine*, believes that governments must get involved to avoid a tragedy of the commons: "The best news in the fight against climate change is that business is starting to invest in clean energy seriously. But these investments will flourish only if governments are prepared to put a price on carbon. The costs of doing that are not huge. The costs of not doing so might be."[6]

The Flaw of Averages in Health Care

The great radio comedian Jack Benny was confronted in one of his skits by a mugger who demands, "Your money or your life!" Benny, whose stage persona was notoriously stingy, does not respond immediately. "Your money or your life," repeats the robber.

"I'm thinking it over," responds Benny.

This story highlights a dilemma concerning the U.S. health care system. Although most of us would spend anything to save our own life or the life of a loved one, universal health care is viewed by some as a mugger who demands, "Your money or someone else's life." As a nation, we're still thinking it over.

But regardless of which side of this debate you are on, you can hardly object to getting more health care benefits for the buck. One way to accomplish this is through more precise targeting of treatment.

Treating the Average Patient

That the average adult patient has one breast and one testicle should be ample warning not to apply health care with too broad a brush. A more subtle example involves Simpson's paradox and the kidney stone treatment presented earlier. When you averaged results over the entire population, treatment A was worse than treatment B. But when you zoomed in to focus on groups of patients with either large or small kidney stones, treatment A was found to be *superior* to treatment B in both groups. Here the treatment that was best for the average patient was worst for every individual patient!

Poorly targeted treatment is common. In preparation for a workshop on medical decision making, I once informally interviewed several physicians on this subject and was particularly struck by the comments of a doctor in a cardiac unit of a large hospital. He described how treatment was specified for patients with blocked coronary arteries. The two primary choices are coronary artery bypass graft (CABG), which transplants a vein from the patient's leg into the heart, and angioplasty, which inserts a small balloon into the offending artery and inflates it to create greater blood flow. "It works like this," said the physician, "If the admitting doctor is an open heart surgeon, the patient gets a CABG. If the doctor specializes in angioplasty, the patient gets the balloon." If you ever go to the hospital with chest pains, just hope you aren't admitted by a proctologist.

Recall the problem of false positives discussed in the context of detecting terrorists. The same issue occurs when detecting rare diseases. For example, in spite of the seriousness of HIV, the percentage of the U.S. population that is infected is still small. Thus, universal HIV testing would likely result in many more false positives (uninfected people who tested positive) than true positives. As a further example, a recent study reported in *Time Magazine* indicates that women who perform self-exams to detect breast cancer may be doing themselves more harm than good.[1] How? They end up having nearly twice as many biopsies with benign results, which are expensive and present their own risks. On a similar note, the U.S. Preventive Services Task Force, a panel of medical experts, has now recommended that men over age 75 not be routinely screened for prostate cancer.[2] Why? If the test detects cancer, they probably would have it, but the treatment is no picnic, and the cancer is slow growing, so they would likely be dead of other causes by the time the therapy did any good.

Need more examples? *More Harm Than Good*, by Alan Zelicoff (an MD), and Michael Bellomo (who works for Baxter Biosciences), is full of them.[3] The book stresses the importance of the statistically attuned patient. For example, they discuss a hypothetical 59-year-old athletic male patient with no signs of cardiovascular disease who is nonetheless worried because a relative had a heart attack. Through a sequence of ill-advised tests, each of which has a high rate of false positives, they show how the patient could ultimately be led, at great expense, to an invasive cardiac catheterization, which has about the same chance of killing him as a heart attack did in the first place.

In 1982 Stephen Jay Gould, the naturalist quoted in Chapter 1, was diagnosed with a rare "incurable" form of cancer for which the median life span was eight months. In a 1985 article in *Discover Magazine*, entitled "The Median Isn't the Message," he describes how looking at the *distribution* of outcomes instead of a single number helped him maintain hope, which in turn helped save his life.[4] The median is the point in the distribution that divides the population in half, so he reasoned that he had at least a 50 percent chance of living more than eight months. Furthermore, the literature indicated that, given his age (40) and the early stage at which the cancer had been discovered, he was more likely to live for more than eight months rather than less. Then he realized that the distribution of time to mortality must be skewed to the right. That is, the soonest any patient could die was immediately, but the longest one could live might be considerable, as shown in Figure 38.1. Finally he was put on experimental drugs, whose results were not reflected in the current statistics, so this further pushed his chances out to the right. All these things helped Gould maintain a positive attitude, which is now acknowledged as a significant factor in cancer survival.

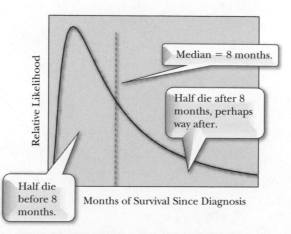

Figure 38.1   A skewed distribution of survival times.

In his 1996 book, *Full House*, he recalled the experience:[5]

> I was able to make such an analysis because my statistical training, and my knowledge of natural history, had taught me to treat variation as a basic reality, and to be wary of averages—which are, after all, abstract measures, applicable to no single person, and often largely irrelevant to individual cases.

He survived for two decades after the diagnosis before succumbing to an unrelated disease. During this time he wrote 20 books and hundreds of papers, as well as serving as an ongoing inspiration to countless cancer survivors.

Gould's inspirational story should be kept in mind when doing cost/benefit analysis of expensive therapies. Do we really want to measure costs and benefits in terms of average years of life gained? Consider a hypothetical drug that has no effect in eight out of ten patients, but extends the life of the other two in ten by 36 months. If you were the patient, would you look at the treatment as offering you a guaranteed 7.2 months of increased life expectancy? It wouldn't. What it would do is provide a one-in-five chance for three more years of life, during which you might attend your daughter's wedding and live to see your grandchildren.

Medicine Meets Mathematics

In the 1970s, a Stanford Hospital heart surgeon named David Eddy started questioning how medical decisions were made. "I concluded that medicine was making decisions with an entirely different method from what we would call rational," he recalls in a 2006 cover story in *BusinessWeek*.[6] At some point Dr. Eddy discovered that he was within walking distance of one of the world's great epicenters of decision analysis: Ron Howard's department in Stanford University's School of Engineering. Eager for a challenge, Eddy proceeded to get a PhD in the mathematical analysis of medical decision making. Here he discovered Markov chains. These were presented earlier as a potential approach for modeling the evolution of the states of militancy within a population. In health care, instead of states of peaceful, militant, terrorists, or killed, members of the population might have states such as disease free, infected with a particular disease, symptomatic for the disease, contagious, or dead. In the terror example, one could view a foreign policy strategy as an attempt to control the rate at which people moved among the various states of militancy. In the health care arena, a treatment strategy would attempt to control the transition rate between various states of health. Dr. Eddy, who has championed the use of similar mathematical models in health care, has devoted a web page to this important area.[7]

Eddy, now an advisor to Kaiser Permanente health care, pioneered the idea that medical decisions should be based on actual evidence of effectiveness, not just the beliefs of physicians. He coined the term "evidence-based medicine" to describe this approach. "The history of medicine, both in the past and very, very recently, is filled with examples where experts were dead sure that a treatment was effective," Dr. Eddy said on a PBS presentation on health care.[8] "But when we finally got around to doing the studies, we found out the treatment wasn't effective, or might even be harmful." Anyone for a quick lobotomy before lunch?

Based on Your Average Breath, You'd Probably Be Dead

While soliciting examples of mathematical applications to health care, I learned that JENSEN'S INEQUALITY (the Strong Form of the Flaw of Averages) had been explicitly recognized and exploited in the design of ventilators, mechanical devices that assist patients who cannot breathe on their own.

A statistician and two anesthesiologists from the University of Manitoba describe the case in a 2005 paper in the *Journal of the Royal Society Interface*.[9] Figure 38.2 represents the relationship between oxygen delivered to the blood and the air pressure in the lungs. Notice that in the normal breathing range, oxygen delivery is a smiling (CONVEX) curve with respect to air pressure. This is because of how the little sacks in the lungs, known as alveoli, expand under increased pressure.

This presents a problem for patients on ventilators. According to the authors, "Most ventilators monotonously deliver the same sized breaths, like clockwork; however, healthy people do not breathe this way." If the ventilator delivers the correct average pressure, the patient does not get enough oxygen. On the other hand, if the pressure is increased, it can potentially cause lung damage.

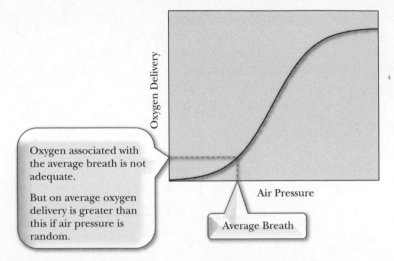

Figure 38.2   Oxygen delivery to the lungs versus air pressure.

The solution? Design the ventilator so that it randomizes the air pressure around the desired average. In this case, the Strong Form of the Flaw of Averages implies that the average oxygen delivery will be greater than the delivery for the average breath. Thus, adequate oxygen is provided without injuring the lungs. Note that at higher-than-normal pressures, where the curve begins to frown; randomizing would reduce the amount of delivery instead of increasing it.

Such models of human biology have the potential to be expanded well beyond ventilators. For example, Dr. Eddy and his colleagues have developed a system called the Archimedes model that simulates the response of a patient suffering from multiple maladies under various treatment regimens.

BusinessWeek quotes a Kaiser advisor, Dr. Paul Wallace, on applying the model to combinations of ailments: "One thing not yet adequately embraced by evidence-based medicine is what to do for someone with diabetes, hypertension, heart disease, and depression." According to the article, it took only a half hour of Archimedes time to simulate thousands of patients over a 30-year trial. As a result, Kaiser adopted a new protocol for diabetes patients with the complication of cardiovascular disease.

Archimedes is a highly complex system requiring special training to use effectively. But according to Dr. Eddy, a web-based version is under development to make the model directly available to a broad group of health care decision makers.

Unintended Consequences

In a 1996 article in *Slate*,[10] Michael Kinsley describes how well meaning policies to protect our well-being can sometimes have the opposite effect. "In recent years, the FAA has been struggling with the question of whether to require small children to fly in safety seats." Currently those over two years of age must wear a belt, but those younger can sit on their parent's lap. Kinsley continues, "Flight attendants and other supporters of safety seats make a good argument that it's a bit odd for the government to require that coffee pots, and adults, be strapped down, but not little children." He explains, however, that forcing toddlers into airplane safety belts would cost lives, not save them. Most young lap passengers do not have a ticket. Requiring them to purchase a seat would increase the price of the trip for the parents, who would then be more likely to drive, which is significantly more dangerous than flying. One study estimates that this would result in nine additional babies killed on highways per decade, while saving one baby in plane crashes over the same period.

A similar unintended consequence of expensive health care is that many people will not make use of it until they are so ill that they need to go the emergency room or, worse, have spread their illness to others. In either case, the costs to society are greatly increased.

I'm Not Dead

Near the beginning of the flim *Monty Python and the Holy Grail*, we hear the call of "Bring out your dead. Bring out your dead," as a corpse-laden cart is slowly pushed through the mud and raw sewage comprising the streets of a medieval town.

"Here's one," says a man walking up with a body slung over his shoulder.

"Ninepence," says the man pushing the cart.

"I'm not dead," says the body slung over the shoulder.

The major costs in health care usually occur near the end of life, and multiple stakeholders are always involved in the decisions. The man with the cart wants his ninepence, the man slung over the shoulder wants to stay off the cart, and the man carrying him wants to get the load off his back. After some bickering and negotiation, a coalition forms, a decision is reached, and a course of action is arrived at. (You can easily find this priceless scene by searching the web for the phrase "Monty Python bring out your dead.")

Today, end-of-life costs still dominate health care expenditures, and there are even more stakeholders in the mix. Medical specialists all promote their own procedures. Pharmaceutical and health care equipment firms hawk their expensive potions and devices. Academic researchers have their own intellectual axes to grind. Insurance companies control much of the scene. And then there are the patients, a few in vegetative states, along with their families, perhaps irrational with fear.

Yet in the past few decades, out of this chaos has sprung unprecedented basic medical knowledge, perhaps analogous to the metallurgy and chemistry that began the Industrial Revolution. But just as it was not obvious how to turn metal and chemicals into useful items for consumers, there is a continual struggle to turn medical knowledge into effective health care.

As in the Monty Python scene, the patient still has the most to gain or lose in this struggle and continues to be in the weakest negotiating position among the stakeholders. As a patient, you do not want the *average* treatment for your condition; you want the best treatment for your specific *set* of conditions, which may, in fact, be unique. When you are in this unfortunate position, a good defense is to use the tools of the Information Age to explore the options and trade-offs you face. Or, as Zelicoff and Bellomo put it, "Our philosophy is that to effect rational change, individuals must—and can—understand the basic medical facts and biology behind the common diseases that account for the vast majority of long-term suffering and the lion's share of health care costs." And I believe that this will be true regardless of whether you are ultimately cared for by a heartless, profit-motivated commercial health care provider, or an incompetent, unmotivated government bureaucracy.

CHAPTER

39

Sex and the Central Limit Theorem

Have you ever wondered why there is sex in the first place? One theory is that animals that reproduce asexually have non-diversified immune systems. Therefore they are easy pickings for parasites, such as bacteria, which do not need to evolve much themselves to stay comfortable in their hosts. On the other hand, organisms whose genes get scrambled sexually every generation present parasites with a moving target. If this theory is correct, you would expect that one factor in selecting a mate would be to maximize the diversification of your offspring's immune systems by adding genes unlike your own. In fact, incest *is* frowned upon in virtually all cultures, and scientists have shown that women prefer further genetic dissimilarities in choosing a mate. A set of genes known as the major histocompatibility complex (MHC) seems to be involved in both odor preferences and mate selection. Studies have shown that when women are asked to smell T-shirts that have been slept in for a couple of nights by men, they prefer those worn by men whose MHC genes are dissimilar to their own.[1] But even if some aspects of mate selection are in fact driven by the CENTRAL LIMIT THEORM, I still don't recommend this term in pickup lines.

Just as investors use their money to make more money, organisms invest their genes to make more genes. But as Richard Dawkins pointed out in his 1976 book, *The Selfish Gene*, males and females have evolved with very different biological risk/return profiles. For both men and women (and other vertebrates, for that matter), the genetic return for either parent is a 50 percent share in all offspring produced because they share an equal number of genes with each parent. Sounds fair so far.

Now let's examine the risk side of the equation. The woman suffers the hardship of pregnancy, which during prehistoric times could turn her into saber tooth tiger bait if she did not choose a mate who was nimble with a club. Then, of course, there is childbirth itself, which I have heard from reliable sources is no piece of cake and in our evolutionary past often resulted in death. Furthermore, if you think of each pregnancy as an investment, a woman gets a maximum of only about a dozen in her lifetime portfolio. The biological risks for men are negligible in comparison, and in theory their lifetime portfolio of caused pregnancies could be in the hundreds. With men being so diversified in their potential reproductive investments and women so undiversified, one cannot expect them to see eye to eye on all facets of the partnership.

There are other aspects of reproduction, however, in which *women* are the beneficiaries of higher diversification. My father Jimmie and my Uncle Richard were both born with congenital nystagmus, a disease that causes involuntary eye movement and very poor sight in general. Playing baseball and other sports was out of the question for them, but they could read by taking off their thick glasses and holding the material very close to their eyes. Books were their only clear window to the world. They both read prodigiously and became prominent academicians.

As is the case for hemophilia, color blindness, and adrenoleukodystrophy (which leads to total debilitation), the defective gene that causes nystagmus resides on the X chromosome. Girls receive two Xs, one from each parent, whereas boys get one X from their mother and one Y from their father, as shown in Figure 39.1.

> If a female has the defective gene on the one of her Xs, she is a carrier and can pass the disease to her male offspring. But since her other X will come to her rescue, she won't display the disease herself.

> If, however, a male has the defective gene on his only X, as in the case of my father and uncle, he displays the disease.

Figure 39.1   Inheritance of X and Y chromosomes.

Such males can pass on the defective X to their daughters, but not to their sons, so my branch of the family tree is off the hook.

The Results of Diversifying Your Portfolio of X Chromosomes

Recalling how uncertainties combine, when it comes to X chromosomes, males are playing with only one die, while females get to roll two Xs. In this context, genetic disorders can be explained as follows. The genes that carry hemophilia and other conditions are *recessive*; that is, if you have a backup gene that is *not* defective, it will override the bad one. If a man rolls a 1 on his X die, he is in trouble, but a woman gets the better of two rolls and displays the disease only if she gets snake eyes. Thus the number of cases of X-linked diseases is much higher for men than for women. And unlike six sided dice, genetic dice have more like a thousand sides. This means that the chance of roling a 1 is on the order of one in a thousand, and the chance of snake eyes is something like one in a million.

In these examples, a female displays only the trait associated with one of her two X chromosomes. But one can also imagine traits in women that are based on combinations of genes from both X chromosomes. These traits in men would still be the result of rolling a single X die, but in women it would be more like averaging the results of two X dice. Men and women would be expected to have the *same* average value of these traits (3.5 in terms of dice), but because of their diversification, women would display *lower* variation than men (fewer 1s and 6s). Several years ago I had heard that this might explain higher variation in certain male traits, but until recently I had not seen a credible reference.

Then in the draft of Howard Wainer's *Picturing an Uncertain World* I found a reference to a *New York Times* article that states, "It so happens that an unusually large number of brain-related genes are situated on the X chromosome."[2] The article goes on to say, "Several profound consequences follow from the fact that men have only one copy of the many X-related brain genes and women two." University of California–Los Angeles physiology professor Arthur Arnold is quoted as stating that "men, as a group, will have more variable brain phenotypes because women's second copy of every gene dampens the effects of mutations that arise in the other."

Then Wainer discusses relative intelligence from the perspective of educational testing. "Over the last few decades however most enlightened investigators have seen that it is not necessarily a difference in level, but a difference in variance that separates the sexes."

And, of course, being a statistician, he backs this up with statistics. It consists of numerous eighth-grade test results from the National Assessment of Educational Progress and covers various subjects over various years. In some areas, such as reading, girls have consistently higher averages in every year of data than boys, and in others, such as science, it's the other way around. Revealing my own biases, however, I was surprised to see that in math there was very little difference in average scores between the sexes. But in *every* subject for *every* year of data, the variation in boys' scores *exceeded* those of girls.

That difference in variation could not have happened by chance. However, at first glance I thought it was too small to be material. I was wrong. Let's look at the data Wainer presents for the 1994 eighth-grade U.S. history test. The mean score for both boys and girls was an identical: 259. But the STANDARD DEVIATION for boys and girls was 33 and 31, respectively. This is reflected in Figure 39.2, which shows that the distribution for girls is slightly higher in the center and that the distribution for boys is slightly higher in the tails.

Which Tail Are You Looking At?

But when you look at the extremes of the population, things are amplified. Consider the 1st and 99th percentiles of 184 and 334. Regardless of sex, only one student out of a 100 gets a score of 184 or less, and one out of 100 gets a score of 334 or greater. The tails of the graphs tell the story, as shown in Figure 39.3. Once you reach

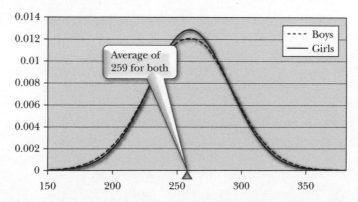

Figure 39.2   Distribution of eighth-grade U.S. history test scores.

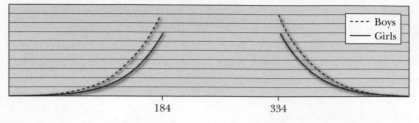

Figure 39.3   Tails of the distribution: the top 99th and bottom 1st percentiles.

these extreme tails of the distribution, the number of boys is clearly greater than the girls—almost 50 percent greater, to be exact.

The Myth of the Myth of the Math Gender Gap

This difference in test score distribution between boys and girls was also recently confirmed in a large study that ironically spawned nationwide headlines that ran afoul of the Flaw of Averages: "Girls Match Boys on Tests in Math" (Reuters, July 24, 2008), "Math Scores Show No Gap for Girls, Study Finds" (*New York Times*, July 25, 2008), and "*The Myth of the Math Gender Gap*" (*Time*, July 24, 2008). Naturally these headlines all referred to *average* scores. *The New York Times* starts out by saying that

> Three years after the president of Harvard, Lawrence H. Summers, got into trouble for questioning women's "intrinsic aptitude" for science and engineering . . . a study paid for by the National Science Foundation has found that girls perform as well as boys on standardized math tests.

No, it didn't. What Summers had argued was that there is greater variation in men than women, not that they have greater ability on average. And this was indeed confirmed by the math score study. In the Reuters article, Janet Hyde, the University of Wisconsin author of the study, says that "we did find more boys than girls above the 99th percentile at a 2-to-1 ratio," which is even greater than that found in Wainer's history scores.

How should this greater variation in test scores be interpreted? As a result of researching this chapter, I suspect that men and women have physiologically different brains and that each requires his or her own interpretation of the results. I will provide the one for men, but due to my brain structure I am not qualified to interpret the results for women. I have left that task to my wife Daryl, a professional writer who did *not* get Ds in English.

> Interpretation for men only by Sam Savage. Guys it's pretty much what you knew all along. If you define a genius as someone who is in the top 1st percentile, men in this category significantly outnumber women.

> Interpretation for women only by Daryl Savage. Hey ladies, don't listen to my husband, it's pretty much what you knew all along. If you define a moron as someone who is in the bottom 1st percentile, men in this category significantly outnumber women.

But regardless of the ultimate resolution of the statistical genetic argument, history has shown us repeatedly that people of either sex can change the world. I have no more tolerance for those who discourage girls from being mathematicians, astronauts, or presidents than I do for the high school teachers who discouraged me and my father from going to college.

On Rethinking Eugenics

In 1883, Francis Galton (1822–1911), a cousin of Charles Darwin, coined the term "eugenics" to describe the practice of attempting to improve human heredity through intervention. We do this when we breed domesticated animals, so why not humans? The problem lies in the definition of the word "improve." Eugenics was widely used in the United States in the early twentieth century, for example, as a basis for sterilizing so-called imbeciles, which according to my English teachers may well have included me. But the most famous proponents of eugenics were the Nazis, who thought they could improve the human race by killing as many Jews, gypsies, and homosexuals as possible. Meanwhile, much of the rest of the world believed that humanity would be improved by killing as many Nazis as possible, and in the end eugenics was not the panacea that Galton had envisioned.

When humans mess about in this area, they are asking for trouble. Ultrasound can determine the sex of a child before it is born, and in some parts of the world parents are practicing their own eugenics by using this technology to selectively abort daughters. This practice has resulted in significantly more male births than female and could lead to severe unintended consequences. It has been suggested that when the ratio of adolescent boys to girls reaches a critical level, it increases the propensity for war, and, given the size and proximity of the countries involved, the wars could be bloody ones. As another example of misguided eugenics, royal families have traditionally tried to keep their blood pure by intermarrying. This flagrant disregard of the smelly T-shirt imperative leads to an undiversified gene pool with higher rates of, you guessed it, X-linked genetic defects like hemophilia.

Despite the historical evidence, if you still believe that humans should be actively tinkering with their own gene pool, then let's at least base it on our current understanding of genetics. As in finance, diversification is good unless you're fond of bleeding, bad eyes, and persistent parasites. Its benefits are prominently borne out by the success of golfer Tiger Woods, actress and model Halle Berry, and President Barack Obama. Eugenics enthusiasts, I offer you a new goal: Have you considered banning marriage between people of the same race?

PROBABILITY MANAGEMENT

I will now present a new approach to risk modeling: Probability Management. It is modular in that it is built up from "Uncertainty Objects" that can be combined to model combined uncertainties. This will not be an unbiased assessment because I have spent the past decade participating, with others, in its development. But the approach is still so new that it is not yet a zero-sum game among its purveyors. Thus, some potentially competitive organizations have found it mutually beneficial to establish industry standards to advance the cause of transparency in the communication of uncertainty and risk. This is a problem that must be solved if we are to improve the stability of our economy, as we have now witnessed the consequences of applying Steam Era statistics to Information Age risks.

So how revolutionary is Probability Management? History will tell. It is not based on fantastic breakthroughs like X-rays or atomic energy, although it has pushed the limits of current technology. The typical manager has never seen anything like it before, yet it does not have a steep learning curve. Most importantly, it evolved quickly and organically in the heat of strategic decision-making in large organizations. So from a technological and intellectual perspective, I would characterize Probability

Management today as being on the cutting edge of the mundane. That is why it can be so easily adopted. My hope is that tomorrow, it will become a useful standard for helping us manage risk better than we have in the recent past. That is, it will have become just *plain* mundane.

TOWARD A CURE FOR
THE FLAW OF AVERAGES

The story that I have to tell is marked all the way through by a persistent tension between those who assert that the best decisions are based on quantification and numbers, determined by the patterns of the past, and those who base their decisions on more subjective degrees of belief about the uncertain future. This is a controversy that has never been resolved.
—Peter L. Bernstein, *Against the Gods: the Remarkable Story of Risk*

The point of view based on "patterns of the past" is classical statistics, somewhat analogous to classical music. It is historical and based on rigid and elaborate rules. Although mathematically aesthetic (I cannot imagine life without Bach), it cannot be expected to keep up with the quickly changing rhythms of our uncertain world. Classical statistics shines at determining the average lengths of swan beaks to three decimal places given thousands of white swans. But it will never predict a black one from purely white data.

The form of reasoning based on "subjective degrees of belief about the uncertain future" is like improvised jazz, in which the musicians commit to their own notes in advance of knowing with certainty what the others are going to play. If there were a field of statistics to deal with black swans, it would be this improvisational form.

The instruments played by the improvisational statistician are based on interactive visualization. Those wishing to join in will not wait for classical training in these instruments but will start playing with them right out of the box. Furthermore, they must be adept at the performing arts, or no one will listen.

But let's not forget that many jazz musicians have had classical training and also that if Bach were brought back to life and deposited in New Orleans, he would probably improvise circles around anyone alive today.

In this analogy, Probability Management should be eclectic and support good music of any kind.

CHAPTER

The End of Statistics
as You Were Taught It

F rancis Galton, introduced in the last chapter as the father of
eugenics, should not be blamed for the horrors committed in its
name any more than Einstein was responsible for the bombing of
Hiroshima. Galton was also central in the development of the field
of statistics. He recently received some well deserved good press
in the opening scene of James Surowiecki's *Wisdom of Crowds*, in
which he appears at an English county fair in 1906 and marvels that
the average guess in a contest to estimate the weight of an ox was
extremely close to the true value.[1] "The result seems more creditable to the trustworthiness of a democratic judgment than might
have been expected," he wrote upon observing this early prediction
market.

Stephen Stigler, a prominent University of Chicago statistician
and son of the economist George Stigler, has written extensively
on the history of statistics,[2] including early attempts by Galton
and others to generate random numbers through mechanical
means. Stigler's paper on "Stochastic Simulation in the Nineteenth
Century"[3] shows that even as these pioneers were at work on the
foundations of classical (Steam Era) statistics, they were testing
their theories with simulation methods.

Galton's Dice

My favorite part of Stigler's paper quotes directly from a Galton
paper of 1890, in which he discusses his latest random number
generator based on dice:

> Every statistician wants now and then to test the practical
> value of some theoretical process . . . [4]

then displaying his keen marketing instincts,

> The assurance for a real demand for such things induced
> me to work out a method for supplying it . . .

and the sell,

> which I have already used frequently, and finding it to be
> perfectly effective, take this opportunity of putting it on
> the record.

Next he covers the technical superiority of his invention:

> As an instrument of selecting at random, I have found
> nothing superior to dice. It is most tedious to shuffle
> cards thoroughly between each successive draw, and the
> method of mixing and stirring up marked balls in a bag is
> more tedious still.

Right you are, and speaking of tedious, Francis, you would be
shocked to learn that governments today are reaping billions of dollars
of regressive tax revenue through lotteries based precisely on the mix-
ing and stirring up of marked balls. When he goes on to describe the
randomizing action of dice, Galton can barely contain his enthusiasm.

> When they are shaken and tossed in a basket, they hurtle
> so variously against one another and against the ribs of
> the basket-work that they tumble wildly about, and their
> positions at the outset afford no perceptible clue to what
> they will be after even a single good shake or toss.

And his were no ordinary dice with 6 numbers per die. Instead
they had 24 markings, one on each of the four edges of each face and
were designed to generate numbers from a **NORMAL DISTRIBUTION**.

The Bad Boys of Statistics

The statisticians of Galton's era developed powerful theories around their experiments with dice, cards, and marked balls.
Computational Statistics bypasses the theory altogether and simply

simulates more dice, cards, and marked balls on the computer than Galton could have dreamt of.

Recall that Rick Medress and I resampled the box office receipts of a set of movies to investigate the effects of a diversified portfolio. In effect, this was a computerized version of writing the revenues of the films on balls, stirring them up in a bag, and then repeatedly sampling them with replacement.

Brad Efron (1938-)

Brad Efron, one of the founding fathers of Computational Statistics, has never been an average statistician. As a PhD student at Stanford in the early 1960s, he was editor of Stanford's satire publication, *Chaparral,* where his spoof of *Playboy* magazine got him suspended for four months.[5]

In 1979 Efron showed that the brute force computational approach of simulating balls and dice could be integrated into a technique that was actually more robust than the classical theoretical approach to statistics. He called his method the "bootstrap."[6] The name comes from the fact that in classical statistics you assume some particular theoretical form of distribution, say NORMAL, then estimate its parameters: the average and SIGMA. In the new approach you pull yourself up by your bootstraps, by resampling from the raw data. This method has greatly influenced the field of statistics, and in 2007 Efron was awarded the National Medal of Science.

Efron is one of those rare individuals who straddle a technological divide. He was good at classical statistics, yet he inspired a revolution that supplanted it. Here are his views on modern statistics. "From a pre-World War II standpoint our current computational abilities are effectively infinite, at least in terms of answering many common questions that arise in statistical practice. And no, this has not spelled the end of statistical theory—though it certainly has changed (for the better, in my opinion) what constitutes a good question and a good answer."[7]

Julian Simon (1932-1998)

Julian Simon was a controversial professor of business administration at the University of Maryland. He is perhaps best-known for a famous wager with Paul Ehrlich, Stanford author of the *Population Bomb.* Simon was a Boomster, who believed that technology would grow fast enough to counter the adverse effects of the rapidly expanding population. Ehrlich was a Doomster, who believed the earth was running out of resources and that the prices of scarce materials would be driven up accordingly.

In their 1980 wager, Ehrlich picked a bundle of commodities at the then current prices with the understanding that if the total price of the bundle went up by 1990, Simon would pay him the difference, but if they went down, he would pay Simon the difference. Simon won.

Although he wrote numerous books, mostly on economics, Simon became fascinated with statistical resampling and in the late 1960s began experimenting with it as a way to teach statistics.[8] In the 1980s he developed the Resampling Stats software package with Peter Bruce, and in 1993 wrote *Resampling: The New Statistics*.[9] He was also prescient enough to grab www.Statistics.com, which is still marketing professional development in the area of statistics.

Fibonacci (1170–1250): The Bad Boy of Numbers

Fibonacci, the great Italian mathematician, lived centuries before any serious thought was given to modeling uncertainty. Rare among mathematicians, he was apparently good at public relations as well. He had learned Arabic numerals as a child in Algeria while his father was there on business. When he returned to Italy, he had a competitive advantage in working out business deals because he could calculate circles around people who were using Roman numerals. His famous Fibonacci series can be viewed as sort of a PR splash with which he was challenging people: "Try this with Is, Vs, Xs, Cs, and Ms, you numerical Luddites!" Can you imagine the public relations challenges involved in replacing a culture's number system? Fibonacci did it, and prospered greatly through his efforts to make arithmetic more transparent. He consulted extensively with people who needed to use numbers in commerce, which turned out to be a pretty big market.

. . . And of Probability Management

Those of us who work in the area of Probability Management are constantly grappling with a description of our field. I have presented several so far in this book, and here is another from a different perspective.

Galton and others of his generation modeled uncertainty with balls and dice to calibrate their powerful steam era theories of probability and statistics. Simon realized that a computerized version of this approach provided an intuitive way to model and manage uncertainty in the real world, bypassing the theory altogether. Efron used similar principles to establish a whole *new* body of theory that revolutionized the field of statistics. Recent advances in both computation and data storage have carried these ideas to the point that probability distributions, in the form of DISTs, may now be manipulated like everyday numbers instead of their cumbersome predecessors. In this light, the goal of Probability Management is to do for probability distributions what Arabic numbers did for Roman numerals. Galton, Simon, Efron, and Fibonacci are its patron saints.

CHAPTER 41

Visualization

Two very young kittens are harnessed in a vertical drum with patterns painted on the inside. One kitten is able to walk on the floor of the drum, and the other is suspended just above it. Both kittens are presented with the same visual environment, but only the one on the floor can *interact* with it; that is, the drum rotates when it walks. By the end of the experiment, the suspended kitten requires a seeing eye dog. It has not learned how to process visual information and is effectively blind.

This experiment is described in *Action in Perception* by the philosopher Alva Noë, who argues that without action on the part of the observer, there can be no perception.[1] The retina is not just a digital camera that sends multi megapixel snapshots off to the brain for interpretation. According to Jeff Hawkins and Sandra Blakeslee, in *On Intelligence*, the eye explores a scene by moving its gaze around, much in the way your hand would explore the top of your desk in a darkened room by groping around and bumping into things.[2]

Visual Statistics

So how should one explore statistical data? That's easy, because there was an undisputed master of the subject. In 1977 John W. Tukey (1915–2000) published *Exploratory Data Analysis*, a book on interpreting statistical data.[3] Tukey was the author of many enduring Mindles, including the Box Plot, Stem and Leaf diagram, and even the words "bit" and "software."

Today, powerful visualization software continues in the Tukey tradition. When Daniel Zweidler generated a new scenario library at Shell, for example, the first thing he did was to run it into a visualization program so that the right side of his brain could detect patterns that would be invisible in the underlying numbers.

One such program is JMP, from the analytical software company SAS.[4] I recently applied it to the scenario library of the Shell demo model posted at ProbabilityManagement.org. The library contains simulation trials of a number of interrelated uncertainties, including various economic factors and the resulting profits of the exploration projects. JMP is able to display a picture of these interrelationships (Figure 41.1) that is worth a thousand words. Think of this as a scatter plot of scatter plots. I generated it from the data in the Excel file with just a few keystrokes. The uncertainties scattered on the x axis represent global economic factors, such as world oil price and various regional gas prices. Those on the y axis are the economic outputs of the hypothetical ventures under consideration for the portfolio.

Can you spot the real option? It is Venture 1, in which the underlying asset is World Oil Price (upper left square). For each point in this scatter plot, the x value is an oil price, and the y value is the economic output of Venture 1. This prospect is mathematically equivalent to the gas property with the option not to pump. That is, it is a call option on a known quantity of oil, where the fixed production cost serves as the strike price. Now observe the relationship between Venture 5 and Region 1 Gas Price. The two straight lines in this graph reflect the fact that Venture 5 was modeled as a tree in the decision forest with two branches corresponding to a high volume or low volume of gas. Whichever volume occurs, it gets multiplied by the Region 1 Gas Price, one of the winds of fortune. If a high volume occurs, the point will be on the upper line. If the low volume occurs, it will be on the lower line. The plot between Venture 7 and Region 6 Gas Price is a blob indicating no relationship, which is important information in its own right. Such graphs are of great benefit both in verifying that a scenario library has been correctly generated and in analyzing the output of a simulation based on such a library.

In Steam Era statistics you win arguments using Red procedures with names like F-TEST and T-TEST. Joe Berkson, a statistician at the Mayo Clinic, developed his own criterion, which he termed the IOT Test, or Inter Ocular Trauma Test, requiring a graph that hit you between the eyes.

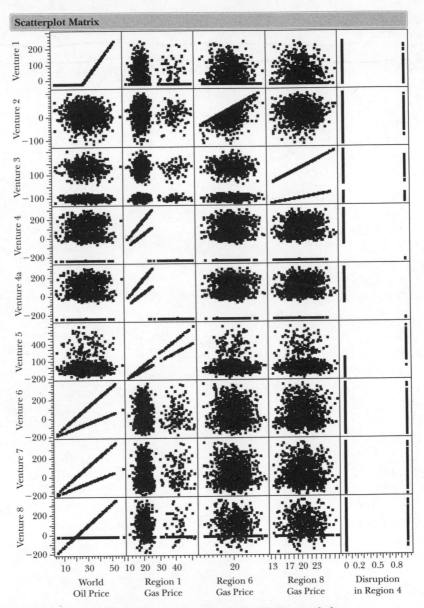

Figure 41.1 JMP scatter plot matrix of Shell demo data.

I recommend two resources in this area. First, *The Visual Display of Quantitative Data* by Edward Tufte is a classic in informational design that should be on everyone's bookshelf, if not coffee table.[5] Second, *How to Lie with Statistics* by Darrell Huff is a classic on *dis*informational design, first published in the 1950s, which is no doubt treasured by politicians and government bureaucrats worldwide.[6]

Toward a Theory of Irrational Expectation

So how do humans really perceive risk and uncertainty? In Tom Robbins' novel, *Even Cowgirls Get the Blues*, the human brain is referred to as that organ of the body possessing a high opinion of itself.[7] So how like a brain it is, then, to invent the theory of rational expectation. And upon realizing, to its chagrin, that humans aren't exactly rational, the brain went on to develop behavioral finance to study how people really make decisions. The real problem here is that you can't trust a brain to tell you how a brain works.

To see what the brain is doing, you need an MRI machine, which is the basis of the new field of neuroeconomics. A recent article in *The New Yorker* by John Cassidy describes how actual brain activity is tracked during economic decision making.[8] A spot of particular interest is the amygdala, the fight-or-flight center. Researchers can directly detect a subject's perception of risk by monitoring this fear-mongering, almond-shaped region at the base of the brain, which is intimately connected to the seat of the pants.

In the end this new area of research will undoubtedly increase our understanding of the irrational ways in which people perceive uncertainty and risk, and how they make decisions in the face of it.

CHAPTER

42

Interactive Simulation: A New Lightbulb

I hope the last chapter got your eyes engaged. But you will still end up as blind as the suspended kitten if you can't interact with your visual environment. In the mid-1990s I began to experiment with what I call interactive simulation, in which, from the perspective of the user, thousands of Monte Carlo trials occur instantaneously when some input to the model is changed.

I coined the term "blitzogram" to refer to an interactive histogram. This is described with animations and downloadable Excel models in an online article at the Informs Transactions on Education.[1] You may link to it at FlawOfAverages.com.

Today, the continued improvement in computers and recent software developments have brought interactive simulation tools to the marketplace. Tied to computer graphics, these applications are providing Mindles that would have tickled Tukey.

The Return of a Pioneer

In the winter of 2005, in a picturesque mountain village on the shore of a serene lake, a world-class entrepreneur and software engineer tirelessly leads his small team of mathematicians and programmers toward achieving a daunting goal. The village is Incline, the lake is Tahoe, the entrepreneur is Dan Fylstra. The team is international, including Americans, Dutch, and Bulgarians, and the goal is to do for probability distributions what the spreadsheet did for numbers.

If you don't recognize the name, you could be forgiven for considering such an aspiration to be delusional. But Fylstra was a key player in the development of the *first* spreadsheet. He is one of a handful of pioneers, including Bill Gates of Microsoft and Steve Jobs of Apple, who helped launch the personal computer revolution in the late 1970s. He was a founding editor of *Byte Magazine* in 1975 and had his own personal computer software firm, marketing a chess program, almost before there *were* personal computers.

Then in 1978 Fylstra met Dan Bricklin, who had an idea for a program that would function like a Texas Instruments calculator, but for a screen full of numbers at once. The collaboration between fellow MIT grads Fylstra, Bricklin and Bob Frankston led to VisiCalc, the first electronic spreadsheet for personal computers, published by Fylstra's young software company. In 1979 VisiCalc, running on Steve Jobs's Apple II computer, initiated the spreadsheet revolution. "We were children of the sixties," says Fylstra, "we wanted to change the world, and in fact we did. What made VisiCalc irresistible is that it performed instantaneous interactive calculations on the numbers in business plans."

In spite of a head start, the introduction of the IBM PC offered an opportunity in 1982 for Lotus 1-2-3 to leapfrog VisiCalc. Lotus remained the dominant spreadsheet for over a decade, whereupon it too was leapfrogged by Microsoft Excel in the Macintosh and Windows environments.

In 1987 Fylstra founded his current company, Frontline Systems. In 1990 Frontline provided the Solver for Microsoft Excel that brought mathematical optimization capability to millions of computers. For customers requiring added horsepower, Frontline provides an array of more powerful optimization engines.

Although trained in computer science rather than mathematics, "Dan's knowledge of the literature of mathematical optimization is on a par with most academicians," according to the late Professor Richard Rosenthal, former chairman of the renowned Operations Research Department of the Naval Postgraduate School. "On top of this," Rick goes on, "he has implemented much of what he learns into robust, user-friendly software."

Polymorphic

According to *Merriam-Webster's Collegiate Dictionary, 11th Edition, polymorphic* means: "the quality or state of existing in or assuming different forms." By 1998, Dan had learned a great deal about Excel. He'd learned so much, in fact, that he told me about a plan to enhance Excel's calculation engine by, in his words, "assigning new and more powerful 'meanings' to all the operators and functions in spreadsheet formulas." He was going to make Excel polymorphic!

I had long respected Dan's technical skills and marketing ability, but this time I had my doubts. It looked like a massive undertaking that might be appreciated by only a few propeller heads.

Fast forward six years. I had worked out some of the basic elements of what has now become Probability Management and had even prototyped a primitive interactive simulation add-in for Excel without having any idea how to implement it in a general way. It was then that I remembered Dan's claim that he was going to make Excel polymorphic. The particular morph I had in mind was to replace each numeric cell with a thousand or more values going back into the computer screen in a third dimension, with each value representing a single trial of a simulation.

In December of 2004 I gave Dan a call. Thankfully, my pessimistic assessment of his approach had been wrong. What he now calls the Polymorphic Spreadsheet Interpreter (PSI) technology had already proven itself, speeding up Frontline's optimization software. I scheduled a visit to Incline to show him my interactive simulation prototype. I didn't know what his reaction would be, but in case he wasn't interested, I just planned to go skiing. Dan *was* interested, however, and we went skiing together. Between runs we discussed the possibilities.

Tip of the Iceberg

Within a few months, Dan had proven the feasibility of interactive simulation in Excel, and the results were astonishing. On my laptop computer, which was not even state-of-the-art, the software could simulate 100,000 trials of a spinner and draw a histogram before my finger had left the <Enter> key. The final product, called Risk Solver, is now in use in industries as diverse as energy, finance, and pharmaceuticals. At Shell, it sped up our interactive simulation model and allowed us to reduce the number of formulas by a factor of roughly 1,000.

To demonstrate the broad implications of this technology, I have created some Excel demonstration models at FlawOfAverages.com.

In case you haven't noticed, in the long run computers aren't getting any slower, and interactive simulation is bound to grow. Beyond the spreadsheet, JMP, the visualization software from SAS, also provides this capability. And Vensim from Ventana Systems does interactive dynamic simulation of the type popularized by MIT's John Sterman with the beer game.[2] "When you activate it, all parameters and nonlinear relationships become sliders that you can move," says Sterman, "and as you do, the model is re-simulated," he continues. "It really makes it easy to explore the parameter space of a model, tune to data, and test policies."

Fylstra sums it up this way. "What we are doing with Interactive Simulation is a close parallel to what we did with VisiCalc, but this time the calculations are on the *uncertainties* in business plans," he says, "and I expect this to be just as revolutionary."

It is easy to picture interactive simulation as a new lightbulb for illuminating uncertainty, with Dan as a latter-day Edison. While keeping his current software business up and running, he worked around the clock on this project, involved in every detail from programming to documentation. Perhaps the adjective "polymorphic" applies best to Fylstra himself.

Scenario Libraries: The Power Grid

In the mid-1950s, in the spirit of Francis Galton's dice, the Rand Corporation published a book containing 1 million random digits for use in simulating uncertainty.[1] I understand it was a great hit among insomniacs. Ironically, this simple idea is very close to the scenario libraries in use at Shell, Merck, and Olin today to maintain enterprisewide databases of uncertainties. Such libraries form the power grid of Probability Management.

Modular Risk Models and Age of the Scatter Plot

When Fred retrieves the number 2 from an information system and Joe retrieves the number 3, their results are *modular* (as in modular furniture) in that they can be consolidated. Just add them together, as in 2 + 3 = 5. But if Fred retrieves the distribution of petroleum prices and Joe retrieves the distribution of an airline stock, how do we consolidate these into a portfolio? Recall from the ladder analogy of Chapter 3 that the simulation of the sum is *not* the sum of the simulations.

In general, probability distributions don't add up like numbers for two reasons. First, there is the diversification effect described in terms of the movie portfolios; that is, the sum of two dice or spinners goes up in the middle. Second, there are the interrelationships to worry about, as discussed in terms of the investment examples. When petroleum prices go up, airline stocks tend to go down.

When Markowitz added the distributions of a set of stocks to get the distribution of the resulting portfolio in the 1950s, it was limited to the special case in which:

1. The distributions were bell-shaped, and
2. The interrelationships measured by the **COVARIANCE** were limited to scatter plots shaped like ovals.

This method could not handle the sorts of interrelationships displayed in the Shell demo model (Figure 41.1). And although the scatter plots of stock prices may look like footballs over the short term, over the long haul, they are anything but. My student, Jake Johnson, created a JMP scatter plot of various Nasdaq indices running from 1996 to 2009, as shown in Figure 43.1. **COVARIANCE**

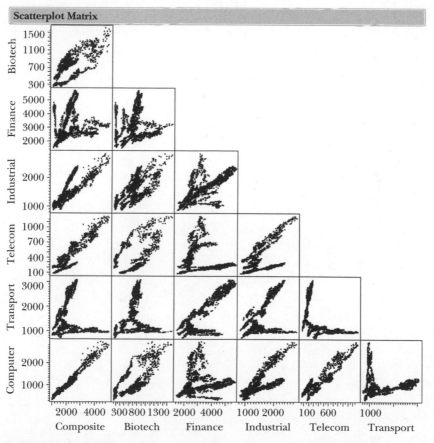

Figure 43.1   Scatter plot of Nasdaq indices from May 1996 to January 2009.

cannot adequately express these interrelationships, except for Computers versus the Composite in the lower left.

Not only can scenario libraries represent the nonfootball-shaped interrelationships of Figures 41.1 and 43.1, but they are modular; that is, the distribution of the sum of any two uncertainties in the library is just the sum of the distribution. Through the brute force of computers, the Age of COVARIANCE has evolved into the Age of the Scatter Plot. Does this mean that Markowitz and Sharpe were wrong? That would be like saying that the jet engine invalidated the Wright Brothers. In fact, Markowitz and Sharpe are two of the most simulation-centric people on the planet. But many of the VaR models that flew us into the ground in 2008 are still based on COVARIANCE. I will demonstrate the concept of scenario libraries with a simple example.

The Subprime Mortgage Fiasco

Long before 2008, people were discussing not *if* the housing bubble would burst, but *when*. Yet some major banks were still investing in mortgage-backed securities with one hand, while making housing loans with the other. As a banker described it to me: "If the housing market tanked, the investment side of the business would clearly take a hit. But this same event would also increase the default rate on the loan side of the business. So taken as a portfolio, the risks were huge." When the inevitable happened, one bank blamed its losses on "two factors": write-downs in the real estate investment market and credit problems in their loan portfolio.

The point is that there weren't *two* factors; there was just *one* factor: the housing market! This was the plank that held the fixed income and credit sides of the business together, so that if either ladder fell over, the other was very likely to go with it.

To get the gritty details of this sort of financial havoc, I suggest *Structured Finance and Collateralized Debt Obligations* by Janet Tavakoli.[2] According to Tavakoli, "If you put too much at stake in a model's ability to predict future prepayment rates, or anything else for that matter, you are asking for trouble." Worse than that, people were using models to help *sell* unsafe investments. *Buyers* need their own models, and should never rely on the sellers' models.

Most large financial organizations spend millions of dollars on complex risk models, like huge Lego block jetliners that may actually mask what's going on. As Stefan Scholtes told us in Chapter 4, what they need are simple models that everyone understands.

A Paper Airplane Model

In Figure 43.2, I have outlined a paper airplane model of a bank with exposure to both direct real estate investments and home loans to demonstrate the scenario library approach. Banks are already quite good at modeling the response of individual business units to underlying market conditions. Figure 43.2 contains a highly simplified representation of the response of two banking divisions to the value of the housing market, which I have modeled as the roll of a die. Too simplistic to be of use, you say? Well, at least it allows the housing market to get better or worse, which is more than some models I have heard of. Note that, although the divisions do not react identically to market conditions, they do move in the same direction, which imposes a hidden risk.

Suppose the CEO asks each division to do its own risk analysis. Using the table in Figure 43.2, it is easy to calculate that Division 1 has two chances in six of losing money, whereas Division 2 has only one chance in six of losing money. If you ignore the interrelationships, you would calculate the chance that both divisions lose money at the same time as $2/6 \times 1/6 = 2/36 = 1/18$. But this grossly underestimates the risk, as we shall see. Here is how Probability Management would have properly consolidated the two risk models.

Housing Market, 1 = Worst, 6 = Best	Division 1, Real Estate Investment Profit	Division 2, Home Loan Profit
1	−$2 million	−$3 million
2	−$1 million	0
3	0	0
4	$1 million	$2 million
5	$2 million	$2 million
6	$3 million	$2 million
Average	$500,000	$500,000

Figure 43.2   Profit by division for each housing market condition.

First, the chief probability officer (CPO) generates the distribution of housing market conditions. This is provided as a _stochastic information packet_ (**STOCHASTIC** is a Red Word meaning uncertain). In honor of John Tukey, who coined the term "bit," I call this a _"SIP."_ The SIP takes the form of, say, 1,000 possible future scenarios of housing market values, generated by Monte Carlo simulation, as shown in Figure 43.3. So far, this is no different from Rand Corporation's soporific book of numbers.

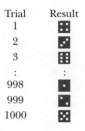

Figure 43.3   The housing SIP.

If you think of the elements of CPO's SIP as machine gun bullets, then the second step is to deliver two identical belts of ammunition to the two divisions, who fire them through their own models to produce SIPs of their profits, as shown in Figure 43.4.

Note that the first element in each output SIP corresponds to rolling a four in the housing market, the second one a three in the market, and so on. In this example, we have determined the output SIP for each division by running the input SIP through the appropriate column of the table in Figure 43.2, but in general each division's model could be created in a spreadsheet or more sophisticated modeling environment.

So, to review, one input SIP went in, and two output SIPs came out. But these aren't just two SIPs anymore. They now form a _scenario library unit with relationships preserved_ (or a _SLURP_), which maintains the dependence of each division on the housing market. The final step is just to add the output SIPs of the two divisions together to create the SIP of total profit, as shown in Figure 43.5.

With SLURPs, the simulation of the sum _does_ equal the sum of the simulations because it preserves the interrelationships. In other words, for each element of the output SIP of total profit, each division faced the same market scenario: four, three, six, etc. If a traditional Monte Carlo simulation had been run on each division, one

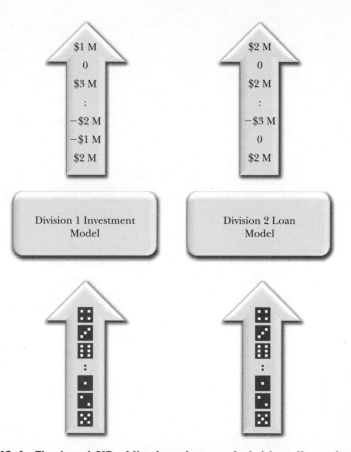

Figure 43.4   The input SIP of the housing market drives the output SIPs of both divisions.

might have rolled a two while the other had rolled a four on the same trial. This is the critical step that makes stochastic libraries modular. The way to accomplish this with traditional Monte Carlo simulation is to build everything into one humongous model. With modularity you can build small risk models independently and hook them together later.

In this example, we consolidated the distributions across two divisions and then rolled the sum up to headquarters—and guess what. As you can see in Figure 43.5, the chance of losing money is not 1 in 18 after all, but 1 in 3, six times greater!

Through such scenario libraries, Shell is able to assemble the simulation of its exploration portfolio from the simulations of its

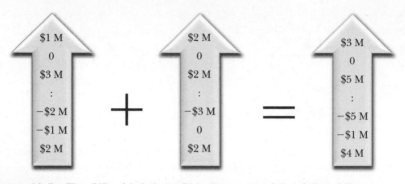

Figure 43.5   The SIP of total profit is the *sum* of the SIPs of the divisions.

individual projects. With real-world problems, it is not as easy as rolling dice, and there is no guarantee that a credible scenario library can be generated at all. But today there are hundreds of industries where simulation packages such as @Risk, Crystal Ball, XLSim, and Risk Solver are already in regular use by thousands of skilled analysts. Currently the scenarios they generate are used to calculate some numbers and graphs, then vanish from their computer's memories. With a bit of coordination by a good CPO, some of them could be stored in libraries and put to good use in creating enterprisewide models of uncertainty and risk.

History

One of the most severe limitations of spreadsheets is that they are fundamentally two-dimensional. So, say you are selling multiple products and decide to allocate one row for each one. That's one dimension. Now you wish to keep track of various accounting items for each product, such as revenue, cost, and profit, which you put into columns. That's your second dimension. Hmm. . . . You also have branches in multiple locations (that's three dimensions), and now you are scrambling to create multiple worksheets, one for each branch. Now suppose that you want to keep track of the figures by month. Is it too much to ask that your firm plans to stay in business for more than one time period? Yes, it is. You now have a four-dimensional model and will have a devil of a time shoehorning it all into a spreadsheet.

   To address this issue, in 1993, Lotus Development Corp. released a Windows version of a program called Improv, which was in effect a 12-dimensional spreadsheet. I was immediately smitten. One of the great thrills of flying a plane is to move freely in three dimensions above the earth as opposed to the two dimensions of its surface. Now I had 12 dimensions, and I couldn't imagine going back. In 1994 I led a team in developing analytical tools for Improv, as I had for Lotus 1-2-3 a decade earlier. I had recently been exposed to Mark Broadie's scenario optimization spreadsheet model, as described in Chapter 28. And as I began to tinker with Monte Carlo simulation in the Improv environment, it dawned on me that I could add a new dimension called "Scenarios" to an Improv file, say with 100 sheets, whereupon the original model would be cloned 100 times, once for each of a 100 different sets of assumptions. So, instead of sequentially shaking your ladder 100 times, you would shake each of 100 identical ladders one time. The beauty was that Improv did this automatically.

Our first Improv-based product was optimization, and we had mailed out 250 demo disks when the news came that Lotus had taken Improv out behind the barn and shot it unceremoniously in the head. Apparently it was so good that it was now competing with Lotus 1-2-3, which by that time was doomed anyway due to the dominance of Microsoft Excel. In any event, these ideas ultimately led to my design of scenario libraries, but I was by no means the first or only person to think along these lines. Two others are discussed shortly, and there must be many more as well. I hope my readers will let me know of other examples, which I will post at FlawOfAverages.com for a more complete history.

When Max Henrion studied physics as an undergraduate at Cambridge University, he reports, "My professors drummed into me that any number is worthless unless you report the uncertainty attached to it." Then as a PhD student in policy analysis at Carnegie Mellon in the 1970s, he noticed that "analysts in public policy and business usually ignored that principle—even though their numbers were generally many orders of magnitude more uncertain than the physicists'." So he started to develop a software tool to explicitly use probability distributions in 1978, a year before the launch of the first spreadsheet, Visicalc. He became a professor at Carnegie, but now infected with the software developer's virus, Max eventually moved to Silicon Valley and started up Lumina Decision Systems. The company launched the first commercial version of the software, now called Analytica,[3] in 1994. From its inception, Analytica has been based on what Max calls the "intelligent array" representation of uncertainty; that is, <u>uncertainty is just another dimension</u>, as I later envisioned it in Improv. Each uncertain variable is essentially a SIP, and an array of such variables is a SLURP. So without using the terminology, Analytica has been providing what I would call a full Probability Management solution from the beginning.

At roughly the same time that I discovered Improv, Kevin Hankins, currently a civilian analyst at U.S. Marine Corps Headquarters in Quantico Virginia, was tunneling out from the restrictions of the spreadsheet on his own. He was doing quality control statistics on engine computer circuits for Delco Electronics, and he needed to analyze vast quantities of multidimensional test data. This was in effect a scenario library of results on numerous types of circuits under many operating conditions, and just storing it in Excel, let alone analyzing it statistically, was impossible. So Kevin wrote an add-in for Excel that compressed the library into a form that he could access in true multidimensions and then analyze with graphical statistics to determine how likely a new application was to fail in the field. This work is in the public domain and available at the Automotive Electronics Council's web site.[4]

In a sense, scenario libraries of numerical results were perhaps inevitable as computers became faster and disk storage cheaper. Now is the time to start using them on a broad scale to cure the Flaw of Averages.

Things to remember:

- Scenario Libraries form the power grid of Probability Management.
- SIPs and SLURPs allow probability distributions to be consolidated in a wide variety of applications even if their scatter plots don't look like footballs.

Things to forget:

- COVARIANCE.
- CORRELATION—Use "Scatter Plot" instead of either of these. I know I already asked you to forget this stuff in Chapter 13, but I was afraid you might have remembered it again by now.

CHAPTER

The Fundamental Identity of SLURP Algebra

What's genuinely new about Probability Management is that SIPs and SLURPs allow probability distributions to be operated on *just like numbers* in a wide variety of applications. I call this property the FUNDAMENTAL IDENTITY OF SLURP ALGEBRA.

RED WORDS
AHEAD

A Note from Your Author

Unless you like Red Words, I suggest that you jump to the next chapter, which describes how to actually apply this stuff. In deference to those who remain, I will forgo the aggravating Dracula font for the rest of this chapter.

As we have seen, the algebra of probability distributions is very different from that of numbers. But by keeping track of thousands of simulation trials at once, SLURP notation makes distributions much easier to think about. For example Jensen's inequality, the central limit theorem, and interrelated uncertainties all work their way out in the wash once the CPO has set up a valid scenario library.

For this to work, all the distributions involved must pay homage to the central limit theorem, that is, the results must converge. But if they don't, simulation doesn't work in the first place.

$$P(X, Y)$$

$$
\begin{array}{ll}
X \text{ Trial 1} & Y \text{ Trial 1} \\
X \text{ Trial 2} & Y \text{ Trial 2} \\
X \text{ Trial 3} & Y \text{ Trial 3} \\
\quad \vdots & \quad \vdots \\
X \text{ Trial N} & Y \text{ Trial N}
\end{array}
$$

Figure 44.1   *P(X, Y)* **the SLURP of the joint distribution of** *X* **and** *Y* **is a matrix.**

Let X and Y be random variables with joint distribution represented by the SLURP $P(X, Y)$, consisting of N realizations of X, Y pairs. $P(X, Y)$ is a matrix, with one column for each variable and a row for each trial, as shown in Figure 44.1. This is very different from conventional definitions of probability distributions, but it is valid when used in simulations.

The Identity

Let F be a function of X and Y. Then
$$P(F(X, Y)) = F(P(X, Y))$$
Where $P(F(X, Y))$ is the SIP of $F(X, Y)$

In the normal notation of Probability Theory, this expression would be nonsense. But in SLURP notation, it is just fine.

$P(F(X, Y))$ is a vector, as shown in figure 44.2, found by applying F to each row of $P(X, Y)$.

$$P(F(X, Y)) \qquad\qquad F(P(X, Y))$$

$$
\begin{array}{l}
F(X, Y) \text{ Trial 1} \\
F(X, Y) \text{ Trial 2} \\
F(X, Y) \text{ Trial 3} \\
\quad \vdots \\
F(X, Y) \text{ Trial N}
\end{array}
\quad = \quad
\begin{array}{l}
F(X \text{ Trial 1}, Y \text{ Trial 1}) \\
F(X \text{ Trial 2}, Y \text{ Trial 2}) \\
F(X \text{ Trial 3}, Y \text{ Trial 3}) \\
\quad \vdots \qquad \vdots \\
F(X \text{ Trial N}, Y \text{ Trial N})
\end{array}
$$

Figure 44.2   The distribution of *F(X, Y)*, **denoted by** *P(F(X, Y))* **is a vector of** *N* **trials.**

One more thing: To model interrelated time series, a third dimension is added to $P(F(X, Y))$ to represent time periods. In this case, the SLURP would be a three-dimensional array containing realizations of sample paths through time.

CHAPTER

Putting It into Practice

The technology surrounding Probability Management is improving fast, and recent breakthroughs promise to make it more accessible than ever. For perspective, I will review the evolution to date. The first-generation models, like the Bessemer and Shell demos at ProbabilityManagement.org, displayed the two revolutionary hallmarks of this approach. First, they were based on scenario libraries; so they were modular, meaning their results could be consolidated, or added together. Second, they were interactive, connecting the seat of users' intellects to the seat of their pants.

What was *frustrating*, on the other hand, was that the models, as implemented in practice, required literally 20,000 to 40,000 spreadsheet formulas. This was because they were actually comprised of a thousand identical models, one for each of 1,000 potential scenarios stored in the SLURP. Then in 2007, with the introduction of Frontline Systems' Risk Solver, we were able to greatly reduce the number of formulas in our clients' models. Instead of requiring one submodel per row of the SLURP, we needed just a single model, through which the Risk Solver fired all 1,000 scenarios like bullets through an Uzi. When people say that size doesn't matter, they are not talking about factors of 1,000. A spreadsheet with 40 formulas is easy to build and maintain, whereas one with 40,000 formulas, even if highly repetitive, is a nightmare. In addition, the new technology made the models even faster than before.

Although the Risk Solver represented a great improvement in the area of model development and speed, there was still a big problem, a really big problem: The SLURPs themselves were huge. For example, in one application we were modeling roughly

100 projects, each with ten metrics (revenue, cost, etc.), and 50 time periods. Multiply that by the 1,000 trials, and you have 50 million numbers to manage and drag around.

The DIST Distribution String

In late 2007 I arrived at a solution: the Distribution Strings (DIST), which encapsulates the 1,000 or even 10,000 numbers in a SIP into a single data element. Consider the SIP of the hypothetical housing market. It contained 1,000 rolls of a die, each one of which would require a separate cell in a spreadsheet or element in a database for storage. Now imagine encoding the numbers on a die into characters of the alphabet, for example 1 = A, 2 = B, and so on up to 6 = F. Then the 1,000 data elements required to store the original SIP can be packed into a single data element: a character string with 1,000 characters. Figure 45.1 displays the first three and last three elements of the housing market SIP and its equivalent DIST.

For every 1,000 separate data elements we had been storing in the Shell application, we now store a single string of 1,000 characters. Instead of requiring a structured query language (SQL) database with 50 million rows, all we need is a single page of a spreadsheet with 50,000 rows. Furthermore, retrieving the data is much faster because we do only one query per SIP instead of the previous 1,000 queries.

So in summary, in 2006, with the help of the Risk Solver, we reduced the number of formulas in our models by a factor of 1,000, and in 2007, by using DISTs, we reduced the number of data elements by another factor of 1,000. To paraphrase the late Senator Everett

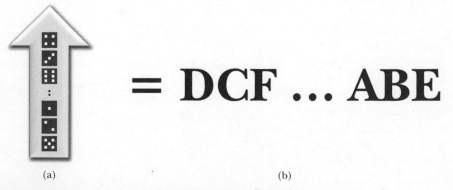

(a)   (b)

Figure 45.1   (a) The market SIP and (b) its DIST.

Dirksen, a factor of 1,000 here and a factor of 1,000 there, and pretty soon you have a simpler model. But enough talk, let's hit the road.

At FlawOfAverages.com is an interactive Markowitz portfolio simulator in Microsoft Excel, which is based on DISTs, as shown in Figure 45.2. If you have access to the Internet, you may wish to load it before proceeding.

The DIST-Based Markowitz Model

Every time you change an investment in this model, the DISTs of the assets are blasted through the model instantaneously, resulting in a new output DIST for the return of the portfolio. This in turn changes the interactive histogram, or Blitzogram, on the left and moves the portfolio dot in the risk/return graph on the right. But where are the DISTs? Put the cursor in any cell in the asset row, and you'll get an eyeful, as shown in Figure 45.3. (Note that, in Excel 2007, you must double click the cell to see the whole thing.)

The DIST data type was designed to be universally acceptable to spreadsheet and database software, and for parts of it to be human-readable as well, with the name and average prominently visible. The gobbledygook starting with "ESV" and ending with "wAA" encodes 1,000 Monte Carlo trials of the large-cap investment, generated so as to capture the interrelationships with the other assets.

Open Architecture

The concept of the DIST is simple, but for it to fulfill its potential, an industrywide standard was required. Returning to the lightbulb analogy, the DIST represents a specification for the electric current on the power grid. I felt that the only way to encourage widespread adoption was to make the technology freely available through an open source agreement.

Wikinomics, by Don Tapscott and Anthony Williams, describes how phenomena like Wikipedia, Linux, and YouTube represent a revolutionary new economics based on collaboration.[1] They suggest that this is based on the principles of openness, peering, sharing, and acting globally.

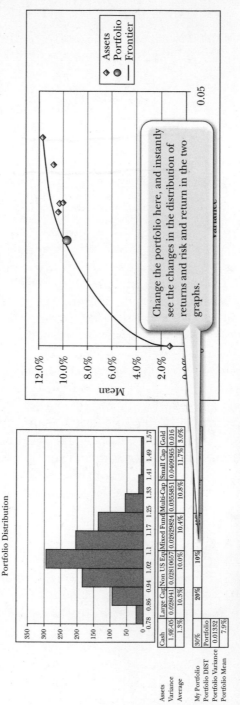

Portfolio Distribution

Assets	Cash	Large Cap	Non US Eq	Mixed Fund	Multi-Cap	Small Cap	Gold
Variance	1.9E-05	0.028041	0.02810657	0.02629824	0.0355851	0.0409365	0.016
Average	1.3%	10.5%	10.0%	10.4%	10.8%	11.7%	3.0%

My Portfolio	30%	20%		10%			
Portfolio DIST							

Portfolio Variance	0.01332
Portfolio Mean	7.9%

Change the portfolio here, and instantly see the changes in the distribution of returns and risk and return in the two graphs.

Mean

Variance

- ◇ Assets
- ● Portfolio
- — Frontier

Figure 45.2 A Markowitz portfolio model based on DISTs.

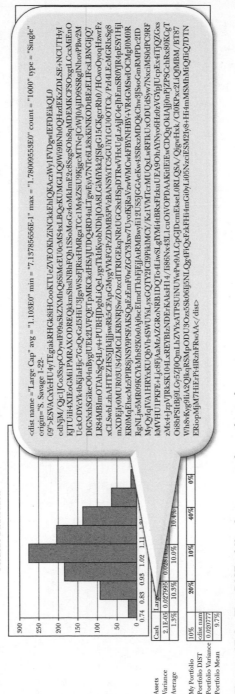

Figure 45.3   The DIST of the large-cap investment.

Openness is beneficial to the development of standards, and a primary purpose of the DIST is to establish a transparent means for sharing and measuring risk and uncertainty.

Peering involves the active participation in the design of a system by its stakeholders. This is the tough part; letting others into the kitchen where you have been cooking up ideas, and standing back while they throw stuff into the stew. I was worried that the result would be inedible. But as it turned out, getting professional chefs involved early on was absolutely the right thing to do. Eric Wainwright, of Oracle, and Harry Markowitz, independently insisted that we define DISTs using a convention known as the XML, extended markup language. This will allow the standard to evolve flexibly in the future. John Sall, of SAS Institute, and John Rivlin, of eBook Technologies, independently urged the use of something called Base64 encoding to generate the actual characters of the DIST. This will ensure compatibility across a broad array of computer platforms. Dan Fylstra, of Frontline Systems, realized that we needed to support multiple degrees of numerical accuracy, which led to the "double precision" DIST. All three of these ingredients turned out to be necessary. But it still would not have been enough without the taste testers at Shell, Genentech, and Merck & Co., who provided much valuable feedback.

As to sharing, the standard is published at www.Probability Management.org, and those who develop improvements are expected to share them with the user community.

Now for acting globally. The only way a standard gets accepted is if a lot of people hear about it. How handy that I was 95 percent done with a book that warned people against the dangers of using numbers instead of distributions when the DIST 1.0 standard was established in July 2008. Perhaps the opportunity to publicize this concept was just the motivation I needed to finally push the manuscript out the door after nine years.

Certification and Auditing

Another major benefit of Probability Management is that it allows risk models to be certified and audited.

At the dawn of the electric age, people regularly electrocuted themselves. But in 1894 a 25-year-old electrical engineer named William H. Merrill founded Underwriters Laboratories, Inc. This nonprofit organization north of Chicago performs product safety tests and certifications to this day, and it is responsible for the label

on my wife's hair dryer that says, "DANGER—ELECTROCUTION POS-
SIBLE IF USED OR DROPPED IN TUB."

Source: Underwriters Laboratories.

The analogous concept in Probability Management is that of
a Certified Distribution, which indicates that a chief probability
officer has signed off on it.

If all distributions are stored in a single library for which the
CPO has preserved the statistical relationships, then the scenario
library is certified as *coherent.* In this case, the outputs of any two
models using those distributions may be consolidated as we did with
the two banking divisions.

The next level of certification involves a *pedigree*, which travels
along with the distribution and describes its evolution like a family
tree. For example, a DIST representing the total profit of a firm
could contain the names and dates of the DIST libraries of the divisions from which it was rolled up, along with the names and dates of
the DIST libraries of the subdivisions from which they *themselves* were
rolled up. And somewhere at the bottom would be a DIST library of
global economic uncertainties generated by the CPO and broadcast
across the enterprize, ensuring that the whole thing is coherent.

Imagine the worst-case scenario in which a CPO committed fraud
by intentionally creating a DIST library in which airline stocks increase
with oil prices instead of decreasing. During an audit, it would be possible to show precisely the point at which the falsehood had been
introduced and the extent to which it had misstated the actual risk.

Software Implementation

So when will such systems be available? Now. You can start doing this today with several current simulation systems. Visit Probability Management.org for a current list of products available.

Risk Solver

I have listed Risk Solver first, because its developer, Frontline Systems, has been a pioneer in the area of Probability Management, being the first to introduce both interactive simulation and functions to process SIPs, SLURPs, and DISTs, directly from user data.[2] In addition it has implemented a facility for certifying distributions up to the pedigree level as defined above. Figure 45.4 displays the Risk Solver's certified distribution menu.

Analytica

Analytica from Lumina Decision Systems, mentioned earlier, has embodied many of the concepts of Probability Management for decades. DIST support should be implemented by the time this is published.

XLSim

XLSim® from Probilitech, is my own Monte Carlo simulation package for spreadsheets. It is less powerful than the others in this chapter, but as a result is easier to learn. This makes it ideal for teaching, building prototypes, and small applications. The latest

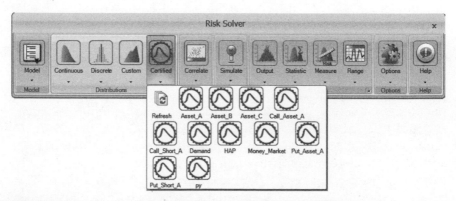

Figure 45.4 The Certified Distribution Ribbon in Risk Solver.

version provides interactive simulation with DISTs. I currently have no financial interest in any software beyond my own, other than the fact that by allowing users to work with probability distributions, they all potentially benefit my consulting activities, and the cause of Probability Management.

Crystal Ball

Crystal Ball® is an industrial strength Monte Carlo package for Excel, now owned by Oracle.[3] As of this writing, full SIP import and export have been implemented with release 11.1.1. As with other distribution types, SIPs can be shared across organizations through the use of Crystal Ball's pioneering publish/subscribe feature. The product has a large user base, supported by educational programs and consulting services. Their affiliation with Oracle ensures that they will be central players in the future of Probability Management. As of this writing Probilitech has developed an Excel add-in to allow Crystal Ball to read DISTs, with more advanced support planned for the future.

JMP

JMP™ from SAS Institute, and other graphical statistics packages, are useful for quickly validating scenario libraries through scatter plot matrices, as displayed in Chapters 41 and 43, and for performing analysis of model outputs. There is support for reading DISTs directly from Excel into JMP to facilitate this process.

The Vanguard System

The Vanguard System is a large-scale multidimensional modeling system with its own internal Monte Carlo simulation support.[4] It is a good deal more expensive than spreadsheet software, but does not have its shortcomings in terms of documentability and scalability. It was designed with enterprisewide risk modeling in mind. As such, it is possible for different groups within an organization to create separate components that can be linked into a larger model. In addition, the system supports stochastic libraries for importing distributions from other systems or exporting them to other systems.

   According to Rob Suggs, Vanguard Software's CEO, "There is a lot of money to be made selling timely market data and the same should be true for forecast data. I look forward to a time when I can get not only the current spot price for oil, but I can link dynamically to an analyst's projection for oil price as a multi-period SLURP."

@Risk

@Risk from Palisade is another major player in the spreadsheet Monte Carlo simulation field, with a large user base and extensive support services.[5] Although as of this writing, it does not yet formally support scenario libraries, it is easy to integrate DISTs into @Risk models, and in fact it plays an important role in the Probability Management application at Merck & Co. This is a distributed environment, in which DISTs created in @RISK are used by others in Risk Solver, as described further in Chapter 46. By the time you read this, DIST support is expected to be available through Probilitech. Visit ProbabilityManagement.org or FlawOfAverages. com for the latest on DIST software support.

The Outlook

According to Brian Lewis, a vice president at Vanguard Software, "Companies are realizing that backward-looking analysis of historical data is insufficient on its own to drive company strategy. They are asking instead for forward-looking planning and analysis through simulation." This will require libraries of probability distributions.

Another perspective comes from Steve Tani, a partner at Strategic Decisions Group (SDG), the consulting company cofounded by Stanford's Ron Howard. "We are seeing increasing interest in enterprise wide risk simulation." Tani has developed a sophisticated Crystal Ball simulation model for a pharmaceutical firm, which not only generates distributions of uncertain demand for each drug, instead of averages, but further can capture important interrelationships between demand for various products as well.

"This is an uncertain business," says Tani. "You have several important compounds under development that may interact with each other in the marketplace. For example, there might be cannibalization, where success of one compound steals sales from another. Or there might be the opposite, which we call the halo effect, in which success of one compound enhances the success of another." Tani exports the results from Crystal Ball to create scenario libraries that can be shared with others in the organization.

Because DISTs allow distributions to be used in spreadsheets and other applications, essentially like numbers, they have the potential to facilitate today's risk calculations much in the way that Fibonacci's beloved Arabic numbers facilitated the business calculations of Medieval Italy. Imagine how hard it would be to buy something in a store for $10.95 with a $20 bill and calculate the change if we didn't have simple arithmetic. Unfortunately, simple arithmetic has not been available for uncertain numbers, even when all parties agree on their shapes and interrelationships. As a result, when one entity purchases a risky asset from another entity, instead of just using a calculator to make change, they send the problem off to a bunch of propeller heads behind the algebraic curtain, thereby *separating* the seat of the intellect from the seat of the pants. Publicly available DISTs of such important uncertainties as housing values, even if not terribly accurate, would provide much needed benchmarks, and a degree of transparency. In such an environment, any model of default rates that did not allow housing prices to fall would be met instantly by howls of "Emperor's New Clothes" derision.

CHAPTER

The CPO: Managing Probability Management

If a man will begin with certainties, he shall end in doubts, but if he will be content to begin with doubts, he shall end in certainties.
—Francis Bacon, English philosopher, 1561–1626

This is the motto of the ideal chief probability officer, or CPO. He or she should not only know something about uncertainty but should ferret out excessive certainty within their organization and replace it with doubt to keep people on their toes.

Let's return once again to the gas property, whose average value was doubled by taking into account the option not to pump. But this time we will extend it to an entire gas company, with hundreds of wells selling into the same market. Should they manage the firm based on a single average price of gas? If they do, they are leaving a lot of money on the table. Should they let the manager of each gas well make their own estimate of the distribution of the price of gas? That would be like letting them estimate the discount rate for the net present value of their own projects or appointing foxes to run the Department of Defense for the hen house. The *chief financial officer* (CFO) should provide the discount rate centrally, or you could never sensibly compare the NPVs of two projects. Similarly, the CPO should provide a DIST of the gas price distribution, whereupon managers can run simulations of their individual properties, which can then be consolidated into a coherent model of the entire enterprise.

The CPO Versus the CRO

To better explain the role of the CPO, a comparison to that of the chief risk officer (CRO) is useful. The CRO has traditionally been in charge of delivering the value at risk (VaR), as defined earlier, from behind its algebraic curtain. But if anything VaR may have become a moral hazard, lulling people into the belief that there was no risk because they were covered by doing "Risk Management." Joe Nocera has noted in a January 2009 *New York Times* article on VaR[1] that:

> There were the investors who saw the VaR numbers in the annual reports but didn't pay them the least bit of attention. There were the regulators who slept soundly in the knowledge that, thanks to VaR, they had the whole risk thing under control. There were the boards who heard a VaR number once or twice a year and thought it sounded good.

As a result, actual investment decisions were *not* based on a clear view of risk. It is not that modern portfolio had failed, but rather that people ignored the very basis of modern portfolio theory; that is, that risk must be genuinely taken into account, not merely presented as an abstract number.

In contrast, the Shell exploration portfolio model interactively displays uncertainty in multiple ways and multiple dimensions to the executives actually committing the money. In contrast to a CRO, a CPO attempts to deliver a coherent library of DISTs, which may be viewed individually as histograms or jointly as scatter plots. They may be used in calculations in place of the uncertain numbers they represent, throughout an organization. People may disagree with some of them and plug in their own DISTs containing black swans if they like. And the DISTs of individual projects may be assembled into portfolios, for which the entire distribution may be viewed or, if you insist, just its VaR.

Well, I got a little carried away there. This won't happen overnight, but the technology is now available, and it can take place at a grass roots level because the software to use DISTs interactively in spreadsheets is already available.

I don't expect companies to suddenly open up new C-level job positions for CPOs either. More likely, over time, chief financial officers and chief risk officers will start spending more time wearing a CPO hat. But if organizations are to conquer the Flaw of Averages, they must start dealing in probability distributions, *not* in single numbers, be they averages or VaRs. As with discount rates, enterprisewide standards should be established, estimating procedures should be calibrated, and probability distributions should be certified. Given the huge impact these estimates have on the strategic management of a firm, the chief probability officer must not be someone in a white lab coat in a basement room without windows. Instead, he or she must be feisty, egotistical, and well paid, like the rest of the management team. They should have an explanation for all the weird shapes that will inevitably show up in the scatter plot matrix of the corporate scenario library, and get fired on the spot if they ever produce a distribution for an investment that cannot go negative.

In the Land of the Averages, the Man with the Wrong Distribution Is King

It has been said that simulations are only as good as the distributions that go into them, but I disagree. Going back to the ladder analogy, I have some bad news for you. The distribution of forces on a ladder when you shake it is different from the distribution when you climb on it. I wonder how many of my readers will now stop shaking their ladders because I've pointed out that they have been using the wrong distribution all these years. With a good simulation model, when you put garbage in, you get valid insight out.

Ironically, I have actually heard people say, "How could I provide you with a distribution for this number? I can't even estimate its *average*." A good CPO would find this statement hilarious. It's like saying, "How do you expect me to learn to use a parachute now? Can't you see the wing is on fire?" Or, "I couldn't possibly shake my ladder today, because I'm setting it up on a surface of broken beer bottles next to a great white shark tank."

If a CPO has no idea of a particular distribution, they should pull several different ones from the seat of thier pants and see how the results differ under each. Today's interactive simulations are so fast that you can actually enter probabilities as variables and discover at what point you would make different decisions.

The CPO must not be tempted to impress the statisticians in the organization with a perfect model, at the cost of confusing the

CEO. In developing Shell's portfolio model, Daniel Zweidler constantly needed to balance the transparency of the results and ease of collecting data against the rigor of the probabilistic models.

Probability Management at Merck & Co.

And speaking of Daniel, he had spent much of his professional career writing Monte Carlo simulations of the volumetric reserves of petroleum exploration sites around the world. Therefore he could detect the probabilistic biases of the reservoir engineers in the field who reported to him. So when he directed the development of the exploration portfolio at Shell, he was the perfect project CPO. But when he moved to Merck & Co. to lead the development of similar models for pharmaceutical R&D projects, he lacked domain-specific expertise. Whereas the entire project at Shell took place in an intimate skunk works environment, at Merck a true team effort was needed, which had not yet been attempted with the Probability Management approach.

This required strong support from the very top. In a December 9, 2008 press release,[2] Peter Kim, former MIT biologist and president of Merck Research Laboratories, clearly articulated the need for effective portfolio management of their R&D projects.

> "We are diversifying our R&D activities, promoting technological changes and bringing together complementary R&D activities to drive innovation at Merck," Kim said. "Our strategy of scientific diversification facilitates innovation and provides a sustainable approach that sets Merck apart in an industry that is increasingly focused on specialty medicines."

When it came to modeling this situation, as usual we started with some quick prototypes to convince ourselves that we were on the right track. For this purpose I teamed up with Andrew Levitch, senior director of business integration, who is located at Merck's San Francisco office. This allowed us to work face to face during the critical first few hours of model development, the stage at which most fatal flaws are introduced. Andrew's high school career was about as successful as that of mine and my father's. He dropped out altogether and joined the U.S. Navy, serving as a quartermaster. After the service he went back to school and got an MBA from Lehigh University. But it is his Navy experience that shaped his approach to simulation.

A Submariner's Philosophy of Simulation

By ANDREW LEVITCH

I first became familiar with the power of simulation while in the US Navy serving on board the USS *Daniel Webster* (a ballistic missile submarine) in the early 1980s. We weren't using computer models to run simulations, but did them manually. The scenarios that we simulated included ones like being detected by an enemy submarine, getting the order to fire our missiles, and dealing with situations in which the submarine sustained damage from fire, flooding, or a host of other possible malfunctions. My exposure to this type of simulation formed the basis for my philosophy in running complex computer simulations. It is not important to get the input variables exactly right. It *is* important that you understand the relationships between the input variables and that you capture all of the possible relationships when modeling the outputs.

Andrew and I built the first prototype of a pharmaceutical R&D portfolio in less than four hours in a two person extreme spreadsheet programming approach that works as follows. The first step is to get out of the office and go for a walk to clear your head and discuss the problem. Once the ideas begin to flow, you rush back to a single computer, trading off the keyboard when necessary to exploit the relative proficiency of the parties at particular tasks. Often the team will reach Knuth's "step five" within the first few minutes, and have to start again from scratch.

I have worked this way with Daniel Zweidler, Stefan Scholtes, and others, and suspect that there are three primary reasons it is so effective. First, by taking the walk, you comply with Gene Woolsey's admonition that "a pencil is a crutch, a calculator is a wheel chair, and a computer is an ambulance," using your brain, instead, to analyze the issues. The computer is then used primarily to chronicle your thoughts rather than to form them. Second, when it comes to the modeling, you don't get stuck unless both of you get stuck, which greatly reduces the chance of getting stuck. Third, you don't make programming mistakes unless you both overlook the mistake, which greatly reduces the chance of making a mistake.

Of course, you make mistakes anyway, and if you have worked with spreadsheets you know what to do when you are clearly getting wrong answers. You systematically work your way back through the model looking at intermediate results to find out where you messed up.

This is much harder with a simulation model, which is what Andrew and I were working on, because the results are not numbers but distributions. Here interactive simulation makes all the difference because you can easily see the shape of any intermediate calculation. Risk Solver pops up a little histogram when you merely hover the cursor over a formula that is involved in simulation.

When Daniel Zweidler and I had taken a similar initial approach at Shell in 2005, the final model actually evolved as a sequence of prototypes for the first few months. At Merck, however, the knowledge was more distributed, and we needed to pass the prototype on to others to convert to a useful management tool. The plan was to start with a very small part of the actual portfolio as a test.

The expertise for the financial simulation of individual projects came from Aaron Rosenberg, director of R&D evaluation and finance. He has an MBA from New York University's Stern School of Business and extensive simulation experience. As the manager of utilities for a national hotel chain, he had even developed simulation models to forecast hotel water usage. These models had input variables around guest toilet bowl flushes, as well as the percentage of those who washed their hands. He developed his distributions via Internet research, as well as surveying coworkers. As Aaron puts it, "certainly not typical water cooler conversation."

Today Aaron simulates a very different kind of flow: projects through the R&D pipeline. He had already developed extensive Monte Carlo models of pharmaceutical projects using @RISK, and to everyone's relief, he was able to quickly integrate these into the Probability Management framework.

So we now had two pieces of the puzzle. The prototype was the blueprint, and Aaron could supply the scenario library for a small set of projects, but the whole thing needed to be assembled into an application. The prototype and library were handed over to a team of analytical modelers comprised of Lifei Cheng, Prasanna Deshpande, and Nakin Sriobchoey. This was the moment of truth and I held my breath. My programmers and I helped them with a few details, but they did the bulk of the work themselves without a hiccup, and with surprisingly little training. It was like the bittersweet experience of seeing a child go off to college. On the one hand you are thrilled at how self sufficient *they* have become. But on the other you are a little shocked at how irrelevant *you* have become.

So unlike the application at Shell, in which a small team runs the model and generates the scenario library based on data delivered by reservoir engineers around the world, at Merck the entire process is far more distributed. The only person who can adequately compare the two is Daniel Zweidler (whose sidebar appears on the next page).

Using the Probability Management Framework at Merck

BY AARON ROSENBERG

Well before commercial simulation packages existed, Merck was an industry leader in applying probability theory and Monte Carlo to understand the risk and return profile of development candidates. Despite tremendous enhancements achieved via technological improvement, supplemented by employee sweat, incorporating inter-relationships between asset models has always been a challenge. Even consolidating a handful of models for concurrent simulation required tremendous computing horsepower and time . . . forget about the entire portfolio of company projects.

It was not until we applied the beautifully simple concepts of Probability Management that we were able to tackle this problem. Within minutes, existing @Risk models were engineered to accept pre-simulated global scenarios and incorporate them via DISTs with virtually no effect on performance. We now have the ability to link every development project simulation without investment in expensive computing horsepower or changing our software. These concepts and tools will certainly take Merck Portfolio Management to the next level.

Calibrating Your CPO

Since the 1970s, psychologists have studied our ability to estimate probabilities, which varies greatly by individual. However, there is evidence that our estimates can be calibrated through training.[3] According to Doug Hubbard, author of *How to Measure Anything* and *The Failure of Risk Management: Why It's Broken and How to Fix It*,[4] bookies are, not surprisingly, better than executives, and unfortunately medical doctors are often quite bad.

Hubbard has spent much of his career as a consultant on risky IT projects. As a regular part of his practice he assists managers in calibrating their estimates of probabilities.

"Most analysts modeling uncertainty rely on probabilities from so called subject matter experts," says Hubbard. Yet in his controlled

Distributed Probability Management at Merck

By Daniel Zweidler

In early 2008, when I joined Merck Research Laboratories, reporting to Peter Kim, it became apparent that an industrialized approach to portfolio modeling was not only possible, but also necessary. The technology had evolved to a degree where the maintenance of large simulation models was greatly simplified and sharing of scenario libraries across the organization was possible. Technology aside, the pull from numerous parts of the organization to implement "portfolio management" was such that a more distributed approach was required than that implemented at Shell. Success in this regard not only involves the development of models by the likes of Andrew, Aaron, Lifei, Prasanna and Nakin, but maybe more importantly rests on the efficacy of the training of Merck's scientists and leaders in concepts such as the Flaw of Averages and portfolio effects. The technology is necessary but not sufficient to create the desired behavioral shift from ranking individual projects, to assessing their impact on a portfolio of opportunities in the broader context of a highly uncertain world.

experiments, executives who express 90 percent confidence are right less than 60 percent of the time.

Ironically, Hubbard notes that "[w]ith a majority of variables in the majority of models coming from overconfident humans, the entire risk analysis industry has been consistently underestimating uncertainty and risk."

Hubbard believes that most managers can improve their skills in just a few hours with calibration exercises. The simplest method involves a series of trivia tests. "I ask subject matter experts to estimate a 90 percent confidence interval for the height of the Sears Tower," says Hubbard, "or the probability that their answer to a True/False question is correct." At first, they are wrong much more often then they thought. But they quickly improve. Hubbard explains that it doesn't seem to matter what the trivia questions are about. "Being calibrated in one domain improves calibration in all domains." After a few rounds of trivia, Hubbard takes the participants to the next level by having them put real money where their mouths are, as in the prediction markets discussed earlier in the book.

"Calibration training should be a basic skill for CPOs," says Hubbard. "More importantly, the CPO needs to understand how to 'certify' others as calibrated estimators as well."

So suppose that you haven't been calibrated yet. Does that mean you should just keep on using single numbers instead of distributions of uncertainties? Heck, no.

To Blow or Not to Blow the Whistle, That Is the Question

In early February of 2009 I visited New York on business. A palpable sense of gloom hung over this normally most vibrant of cities, as the economic news went from bad to worse. As I addressed two groups of executives from the recently devastated financial industry, I wondered how they were coping. I couldn't help but ask the audience how it was that no one had effectively blown the whistle on the S&P risk model that could not accept *negative* numbers (Chapter 1), or on the SEC's evaluation of petroleum properties based on average oil price (Chapter 31), let alone their astounding perpetuation of Bernie Madoff's Ponzi scheme, or on the banks loading up on both mortgage-backed securities and home loans, both of which were tied inexorably to a single inflated asset: housing prices (Chapter 43)? Why hadn't there been an army of whistle blowers, blowing their lungs out?

I didn't expect an answer but I got one. Mark Permann, a senior manager with American Express, whose opinion is informed from years of experience at more than one large and successful organization, raised his hand. After my session we discussed his thoughts on this issue, which are presented below.

But let's not forget that risk is not inherently bad. In fact, risk, clearly presented and understood, is required for people to make investments. And if people don't make investments, society pretty much grinds to a halt. Let's also not forget that risk is in the eye of the beholder and that the risk attitude that a publicly traded firm should take on is the one anticipated by its shareholders. Unlike its employees, who may be more concerned about keeping their jobs than making profit, the shareholders, who are generally diversified across many other investments, want the firm to take the business risks that induced them to invest in the first place.

Hand Raising

By Mark Permann

While every organization faces unknown unknowns, there are also risks somewhere in those organizations that are known, which are nevertheless not managed. It is these risks, perceived but unmanaged, which create most of the destruction.

Why does this happen? Smart people, closest to the risks and caring about the health of the organization, are nonetheless reasonably reluctant to raise their hand, for fear of having it cut off, along with their heads.

I spent a fair amount of time in my career struggling with the idea that one cannot speak truth to power. More recently, I have come to see that fear about speaking the truth merely alerts us that a different, more effective approach may be needed. The trick is to accept the organizational culture as it is, and seek out means of making the risks, and your motives in raising them, more transparent.

It is when risks are clearly not understood or, worse, misrepresented that the whistle needs to be blown. But given the flawed methods of communicating risk and uncertainty in our society, it was unfortunately all too easy to dismiss someone like Harry Markopolos,[5] who whistled non-stop about Bernie Madoff for a decade before the exposure of his fraudulent investment scheme.

A Posthumous Visit by My Father

My father's 1954 book, *The Foundations of Statistics,* is described on its jacket cover as "a critical examination of statistics, viewed as the discipline of rational decision in the face of uncertainty."[1] It took the point of view that probability was subjective and that it was reflected in the gambles a person would make. Although controversial at the time and still not universally accepted, the prediction markets discussed earlier affirm that this perspective is at least widely held today. But the book is so mathematical that I can decipher only snippets.

Thus I was intrigued when Michael Schrage discovered a very readable article of my father's, of which I had been unaware, entitled "The Shifting Foundations of Statistics."[2] It had been hiding under my own nose for years in a 736-page memorial collection of his writings. I presume the paper in question was written shortly before my father's death in 1971 because it was published in 1977 in a collection of various authors. Unlike his mathematical writings, this piece was completely accessible to me. It made me realize how little my father and I had discussed the technical details of statistics, a field that I had studiously avoided with the exception of a required course in college.

I vividly recall one pivotal scientific discussion with him, however. I had just proven the first result in my doctoral dissertation in computational complexity, and we scheduled time to discuss it. I was proud of the proof, and for the first time in my life had arranged to get together with my father for the sole purpose of talking mathematics. The proof had nothing to do with statistics, but it was gratifying for both of us to have a conversation at a technical level. Too bad he unexpectedly dropped dead of a heart attack two weeks later. Lucky for me he didn't do so two weeks earlier. Ironically, a year after his death, my dissertation suddenly took a sharp turn toward the statistical, and I wish I could have discussed that with him as well.

So Schrage delivered this paper in which my father described where he thought statistics was headed in the future, at a time in his future when I had mostly finished a book on where *I* thought it was headed. I can't tell you how great it was to hear from him again, even though I wasn't allowed to ask any questions.

I was struck by several observations that I don't recall hearing him make in person.

First, he recognized the importance of graphs, charts, and other forms of descriptive statistics, which he described as "the art of putting data before the human mind in a way that is humanely comprehensible." The Mindle!

He observed that this trend toward visualization in statistics had "led to a new respect for puttering about with the data in a relatively informal and unstructured way," which I interpret as developing a seat of the pants understanding through interaction.

And he understood the growing importance of computers in statistics, suggesting that "the cost of calculation" must not exceed the value of the information it provided. Remember that his essay was written in the era of Free Love but expensive computing, when they would take a device less powerful than a $49 graphing calculator, build a $10 million building around it, and charge people $1,000 an hour to use it.

He was always deeply aware of technology and usually understood the basic physics behind it as well. I remember asking him once what technological advance would really impress him, and he said the ability to transport things electronically. I am sure he would be tickled to know that probability distributions are now being shipped in just that manner.

I will finish *The Flaw of Averages* by taking up a challenge posed in *The Foundations of Statistics.* Recall the two opposing proverbs from Chapter 14 that my father quoted near the beginning of his book. "Look before you leap" prescribes planning, that is, making the best choice today, given all the potential consequences of your actions in an uncertain world. "You can cross that bridge when you come to it" prescribes living for the moment and not wasting time on conjectured future events that might never occur. After introducing these two points of view, my father goes on to write:

> When two proverbs conflict in this way, it is proverbially true that there is some truth in both of them, but rarely, if ever, can their common truth be captured by a single pat proverb.

In spite of my father's warning, I will try nonetheless.

The more options you have in place for crossing bridges before you come to them, the less looking you need to do before you leap.

Red Word Glossary

Red Word	Definition	Closest Green Equivalent (If Any)
BAYESIAN ANALYSIS	Addresses (among other things) the problem of false positives in testing for diseases or identifying terrorists. See Chapter 36. The approach is based on the chances of hitting a bull's-eye, given that you have hit a target, as shown in Figure 36-1.	No Green Word (NGW)
CALCULUS	A branch of mathematics that describes continuous changes. It was vital in the precomputer era in physics, engineering, statistics, and many other areas of mathematics. It is still conceptually useful in some applications.	NGW
CENTRAL LIMIT THEOREM	The reason the shape of a combination of uncertain numbers goes up in the middle.	Diversification
CONCAVE FUNCTION	A line graph in which the slope is continually decreasing.	Downward curving
CONVEX FUNCTION	A line graph in which the slope is continually increasing.	Upward curving
CORRELATION	A Steam Era measure of the degree to which points in a scatter plot lie along a straight line. Ranges from −1 (if the line is negatively sloped) to +1 (if the line is positively sloped).	Interrelationship

(continued)

Red Word	Definition	Closest Green Equivalent (If Any)
COVARIANCE	Another Steam Era calculation on which the correlation is based.	Interrelationship
DISTRIBUTION	The name of the shape of an uncertain number. Note, this is the only formerly Red Word I believe we must adopt to cure the Flaw of Averages	Distribution
F-TEST	A type of method for testing whether something happened by chance.	NGW
FUNCTION	A set of calculations into which numbers are input and from which numbers are output.	Spreadsheet model
FUNCTION OF RANDOM VARIABLES	A set of calculations into which uncertain numbers are input and from which uncertain numbers are output.	Spreadsheet model with uncertain Inputs
FUNDAMENTAL IDENTITY OF SLURP ALGEBRA	Describes why simulation models may be consolidated, if based on scenario libraries.	NGW
HYPOTHESIS TESTING	Determining the probability that some event simply happened by chance.	Did it happen by chance?
JENSEN'S INEQUALITY	The reason that average inputs don't result in average outputs in many spreadsheet models.	The Flaw of Averages (Strong Form)
LINEAR FUNCTION	A line graph in which the slope is constant.	Straight-line relationship
LINEAR PROGRAMMING	A powerful mathematical technique to optimize resources, if you can figure out how to formulate your problem using straight-line relationships. Available in the spreadsheet environment since the mid-1980s.	Optimization

Red Word	Definition	Closest Green Equivalent (If Any)
MARKOV CHAIN	A type of mathematical model that describes how the proportions of various segments of a population evolve over time.	NGW
NONLINEAR PROGRAMMING	Like linear programming, but without the restriction of linear relationships. Available in the spreadsheet environment since the early 1990s.	Optimization
NORMAL DISTRIBUTION	The distribution that results when a sufficiently large number of identical independent uncertain numbers are added or averaged.	Bell-shaped distribution
NULL HYPOTHESIS	The assumption that something happened by chance.	Devil's advocate's position
P VALUE	The probability that something happened by chance.	Likelihood of chance occurrence
RANDOM VARIABLE	A mathematical construct used in the theory of probability.	Uncertain number
REGRESSION	Fitting a line to data points so as to minimize the errors.	Straight line fit through a scatter plot
SCENARIO OPTIMIZATION	A form of optimization that takes into account hundreds or thousands of possible future scenarios.	NGW
SEQUENTIAL ANALYSIS	A form of analysis that is halted when the value of the information that could be gained is less than the cost of continuing.	NGW
SIGMA	A Steam Era measure of the degree of uncertainty of an uncertain number.	Degree of uncertainty
SIX SIGMA	A set of quality management methods for improving the consistency of products and services.	Quality control
STANDARD DEVIATION	Sigma	Degree of uncertainty

(continued)

Red Word	Definition	Closest Green Equivalent (If Any)
STATISTICAL DEPENDENCE	The degree to which the change in one variable is statistically likely to imply a change in another variable.	Interrelationship
STOCHASTIC	Pertaining to uncertainty.	Uncertain
THEORY OF RATIONAL EXPECTATION	A theory of behavior that assumes that people are able to calculate optimal strategies in the face of uncertainty (which they clearly can't always do) and then act on them.	Acting in one's best self-interest, if it can be determined
T-TEST	A type of method for testing whether something happened by chance.	NGW
UTILITY THEORY	The economic theory addressing risk attitude.	Risk attitude
VARIANCE	A Steam Era calculation on which the standard deviation is based.	Degree of uncertainty

Notes

Preface

1. A. F. M. Smith, *The Writings of Leonard Jimmie Savage—A Memorial Collection* (Washington, DC: American Statistical Association and The Institute of Mathematical Statistics, 1981), p. 29.
2. Ibid., p. 14.
3. Sam L. Savage, "The Flaw of Averages," Soapbox column, *San Jose Mercury News*, October 8, 2000.

Introduction: Connecting the Seat of the Intellect to the Seat of the Pants

1. "Daniel Kahnemann: The Sveriges Riksbank Prize in Economic Sciences in Memory of Alfred Nobel 2002," Nobelprize.org, http://nobelprize.org/nobel_prizes/economics/laureates/2002/kahneman-lecture.html
2. Daniel Kahneman, Amos Tversky, and Paul Slovic (Eds.), *Judgment Under Uncertainty: Heuristics and Biases* (New York: Cambridge University Press, 1982).
3. Malcom Gladwell, *Blink—The Power of Thinking Without Thinking* (Boston: Little Brown and Company, 2005).

Chapter 1: The Flaw of Averages

1. Sam L. Savage, "The Flaw of Averages," Soapbox column, *San Jose Mercury News*, October 8, 2000.
2. Sam L. Savage, "The Flaw of Averages," *Harvard Business Review*, November 2002, pp. 20–21.
3. Patrick Leach, *Why Can't You Just Give Me the Number?* (Gainesville, FL: Probabilistic Publishing, 2006).
4. "S&P/Case-ShillerHomePriceIndices,"Standard&Poor's,"http://www2.standardandpoors.com/portal/site/sp/en/us/page.topic/indices_csmahp/0,0,0,0,0,0,0,0,0,0,2,1,0,0,0,0,0.html
5. Benita D. Newton (staff writer), "All-You-Can-Eat Was Too Much," *St. Petersburg Times*, September 26, 2003.
6. William K. Stevens, "When Scientific Predictions Are So Good They're Bad," Tuesday Science Desk, *The New York Times*, September 29, 1998.
7. Philippe Jorion, *Big Bets Gone Bad: Derivatives and Bankruptcy in Orange County* (New York: Academic Press, 1995).

8. Ibid.
9. Daniel H. Pink, *A Whole New Mind* (New York: Riverhead Books, 2005).

Chapter 2: The Fall of the Algebraic Curtain and Rise of the Flaw of Averages

1. "The 3rd Annual Awards," PCMag.com, http://www.pcmag.com/article2/0,1895, 1177271,00.asp
2. Lindo Systems, www.LINDO.com

Chapter 3: Mitigating the Flaw of Averages

1. Palisade Corporation home page, http://palisade.com/
2. Oracle home page, http://www.decisioneering.com/
3. "Monte Carlo Simulation: Get Insight!" AnalyCorp, www.analycorp.com/
4. "Risk Analysis with Interactive Simulation, Stunning Graphics, Lightning-Fast Simulation Optimization," Solver.com, http://solver.com/risksolver.htm
5. Doug Hubbard, *The Failure of Risk Management: Why It's Broken and How to Fix It*, (Hoboken, NJ: John Wiley & Sons, Inc., 2009)
6. Sam Savage, Stefan Scholtes, and Daniel Zweidler, "Probability Management," *ORMS Today*, Vol. 33, No. 1 (February 2006).
7. Sam Savage, Stefan Scholtes, and Daniel Zweidler, "Probability Management, Part 2," *ORMS Today*, Vol. 33, No. 2 (April 2006).

Chapter 4: The Wright Brothers Versus the Wrong Brothers

1. Russell Freedman, *The Wright Brothers, How They Invented the Airplane* (New York: Holiday House, 1991).
2. "Extreme Programming," Wikipedia, http://en.wikipedia.org/wiki/Extreme_ Programming
3. Lego Shop page, http://shop.lego.com/Product/?p=10177
4. Michael Schrage, *Serious Play: How the World's Best Companies Simulate to Innovate* (Cambridge, MA: Harvard Business School Press, 2000).

Chapter 6: Mindles Are to Minds What Handles Are to Hands

1. Perhaps today's most famous informational designer is Edward R. Tufte. See http://www.edwardtufte.com/tufte/
2. Richard Dawkins, *The Selfish Gene* (New York: Oxford University Press, 1976).
3. Vijay Govindarajan and Chris Trimble, *Ten Rules for Strategic Innovators: From Idea to Execution* (Cambridge, MA: Harvard Business School Publishing, 2006).
4. Bradley Efron, "Vignettes," *Journal of the American Statistical Association*, Vol. 95, No. 452 (December 2000), p. 1293.

Chapter 8: Mindle 2: An Uncertain Number Is a Shape

1. Sam L. Savage, "Statistical Analysis for the Masses," *Statistics in Public Policy*, edited by Bruce Spencer (New York: Oxford University Press, 1998);
2. A. Ingolfsson, "Obvious Abstractions: The Spinner Experiment," *Interfaces*, Vol. 29, No. 6 (1999), pp. 112–122;

3. D. Zalkind, "Another Take on the Spinner Experiment," *Interfaces*, Vol. 29, No. 6 (1999), pp. 122–126.
4. Nassim Nicholas Taleb, *The Black Swan, The Impact of the Highly Improbable* (New York: Random House, 2007).
5. Gary Klein, *Intuition at Work: Why Developing Your Gut Instincts Will Make You Better at What You Do* (New York: Random House, 2003).

Chapter 9: Mindle 3: Combinations of Uncertain Numbers

1. Harry Markowitz, *Portfolio Selection: Efficient Diversification of Investments*, 2nd ed. (Malden, MA: Blackwell Publishing Professional, 1991).

Chapter 11: Mindle 4: Terri Dial and the Drunk in the Road

1. Illustration from Sam L. Savage, *Decision Making with Insight* (with Insight.xla 2.0 and CD-ROM Second Edition, 2003), Cengage Learning, Florence. KY, Reproduced with permission of the publisher.
2. "Human cyclone hits Lloyds TSB," *The Sunday Times*, December 17, 2006.

Chapter 12: Who Was Jensen and Why Wasn't He Equal?

1. Johan Ludwig William Valdemar Jensen, http://www-groups.dcs.st-and.ac.uk/~history/Biographies/Jensen.html
2. Personal correspondence.
3. Note that this should not be confused with the volatility smile associated with stock options.

Chapter 13: Mindle 5: Interrelated Uncertainties

1. "Welcome to Applied Quantitative Sciences, Inc.," AQS, www.aqs-us.com
2. Harry Markowitz, "Portfolio Selection," *The Journal of Finance*, Vol. 7, No. 1 (March 1952), pp. 77–91.
3. Felix Salmon, Recipe for Disaster: The Formula That Killed Wall Street, *Wired Magazine*, February 23, 1909.

Chapter 14: Decision Trees

1. Leonard J. Savage, *The Foundations of Statistics* (Hoboken, NJ: Wiley & Sons, Inc., 1954).
2. Daniel Kahneman, Paul Slovic, and Amos Tversky, *Judgment Under Uncertainty: Heuristics and Biases* (New York: Cambridge University Press, 1982).
3. Peter C. Fishburn, "Foundations of Decision Analysis: Along the Way," *Management Science*, Vol. 35, No. 4 (April 1989), pp. 387–405.
4. Ronald A. Howard, "Decision Analysis: Applied Decision Theory," *Proceedings of the Fourth International Conference on Operational Research*, edited by David B. Hertz and Jacques Melese (Hoboken, NJ: Wiley-Interscience, 1966), pp. 55–71.
5. Sam L. Savage, *Decision Making with Insight* (with Insight.xla 2.0 and CD-ROM Second Edition, 2003) Cengage Learning, Florence, KY.
6. "Welcome to DEF," Decision Education Foundation, http://www.decision education.org/

Chapter 15: The Value of Information

1. *Chicago Tribune*, May 28, 1995, section 2, p. 6.
2. Ronald A. Howard, "Information Value Theory," *IEEE Transactions on Systems Science and Cybernetics*, Vol. 2, No. 1 (August 1966).
3. Jack Kneece, *Ghost Army of World War II* (Gretna, LA: Pelican Publishing, 2001).
4. "History," Patten, http://trax4you.com/proofs/patten/pt_history.htm
5. Personal correspondence.

Chapter 16: The Seven Deadly Sins of Averaging

1. "Welcome!" ProbabilityManagement.org, www.ProbabilityManagement.org
2. Sam Savage, Stefan Scholtes, and Daniel Zweidler, "Probability Management," *ORMS Today*, Vol. 33, No. 1 (February 2006).

Chapter 17: The Flaw of Extremes

1. Howard Wainer, *Picturing the Uncertain World: How to Understand, Communicate and Control Uncertainty Through Graphical Display* (Princeton, NJ: Princeton University Press, 2009).

Chapter 18: Simpson's Paradox

1. C. R. Charig, D. R. Webb, S. R. Payne, and O. E. Wickham, "Comparison of Treatment of Renal Calculi by Operative Surgery, Percutaneous Nephrolithotomy, and Extracorporeal Shock Wave Lithotripsy," *Br Med J* (Clin Res Ed) Vol. 292, No. 6524 (March 1986), pp. 879–882.
2. Ken Ross, *A Mathematician at the Ballpark: Odds and Probabilities for Baseball Fans* (New York: Pi Press, 2004), pp. 12–13.

Chapter 19: The Scholtes Revenue Fallacy

1. Special thanks to economists Jack Gould of the University of Chicago and Ward Hanson of Stanford University for their insights into this problem.

Chapter 20: Taking Credit for Chance Occurrences

1. Sam L. Savage, *Decision Making with Insight* (with Insight.xla 2.0 and CD-ROM Second Edition, 2003), Cengage Learning, Florence, KY.

Chapter 21: Your Retirement Portfolio

1. Stephen M. Pollan and Mark Levine, *Die Broke* (New York: HarperCollins, 1997).
2. "Welcome," Financial Engines, www.FinancialEngines.com

3. William F. Sharpe, "Financial Planning in Fantasyland," Stanford University, http://www.stanford.edu/-wfsharpe/art/fantasy/fantasy.htm

Chapter 22: The Birth of Portfolio Theory: The Age of Covariance

1. Gordon Crovitz, "The Father of Portfolio Theory on the Crisis," *The Wall Street Journal*, November 3, 2008.

Chapter 23: When Harry Met Bill(y)

1. William F. Sharpe, "Capital Asset Prices—A Theory of Market Equilibrium Under Conditions of Risk," *Journal of Finance*, Vol. 19, No. 3 (September 1964), pp. 425–442.
2. William F. Sharpe, *Investors and Markets: Portfolio Choices, Asset Prices, and Investment Advice* (Princeton, NJ: Princeton University Press, 2007).

Chapter 25: Options: Profiting from Uncertainty

1. "Learning Center," Chicago Board Options Exchange, http://www.cboe.com/LearnCenter/default.aspx

Chapter 26: When Fischer and Myron Met Bob: Option Theory

1. Peter Bernstein, *Capital Ideas: The Improbable Origins of Modern Wall Street* (New York: Free Press, 1993).
2. Myron S. Scholes, "Derivatives in a Dynamic Environment," Nobelprize.org, http://nobelprize.org/nobel_prizes/economics/laureates/1997/scholes-lecture.html; Robert C. Merton, "Applications of Option-Pricing Theory: Twenty-Five Years Later," Nobel Lecture, December 9, 1997, http://nobelprize.org/nobcl_prizes/economics/laureates/1997/merton-lecture.pdf
3. Fischer Black and Myron S. Scholes, "The Pricing of Options and Corporate Liabilities," *Journal of Political Economy*, Vol. 81, No. 3 (1973), pp. 637–654.
4. Robert C. Merton, "Theory of Rational Option Pricing," *Bell Journal of Economics and Management Science*, Vol. 4, No. 1 (1973), pp. 141–183.
5. "2005 Market Statistics," Chicago Board Options Exchange, http://www.cboe.com/data/marketstats-2005.pdf
6. Roger Lowenstein, *When Genius Failed: The Rise and Fall of Long-Term Capital Management* (New York: Random House, 2000).

Chapter 27: Prices, Probabilities and Predictions

1. Adam Smith (1723–1790), *An Inquiry into the Nature and Causes of the Wealth Nations* 5th ed., edited by Edwin Cannan (London: Methuen and Co., Ltd., 1904). First published in 1776.
2. "Prime Minister Vladimir Putin's Speech at the Opening Ceremony of the World Economic Forum," Davos, Switzerland, January 28, 2009, http://www.weforum.org/pdf/AM_2009/OpeningAddress_VladimirPutin.pdf

3. William F. Sharpe, "Nuclear Financial Economics," http://www.stanford.edu/wfsharpe/art/RP1275.pdf

4. Richard Roll, Richard, "Orange Juice and Weather," *American Economic Review*, Vol. 74, No. 5 (1984), pp. 861–880.

5. James Surowiecki, *The Wisdom of Crowds* (New York: Anchor Books, 2005).

6. "What Is the IEM?" Iowa Electronic Market, http://www.biz.uiowa.edu/iem/

7. Dave Carpenter, "Option Exchange Probing Reports of Unusual Trading Before Attacks," The Associated Press, September 18, 2001. See also "Exchange Examines Odd Jump," *The Topeka Capital Journal*, http://cjonline.com/stories/091901/ter_tradingacts.shtml; Judith Schoolman, "Probe of Wild Market Swings in Terror-Tied Stocks," *New York Daily News*, September 20, 2001, p. 6; James Toedtman and Charles Zehren, "Profiting from Terror?" *Newsday*, September 19, 2001, p. W39.

8. "Welcome to the Options Clearing Corporation," Options Clearing Corporation, http://www.optionsclearing.com/

9. Allen M. Poteshman, "Unusual Option Market Activity and the Terrorist Attacks of September 11, 2001," *The Journal of Business*, Vol. 79 (2006), pp. 1703–1726.

10. 9-11 Research, "Insider Trading: Pre-9/11 Put Options on Companies Hurt by Attack Indicates Foreknowledge," http://911research.wtc7.net/sept11/stockputs.html

11. National Commission on Terrorist Attacks upon the United States, page 499, paragraph 130, http://www.9-11commission.gov/report/911Report_Notes.htm

12. Justin Wolfers and Eric Zitzewitz, "The Furor over 'Terrorism Futures,'" *Washington Post*, July 31, 2003, p. A19.

13. Robin Hanson, "The Policy Analysis Market (and FutureMAP) Archive," http://hanson.gmu.edu/policyanalysismarket.html

14. Michael Schrage and Sam L. Savage, "If This Is Harebrained, Bet on the Hare," *Washington Post*, August 3, 2003, p. B04. See http://www.washingtonpost.com/wp-dyn/articles/A14094-2003Aug2.html

15. "Update," Tradesports, http://www.tradesports.com/; "Iran and the U.S. Will Hold a Summit Meeting in 2009," http://us.newsfutures.com; "The Foresight Exchange Prediction Market," Foresight Exchange, http://www.ideosphere.com/fx/

16. Justin Lahart, "No Future for Poindexter?" CNNMoney.com, http://money.cnn.com/2003/07/30/markets/poindextercontract

17. Justin Wolfers and Eric Zitzewitz, "Prediction Markets," *Journal of Economic Perspectives*, Vol. 18, No. 2 (Spring 2004); Justin Wolfers and Eric Zitzewitz, "Prediction Markets in Theory and Practice," National Bureau of Economic Research Working Paper Series, http://bpp.wharton.upenn.edu/jwolfers/Papers/PredictionMarkets(Palgrave).pdf; Martin Spann and Bernd Skiera, "Taking Stock of Virtual Markets," *ORMS Today*, Vol. 30, No. 5 (October 2003), http://www.lionhrtpub.com/orms/orms-10-03/frfutures.html

18. Joseph Grundfest, "Business Law." *Stanford Magazine*, November 2003, http://www.stanfordalumni.org/news/magazine/2003/novdec/farm/news/bizlaw.html

Chapter 28: Holistic Versus Hole-istic

1. Ben C. Ball, "Managing Risk in the Real World," *European Journal of Operational Research*, Vol. 14 (1983), pp. 248–261.

2. Peter L. Bernstein, *Capital Ideas: The Improbable Origins of Modern Wall Street*, rev. ed. (New York: Free Press, 1993).

3. Hiroshi Konno and H. Yamazaki, "Mean Absolute Deviation Portfolio Optimization Model and Its Applications to the Tokyo Stock Market," *Management Science*, Vol. 37, No. 5 (1991), pp. 519–531.
4. Portfolio Decisions, Inc., www.portfoliodecisions.com
5. Ben C. Ball and Sam L. Savage, "Holistic vs. Hole-istic E&P Strategies," *Journal of Petroleum Technology*. Sept 1999.

Chapter 29: Real Portfolios at Shell

1. Sam Savage, Stefan Scholtes, and Daniel Zweidler, "Probability Management, Part 2," *ORMS Today*, Vol. 33, No. 2 (April 2006), p. 60.
2. Sam Savage, Stefan Scholtes, and Daniel Zweidler, "Probability Management," *ORMS Today*, Vol. 33, No. 1 (February 2009), p. 20.

Chapter 30: Real Options

1. James Scanlan, Abhijit Rao, Christophe Bru, Peter Hale, and Rob Marsh, "The DATUM Project: A Cost Estimating Environment for the Support of Aerospace Design Decision Making," *AIAA Journal of Aircraft*, Vol. 43, No. 4 (2006), pp. 1022–1029.
2. Vanguard Software Corporation, http://www.vanguardsw.com/
3. "California Battered by Storms; Weather Worst in Years," Bloomberg.com, http://www.bloomberg.com/apps/news?pid=20601103&sid=aQI3WxAgwR9c&refer=us

Chapter 31: Some Gratuitous Inflammatory Remarks on the Accounting Industry

1. L. T. Johnson, B. Robbins, R. Swieringa, and R. L. Weil, "Expected Values in Financial Reporting," *Accounting Horizons*, Vol. 7, No. 4 (1993), pp. 77–90.
2. "Summary of Statement No. 123: Accounting for Stock-Based Compensation (Issued 10/95)," Financial Accounting Standards Board, http://www.fasb.org/st/summary/stsum123.shtml
3. Zvi Bodie, Robert S. Kaplan, and Robert C. Merton. "For the Last Time: Stock Options Are an Expense," *Harvard Business Review* (March 2003).
4. "Statement of Financial Accounting Standards No. 123 (Revised 2004)," Financial Accounting Series, http://www.fasb.org/pdf/fas123r.pdf
5. T. Carlisle, "How Lowly Bitumen Is Biting Oil Reserve Tallies," *The Wall Street Journal*, February 14, 2005.
6. Jeff Strnad, "Taxes and Nonrenewable Resources: The Impact on Exploration and Development," *SMU Law Review*, Vol. 55, No. 4 (2000), pp. 1683–1752.
7. S. L. Savage and M. Van Allen, "Accounting for Uncertainty," *Journal of Portfolio Management*, Vol. 29, No. 1 (Fall 2002), p. 31.
8. John Cox, Stephen Ross, and Mark Rubinstein, "Option Pricing: A Simplified Approach," *Journal of Financial Economics*, 7 (1979), p. 229.
9. "Exposure Draft: Proposed Statement of Financial Accounting Standards: Disclosure of Certain Loss Contingencies," Financial Accounting Series, http://www.fasb.org/draft/ed_contingencies.pdf

Chapter 32: The DNA of Supply Chains

1. Sam L. Savage, *Decision Making with Insight* (with Insight.xla 2.0 and CD-ROM Second Edition, 2003), Cengage Learning, Florence, KY.
2. "Jay Forrester, March 1918, Nebraska, USA," http://www.thocp.net/biographies/forrester_jay.html
3. J. W. Forrester, "Industrial Dynamics: A Major Breakthrough for Decision Makers," *Harvard Business Review*, Vol. 36, No. 4 (1958), pp. 37–66.
4. John. D. Sterman, "Modeling Managerial Behavior: Misperceptions of Feedback in a Dynamic Decision Making Experiment," *Management Science*, Vol. 35, No. 3 (1989), pp. 321–339.
5. John D. Sterman, "Teaching Takes Off: Flight Simulators for Management Education: 'The Beer Game,'" http://web.mit.edu/jsterman/www/SDG/beergame.html

Chapter 35: The Statistical Research Group of World War II

1. W. Allen Wallis, "The Statistical Research Group, 1942–1945," *Journal of the American Statistical Association*, Vol. 75, No. 370 (June 1980), pp. 320–330.
2. A. F. M. Smith, *The Writings of Leonard Jimmie Savage—A Memorial Collection* (Washington, DC: American Statistical Association and The Institute of Mathematical Statistics, 1981), pp. 25–26.
3. M. Friedman and L. J. Savage, "Utility Analysis of Choices Involving Risk," *Journal of Political Economy*, Vol. 56, No. 4 (1948), pp. 279–304; M. Friedman and L. J. Savage, "The Expected-Utility Hypothesis and the Measurability of Utility," *Journal of Political Economy*, Vol. 60 (1952), pp. 463–474.
4. W. Allen Wallis, "The Statistical Research Group, 1942–1945: Rejoinder," *Journal of the American Statistical Association*, Vol. 75, No. 370 (June 1980), pp. 334–335.

Chapter 36: Probability and the War on Terror

1. *USA Today*, November 7, 2007, p. 1A.
2. XVIII Airborne Corps and Fort Bragg Provost Marshall Office, *Commander's Handbook—Gangs & Extremist Groups—Dealing with Hate*, http://www.bragg.army.mil/PSBC-PM/ProvostMarshalDocs/GangsAndExtremist.pdf
3. Matt Apuzzo and Lara Jakes Jordan, "Suicide Latest Twist in 7-year Anthrax Mystery," Associated Press, August 1, 2008.
4. "Health Statistics: Suicides (per Capita) (Most Recent) by State," Statemaster.com, http://www.statemaster.com/graph/hea_sui_percap-health-suicides-per-capita
5. Armen Keteyian, "Suicide Epidemic Among Veterans," CBS News, November 13, 2007, http://www.cbsnews.com/stories/2007/11/13/cbsnews_investigates/printable3496471.shtml
6. Sam Savage and Howard Wainer, "Until Proven Guilty: False Positives and the War on Terror," *Chance Magazine*, Vol. 21, No. 1 (2008), p. 55.
7. Lawrence M. Wein, Alex H. Wilkins, Manas Baveja, and Stephen E. Flynn, "Preventing the Importation of Illicit Nuclear Materials in Shipping Containers," *Risk Analysis*, Vol. 26, No. 5 (2006), pp. 1377–1393.
8. "Nunn-Lugar Cooperative Threat Reduction Program," Support Nunn-Lugar, http://nunn-lugar.com/

9. "Cocaine: Strategic Findings," National Drug Intelligence Center, http://www.usdoj.gov/ndic/pubs11/18862/cocaine.htm

10. Personal correspondence.

11. "Rumsfeld's War-on-Terror Memo," *USA Today*, http://www.usatoday.com/news/washington/executive/rumsfeld-memo.htm

12. Mark Mazzetti, "Spy Agencies Say Iraq War Worsens Terrorism Threat," *The New York Times*, September 24, 2006.

13. Paul Stares and Mona Yacoubian, "Terrorism as Virus," Washingtonpost.com, August 23, 2005, http://www.washingtonpost.com/wp-dyn/content/article/2005/08/22/AR2005082201109.html

14. For a discussion of Markov chains, see Sam L. Savage, *Decision Making with Insight*, with Insight.xla 2.0 and CD-ROM, 2nd ed. (Florence, KY: Cengage Learning, 2003).

15. Fareed Zakaria, "Learning to Live with Radical Islam," *Newsweek*, March 9, 2009.

16. Army Field Manual No. 3-24, Marine Corps Warfighting Publication No. 3-33.5, 15 December 2006.

Chapter 37: The Flaw of Averages and Climate Change

1. Harwell, Mark A., *Nuclear Winter: The Human and Environmental Consequences of Nuclear War* (New York: Springer-Verlag, 1984).

2. "Vostok Ice Core Stable Isotope Data," National Oceanic and Atmospheric Administration Satellite and Information Service, http://www.ncdc.noaa.gov/paleo/icecore/antarctica/vostok/vostok_isotope.html

3. Clifford Krauss, Steven Lee Myers, Andrew C. Revkin, and Simon Romero, "The Big Melt as Polar Ice Turns to Water, Dreams of Treasure Abound," *The New York Times*, October 10, 2005.

4. G. Hardin, "The Tragedy of the Unmanaged Commons," *Trends in Ecology & Evolution*, Vol. 9 (1994), p. 199.

5. "MIT Climate Online: Greenhouse Gas Emissions Simulator," http://web.mit.edu/jsterman/www/GHG.html

6. "Cleaning Up," *The Economist Magazine*, June 2, 2007, p. 13.

Chapter 38: The Flaw of Averages in Health Care

1. "Do Breast Self-Exams Do Any Good?" *Time Magazine*, July 15, 2008.

2. Allison Van Dusen, "Do You Need a Prostate Cancer Screening?" Forbes Magazine, August 8, 2008.

3. Alan Zelicoff and Michael Bellomo, *More Harm Than Good* (New York: American Management Association, 2008).

4. S. J. Gould, "The Median Isn't the Message," *Discover*, June 1985, pp. 40–42.

5. S. J. Gould, *Full House: The Spread of Excellence from Plato to Darwin* (New York: Harmony Books, 1996).

6. "Medical Guesswork: From Heart Surgery to Prostate Care, the Health Industry Knows Little About Which Common Treatments Really Work," *BusinessWeek*, May 29, 2006, http://www.businessweek.com/magazine/content/06_22/b3986001.htm

7. "Markov Models," David M. Eddy: Mountains, Math and Medicine, http://www.davidmeddy.com/Markov_modeling.htm

8. Interview with David M. Eddy, "Healthcare Crisis: Who's at Risk?" http://www.pbs.org/healthcarecrisis/Exprts_intrvw/d_eddy.htm

9. John F. Brewster, M. Ruth Graham, and W. Alan, C. Mutch, "Convexity, Jensen's Inequality and Benefits of Noisy Mechanical Ventilation," *J. R. Soc. Interface*, Vol. 2, No. 4 (2005), pp. 393–396.

10. What Price ValuJet? By Michael Kinsley Saturday, July 6, 1996

Chapter 39: Sex and the Central Limit Theorem

1. C. Wedekind, T. Seebeck, F. Bettens, and A. J. Paepke, "MHC-Dependent Mate Preferences in Humans," *Proc Biol Sci.*, Vol. 260, No. 1359 (June 22, 1995), pp. 245–249.

2. Nicholas Wade, "Pas de Deux of Sexuality Is Written in the Genes," *The New York Times*, April 10, 2007.

Chapter 40: The End of Statistics as You Were Taught It

1. James Surowiecki, *The Wisdom of Crowds* (New York: Anchor Books, 2005).

2. Stephen M. Stigler, *The History of Statistics: The Measurement of Uncertainty Before 1900* (Cambridge, MA: Harvard University Press, 1986).

3. Stephen M. Stigler, "Stochastic Simulation in the Nineteenth Century," *Statistical Science*, Vol. 6, No. 1 (1991).

4. Francis Galton, "Dice for Statistical Experiments," *Nature*, Vol. 42 (1890), pp. 13–14.

5. "New Senate Chair Retains Touch of Youthful Rebellion," Stanford Online Report, http://news-service.stanford.edu/news/1998/october14/efron1014.html

6. Bradley Efron, "Bootstrap Methods: Another Look at the Jackknife," *The Annals of Statistics*, Vol. 7, No. 1 (1979), pp. 1–26; B. Efron and R. J. Tibshirani, *An Introduction to the Bootstrap* (New York: Chapman & Hall, 1993).

7. Bradley Efron, "The Bootstrap and Modern Statistics," *Journal of the American Statistical Association*, Vol. 95, No. 452 (December 2000), pp. 1293–1296.

8. Julian L. Simon and Allen Holmes, "A Really New Way to Teach (and Do) Probability and Statistics," *The Mathematics Teacher*, Vol. 62 (April 1969), pp. 283–288.

9. Julian L. Simon, *Resampling: The New Statistics*, 2nd ed. (Arlington, VA: Resampling Stats Inc., 1997).

Chapter 41: Visualization

1. Alva Noë, *Action in Perception* (Cambridge, MA: MIT Press, 2004).

2. Jeff Hawkins and Sandra Blakeslee, *On Intelligence* (New York: Owl Books, 2005).

3. John W. Tukey, *Exploratory Data Analysis* (Reading, MA: Addison-Wesley, 1977).

4. JMP home page, http://jmp.com/

5. Edward R. Tufte, *The Visual Display of Quantitative Information*, 2nd ed. (Cheshire, CT: Graphics Press, 1992), http://www.edwardtufte.com/tufte/books_vdqi

6. Darrell Huff, *How to Lie with Statistics* (New York: W. W. Norton, 1993).

7. Tom Robbins, *Even Cowgirls Get the Blues* (Boston: Houghton Mifflin, 1976).

8. John Cassidy, "Mind Games: What Neuroeconomics Tells Us About Money and the Brain," *The New Yorker*, September 18, 2006, http://www.newyorker.com/archive/2006/09/18/060918fa_fact

Chapter 42: Interactive Simulation: A New Lightbulb

1. http://archive.ite.journal.informs.org/Vol1No2/Savage/Savage.php
2. Vensim, Ventana Systems, Inc., http://vensim.com/

Chapter 43: Scenario Libraries: The Power Grid

1. "Document Information: A Million Random Digits with 100,000 Normal Deviates," Rand Corporation, http://www.rand.org/pubs/monograph_reports/MR1418/index.html
2. Janet Tavakoli, *Structured Finance and Collateralized Debt Obligations*, 2nd ed. (Hoboken, NJ: Wiley, 2008).
3. Analytica, Lumina, http://lumina.com/
4. "DE Histograms," www.aecouncil.com/data_analysis

Chapter 45: Putting It into Practice

1. Don Tapscott and Anthony B. Williams, *Wikinomics: How Mass Collaboration Changes Everything* (Woodlands, TX: Portfolio, 2006).
2. Solver.com home page, www.Solver.com
3. "Oracle and Crystal Ball," Oracle, www.crystalball.com
4. Vanguard Software home page, http://www.vanguardsw.com/
5. Palisade Corporation home page, www.palisade.com

Chapter 46: The Chief Probability Officer

1. Joe Nocera, "Risk Mismanagement," *The New York Times*, January 4, 2009.
2. Financial News, "Merck Outlines Long-Term Prospects and Progress on Strategic Plan at 2008 Annual Business Briefing," Merck home page, http://www.merck.com/newsroom/press_releases/financial/2008_1209.html
3. B. Fischhoff, L. D. Phillips, and S. Lichtenstein, "Calibration of Probabilities: The State of the Art to 1980," in *Judgment Under Uncertainty: Heuristics and Biases*, edited by D. Kahneman and A. Tversky (New York: Cambridge University Press, 1982).
4. Doug Hubbard, *How to Measure Anything: Finding the Value of "Intangibles" in Business* (New York: Wiley, 2009).
5. Allan Chernoff, Sr., "Madoff Whistleblower Blasts SEC," CNNMoney, http://money.cnn.com/2009/02/04/news/newsmakers/madoff_whistleblower/index.htm

Chapter 47: A Posthumous Visit by My Father

1. Leonard J. Savage, *The Foundations of Statistics* (Hoboken, NJ: Wiley, 1954).
2. Leonard J. Savage, "The Shifting Foundations of Statistics," in *Logic, Laws and Life*, edited by R. Colodny (Pittsburgh, PA: University of Pittsburgh Press, 1977).

About the Author

Sam L. Savage is a consulting professor in Stanford University's School of Engineering and a fellow of the Judge Business School at Cambridge University.

He received a PhD in the area of computational complexity from Yale University in 1973, spent a year at General Motors Research Laboratory, and then joined the management science faculty of the University of Chicago Graduate School of Business. Here he quickly realized that an algebraic curtain separated management from management science, and he abandoned the field as moribund. Then a decade later, with the advent of the personal computer and electronic spreadsheet, the algebraic curtain began to fall, and Sam was reborn as a management scientist. In 1985, he collaborated on the first widely marketed spreadsheet optimization package, What's *Best!*®, which won *PC Magazine's* Technical Excellence Award. In 1990 Sam came to Stanford, where he continues to teach and develop management science tools in an algebra-free environment.

His primary research focus is on enterprisewide communication and management of uncertainty and risk. In 2006, in collaboration with Stefan Scholtes (of Cambridge University) and Daniel Zweidler (then of Shell and now with Merck & Co.), Dr. Savage formalized the foundations of Probability Management and is the chairman of ProbabilityManagement.org. Recently he led a consortium that included Frontline Systems, Oracle Corp., and SAS Institute in the development of the DIST™ Distribution String, a new computer data type for storing probability distributions.

He has published in both refereed journals and the popular press, with articles in the *Harvard Business Review, The Journal of Portfolio Management, Washington Post,* and *ORMS Today.* Sam also consults and lectures extensively to business and government agencies and has served as an expert witness.

Index

Nuclear Financial Economics
Bill Sharp — pages PDF

Chance Magazine
StateMaster.com   Statistical Data

Plan of Attack   False Positive Calc XLS

More Harm than Good — Zelicoff
Medical Guesswork BusWeek. com /
Magazine / content / 06_22 / b 39 86001. htm
http:// archive.ite.journal.informs.org / VOl2NO2/
        3 avoge / savage.php
http://
Eversim.com
Risk solver
XLSim
How to measure anything) Hubbard
The failure of Risk Management &
   How to fix it.
www. probability management. org.   XLsim